Conversations with N. Scott Momaday

Edited by
Matthias Schubnell

University Press of Mississippi
Jackson

PS
3563
.O47
Z467
1997

Copyright © 1997 by the University Press of Mississippi
All rights reserved
Manufactured in the United States of America

00 99 98 97   4 3 2 1

The paper in this book meets the guidelines for permanence and durability of the Committee on Production Guidelines for Book Longevity of the Council on Library Resources.

Library of Congress Cataloging-in-Publication Data

Momaday, N. Scott, 1934–
    Conversations with N. Scott Momaday / edited by Matthias
Schubnell.
        p.   cm. — (Literary conversations series)
    Includes index.
    ISBN 0-87805-959-8 (cloth : alk. paper). — ISBN 0-87805-960-1
(pbk. : alk. paper)
    1. Momaday, N. Scott, 1934–   —Interviews. 2. Authors,
American—20th century—Interviews. I. Schubnell, Matthias, 1953–
II. Title. III. Series.
PS3563.O47Z467 1997
813'.54—dc20
[B]   96-35244
                                                                    CIP

British Library Cataloging-in-Publication data available

Books by N. Scott Momaday

The Complete Poems of Frederick Goddard Tuckerman. New York: Oxford University Press, 1965.

The Journey of Tai-me. Privately printed, 1967.

House Made of Dawn. New York: Harper and Row, 1968.

The Way to Rainy Mountain. Albuquerque: University of New Mexico Press, 1969.

Colorado: Summer, Fall, Winter, Spring. New York: Rand McNally, 1973.

Angle of Geese and Other Poems. Boston: David Godine, 1974.

The Names: A Memoir. New York: Harper and Row, 1976.

The Gourd Dancer. New York: Harper and Row, 1976.

The Ancient Child. New York: Doubleday, 1989.

In the Presence of the Sun: A Gathering of Shields. Santa Fe: The Rydal Press, 1992.

In the Presence of the Sun: Stories and Poems, 1961–1991. New York: St. Martin's Press, 1992.

Circle of Wonder: A Native American Christmas Story. Santa Fe: Clear Light, 1993.

Contents

Introduction

N. Scott Momaday has made himself readily available for interviews throughout his career. Among the recurrent issues raised in these conversations are Momaday's multi-ethnic experience, his view of the Indian's place in American society, his synthesis of native oral traditions and the Western literary canon, his concern for ecology and conservation, his theories of language and the imagination, the influences on his academic and artistic development, his work as a teacher and painter, and, of course, his own comments on specific works. Through the years, Momaday's responses to queries on these topics are remarkably consistent.

Momaday makes his perhaps most revealing comment on interviews as a medium for intellectual discourse in his conversation with Lee Abbott, where he asserts that they constitute "Heap Big Medicine, to put it in indigenous terms." This statement acknowledges not only the ceremonial nature of the interviewing process, but its potential for engendering a deeper vision of the writer's work. Momaday is clearly at ease with the questions posed to him, and many of his conversation partners comment on his remarkable voice. Bettye Givens recalls that "Momaday speaks with a deep resonance using cultivated speech, for he cares as much about how language sounds as how his words look on the page." Joseph Bruchac, too, appears mesmerized by Momaday's voice: "The voice with which he greeted me was warm and deep, and the words spoken in a way which gave weight to every syllable. It was a voice which one might expect from a man who wrote and continues to write of the magical nature and power of language." And the students who interviewed him for *Persona* describe him as "a large, impressive man who speaks in a deep, rich voice that immediately makes you feel comfortable and aware that words are valuable things." But the interviews also reveal a side to Momaday which is not always apparent in his published work, namely his exquisite sense of humor.

Among the priceless episodes in these interviews is this response to Givens on how he would rate *House Made of Dawn:* "I think it's a terrific novel. I like it a lot. Pleased to have written it." His account of Georgia O'Keeffe's effort to serve the Momadays a drink on the occasion of their visit to her house at Abiquiu is a delightful example of Momaday's storytelling. The painter, then in her eighties, was without her maid and without the key to the liquor cabinet, which was in the possession of the maid. Refusing to let adversity come between her and her guests' well-being, she eventually took the hinges off the cabinet (Schubnell). Equally amusing is Momaday's story about his diligent efforts to settle his telephone bill before his departure from Russia in 1974: "I thought, 'They can't let me out of the country without the phone money.' And, you know, I thought as I packed and departed for the airport that it's going to happen at the airport: that's where they'll get me. And then I went through customs and got on the plane and then I thought that out over the Baltic, MIGs are going to appear and force us down and say, 'Mr. Momaday, what about the phone bill?' " (Weiler). While these examples illustrate Momaday's delight in capturing life's humorous side, the interviews also offer much insight into his experience as a writer.

When asked about the craft of writing, Momaday frequently speaks to his need for a fixed schedule to ensure a routine of sustained composition. This is important to him not only because, as he puts it to Lee Abbott, his work habits are "lousy," but because he experiences writing as "an isolated and lonely business." Referring to the frustrations of writing, Momaday says in the *Persona* interview that "the machine in my garden is that damn typewriter; it becomes your enemy, and you exorcise all your evil spirits by pounding away at it. The harder you hit the keys, the better. The more pain you inflict on it, the better." What sustains Momaday in the creative process are the workings of the unconscious and the power of inspiration.

In his interview with Gretchen Bataille in 1977, Momaday comments on his delight in having critics point out to him a reading of his work he himself was quite unaware of: "You write out of the subconscious to such a degree that you're not always aware of what the implications and consequent meanings of your expression are. That's one of the most exciting things about writing." To Givens he confesses that only through inspiration can the drudgery of writing be overcome. For Momaday, the creative process is slow and deliberate, requiring much patience and perseverance: "You just live with [poems and novels] as seeds in the mind and then eventually they take shape and that's when you can begin to work them out on the page. But for a thing to germinate it takes a long time, thinking about it, sleeping on it" *(Persona)*. As a result, Momaday reminds his interviewers of a guiding motto that Yvor Winters impressed upon him at Stanford: "Write little and write well" (Abbott).

Numerous interviewers have asked Momaday whether he writes with a mission. On one occasion he claims that his only mission is to satisfy himself as a writer (Bonetti). In his talk with Gaetano Prampolini, he offers a more subtle response by quoting William Gass: "I don't write for an audience, that would be pandering; and I don't write for myself, that would be self-serving. I write for the thing that is trying to be born." On a lighter note, he added, "Wonderful answer. I wish I had said that! I will always hold it against Gass that he said it before I did."

In response to questions as to whether he sees himself as a representative of native peoples, he tells Abbott that he does not view himself as an Indian writer, nor as a writer interested in reform, and he reiterates this point in his conversation with Wm. T. Morgan by saying, "I don't identify with any group of writers, and I don't think of myself as being a spokesman for the Indian people. That would be presumptuous, it seems to me." His creative purpose is perhaps best summed up in this declaration, "This is why I paint and write: I want to astonish God" (Prampolini).

As to the participation of the writer in the process of defining a social consciousness, he assures Louis Owens that he does not intend his readings as political statements, even though they may be read as such, and he shares with Givens that he is not interested in changing attitudes, nor in having his work read as social comment. However, many remarks in Momaday's interviews (and his numerous essays on nature conservation) suggest that his expressions of concern for conservation and interest in ecology are indeed aimed at bringing about change. As early as 1970, in his discussion of "The Man Made of Words," he advocates the development of a land ethic to halt the increasing degradation of the global ecology. He tells Owens in his 1983 interview that "man's relation to the earth" is one of his great themes. When Owens quotes from "The Man Made of Words" essay

that "ecology is perhaps the most important subject of our time,"
Momaday reaffirms his conviction that "not nearly enough is being
done to protect the earth from exploitation," and that the Indian can
serve as an example of ecological responsibility. Responding to Lawrence J. Evers's question about the idea of an American land ethic,
Momaday argues that in the Indian world the relationship to the land
is inevitably moral: "Man understands that he is obligated in certain
ways to the landscape, that he is responsible for it, that he shares in
the spirit of place." Finally, Momaday explains that he pursues his
interest in the natural world around him as "a kind of amateur
naturalist" (Abbott), capturing landscape and animals in precise,
descriptive prose. Yet he is not satisfied with exploring nature's
surfaces alone. As he puts it to Morgan, the landscape must finally be
imagined, for "one's idea of the self involves the environment."

Over the years, Momaday's concern for environmental protection
has led to his active involvement in several causes. In 1981, he
declares to Matthias Schubnell, "Now I think of myself as a conservationist. I have great sympathy for the Sierra Club and such organizations." In 1993, Momaday tells Camille Adkins about his involvement
as a board member of the Grand Canyon Trust, which advocates the
preservation of the Colorado Plateau, and his plan to set up the
Buffalo Trust, "an institute for the preservation of the sacred in
Native American life." This project will include the restoration of the
prairie and the reintroduction of buffalo. These comments indicate
that over the years Momaday's engagement in the cause of conservation has gone well beyond his role as nature writer and advocate for a
new land ethic modeled on native American precepts.

While Momaday eschews the role of spokesman for Indian people,
his answers to questions on the native presence in modern American
culture reveal a deeply held conviction that Americans, in order to
define their cultural identity, must take the Indian into account. In
1970, having deplored that not much attention has been paid to
traditional Indian values, he asserts that "acculturation means a two-
way, a reciprocal kind of thing in which there is a realization of one
world that is composed of both elements," and he adds that the Indian
"ought to educate the white man. We ought to reconstruct our
institutions within the dominant society, so that the Indian values are
available to the dominant society" (Costo). As to the Indian's chal-

lenge in this reciprocal exchange, Momaday urges Native Americans to discover who they are on a comparative basis. To avoid becoming an anachronism, the Indian "has to venture out, I think, beyond the traditional world. . . . But it is possible for him to make that adventure without sacrificing his being and identity" (Costo).

In his conversations with Abbott and Owens, Momaday also points to the Indians' attachment to the land as a model for other Americans to strengthen their cultural identity. He views the land as "a repository of heritage" (Abbott) from which they can draw strength, but he is also aware that his frequent departures from his homeland may have loosened his connection to the Southwest. "I sometimes wonder. In one sense I have driven a kind of wedge between myself and the ancestral land, but in another I've fulfilled the nomadic instincts of that culture [the Kiowas], and I'm not sure what it all means" (Owens). Momaday sees the uprooting of humans from their respective landscapes as "one of the great afflictions of our time, this conviction of alienation, separation, isolation" (Bruchac). While this phenomenon is prevalent in both the Indian and non-Indian context, the Indian appears to be better equipped to overcome this fracture, for "the whole world view of the Indian is predicated upon the principle of harmony in the universe" (Bruchac).

With regard to the native American contribution to American literature, Momaday points to the Indian writer's advantage of having "a very rich spiritual experience." While conceding that this may also be true of writers from other ethnic groups, he claims that in general "the non-Indian writers of today are culturally deprived, I think, in the sense that they don't have the same sense of heritage that the Indian has" (Bruchac). As to the continuing influence of the Indian on American culture, Momaday is optimistic. "The American Indian is indispensable to the soil and the dream and the destiny of America. . . . He always was and always will be a central figure in the American imagination, a central figure in American literature. We can't very well do without him" (Bruchac).

Momaday has frequently been asked how he feels about literary critics. He makes this wry comment to Abbott, "I've been treated very well by the critics. I don't have a great prejudice against them. There are an awful lot of silly critics around." Momaday clearly appreciates those critics who help bring to the surface those meanings

the writer unconsciously incorporates into the text, but he deplores
the fact that these critics are far and few between. Yet he is philosophi-
cal about the writer's relationship to the critic: "So the writer and the
painter, I think, had best ignore the critics as far as they can. Too
much praise is bad . . . , and certainly negative reception of their
work is an impairment, too" (Coltelli).

Momaday also makes no bones about his lack of interest in modern
critical theory. Asked what he thought about "Derrida-ism" and
other current schools of criticism, Momaday replies: "I do not see it
as something that will be taken very seriously by very many people
very long" (*Persona*). In response to Owens's question whether the
experimental form of *The Ancient Child* suggested an awareness of
fictional experimentation by writers such as Robbe-Grillet, Momaday
confesses: "Not at all. Every time I hear contemporary critics talking
about fiction I'm completely confused." And with respect to deconstruction, which Momaday recalls from a Salzburg Seminar in American Studies in 1985, he frankly states, "I wasn't understanding what
was said. I'm not a critic" (Owens). This last statement also applies
to Momaday's own commentaries on his work.

On the whole, Momaday is reluctant to help with specific interpreta-
tions of his writings. He believes that the writer is not a reliable
source of insight into the text because so much of the creative process
is unconscious. As he puts it to Kay Bonetti, "The author is the least
trustworthy person to ask about his work." He often cautions against
overinterpreting his work. For example, he responds to explications
of the protagonist's name in *House Made of Dawn,* Abel, in terms of
biblical allusion by saying: "The name is more suggestive than I
meant it to be" (Bataille 1977 interview). Confronted with questions
concerning the ultimate fate of his fictional characters, he argues that
they take on a life of their own, beyond the control and understanding
of their creator. With respect to Abel's condition at the end of *House
Made of Dawn,* Momaday emphasizes the ambiguity of the final
scene: "That's the question: can he recover his voice? There is no
answer to that" (Bonetti). To Dagmar Weiler, he explains, "The
question of whether or not he makes it is open. I mean a lot of people
want to know what happens after the last page, and I don't know. . . .
I don't want to know." While such comments return the interpretative
challenge to the critic, Momaday provides a host of valuable informa-

tion on the background and genesis of his works, particularly on *House Made of Dawn* and *The Ancient Child*. The entire conversation with the Italian scholar Gaetano Prampolini, for example, is dedicated to the exploration of Momaday's latest novel [*The Ancient Child*].

One of the most frequently addressed issues in the interviews with Momaday is the question of literary influence on his writings. He tells Bonetti, "I don't know who has been an influence on my writing," but adds that "if those people whose work I admire most have been the influence, [Emily Dickinson] would certainly be one of them." On another occasion, Momaday answers the same question by saying, "I can't point to anyone specifically" (Morgan), but then refers to Wallace Stevens and, again, Emily Dickinson, as writers who have had an impact on his work: "I think I have tried here and there to emulate them in certain ways, because I think that's what a writer should do. If he sees something he likes he should try to benefit from being in its presence" (Morgan). In his conversation with Schubnell, he credits Dickinson with teaching him "a little something about the mystery and miracle of language." Other names of writers and works appear in a number of interviews: Faulkner, Hemingway, Joyce's "The Dead" and Isak Dinesen's *Out of Africa* (Abbott); D.H. Lawrence (Owens); André Gide and Albert Camus (*Persona*); and Hart Crane (Schubnell). These references are important clues for scholars interested in placing Momaday into a broader literary context.

Equally important, however, for a balanced understanding of Momaday's writing is his philosophy of language and the imagination. The single most significant statement in this regard is his essay entitled "The Man Made of Words," but many of his statements in the following interviews give the reader and critic further insight into Momaday's appreciation of the power of words. First and foremost, Momaday sees himself as a storyteller who fulfills a sacred duty, since "storytelling is the life's blood of the society" (Morgan). For that reason, "a writer should have that sense of wonder in the presence of words" (Morgan). Emphasizing his roots in the oral tradition, he tells Bruchac that his works are all parts of the same story, an idea he elaborates on in another interview: "It's as if you were writing one story over your lifetime. . . . I think of what I do as telling one story; it's a long one and I can't do it all at once. I can't get it all into one book. So what I do is I write a chapter at a time, as it were, and I publish it as a book. But it's all one story" (Bonetti). This story, composed of elements of the oral tradition, Native American myths and legends, and the themes and techniques of modern literature, is uniquely Momaday's own. He is keenly aware of the significance of such literary expression to human existence: "We do not know what we can do with words. But as long as there are those among us who try to find out, literature will be secure; literature will remain a thing worthy of our highest level of human being" (Bruchac). In his own particular case, writing is a way to create an understanding of self and history through language.

To explain this idea, Momaday has acknowledged the profound impact of the following statement by his Stanford mentor, Yvor Winters: "Unless we understand the history which produced us, we are determined by that history; we may be determined in any event, but the understanding gives us a chance" (Schubnell). Not surprisingly, then, Momaday explains in the *Persona* interview that his writing represents "an invention of history as I see it." This pertains both to Momaday's tribal and racial identity, which he explores in *The Way to Rainy Mountain* and *The Names: A Memoir,* and to his personal sense of self. In his conversation with Schubnell, he notes, "I believe that I fashion my own life out of words and images, and that's how I get by. . . . Writing, giving expression to my spirit and to my mind, that's a way of surviving, of ordering one's life." In the same interview, he adds, "You grow up into an understanding of language and through that to an understanding of yourself. That's how it has to happen. We are determined by our language; it holds the limits of our development. . . . The more deeply you can become involved in language, the more fully we can exist." Statements like these help the reader appreciate that Momaday's work manifests not art for art's sake, but proceeds "out of a tremendous urge" (Abbott) to articulate his sense of self and express his humanity to its fullest extent.

Many of the interviews explore two other aspects of Momaday's work: his teaching and his painting. He is skeptical as to the efficacy of creative writing courses: "One can be taught how to write technically, and one can be taught how to appreciate good writing, but finally it becomes a matter . . . of having the aptitude, or the genius, or the gift of God, whatever it is" (*Persona*). Without that, "a creative writing class is [not] especially useful'' (Abbott). His teaching of literature provides Momaday with an intellectual stimulus and an incentive to write, as well as the necessary time to accomplish it (Abbott). His teaching philosophy centers on student involvement and active learning through discussion. He defines his own role as that of facilitator and mentor. Interestingly, another aspect of effective teaching, according to Momaday, represents a link to his writing. ''I also think of myself as a storyteller. . . . That's what teachers should be, in one sense . . . one learns from stories. We invest ourselves and all our experiences in stories. A class can be taught as if it were a story, and that's good'' (Morgan).

Momaday's painting and drawing have increasingly become an integral part of his artistic expression. Starting with a few drawings accompanying *The Gourd Dancer* and *The Names: A Memoir,* Momaday's visual images constitute an important dimension in his recent works, *Ancestral Voice: Conversations with N. Scott Momaday, In the Presence of the Sun: Stories and Poems, 1961–1991,* and, perhaps most impressively, in the hand-colored, limited edition of *In the Presence of the Sun: A Gathering of Shields,* published by Rydal Press, where the illustrations of the shields gloriously complement the written text.

Not surprisingly, Momaday's painting has drawn numerous questions from interviewers. He explains to Schubnell that the origin of his artistic talent can be traced to his childhood when he was ''watching his father at work on his knees or his drafting board.'' It was during his stay in Russia in 1974 that he began sketching, and this enthusiasm was reinforced by an art class with Leonard Baskin at Stanford in 1976 (Schubnell).

Momaday sees painting as a logical extension of his literary expression, given ''the proximity of the image and the word to things'' (Coltelli). He believes that ''words are artificial in the way that paint on canvas is artificial; it's not the real world, and in some ways the reflection is truer than the things it represents as it passes through the intelligence of the writer or of the painter'' (Coltelli). The relation between Momaday's dual talents is undoubtedly an area for future critical examination.

The reader who joins in the following conversations will find Momaday to be a careful listener and engaging talker, generous in spirit and eager to share his ideas. What emerges from these dialogues is a deeper vision of Momaday, the man and the artist, and, it is hoped, a more precise understanding of the nature and purpose of his work. This introduction, however, would not be complete without the mention of Charles Woodard's book-length dialogue with Momaday, entitled *Ancestral Voice: Conversations with N. Scott Momaday*. This work is essential reading for anyone seeking access to Momaday, the writer and artist, through his own comments. While Woodard's text represents a sustained exchange between Momaday and a single interviewer, the present collection offers a chronological survey of conversations between Momaday and a variety of questioners over a span of a quarter century.

It is the policy of the Literary Conversations series to italicize book titles and reprint interviews uncut and unedited, except where obvious errors require silent editing. As a result, these interviews inevitably contain a certain amount of repetition, which in itself is a measure of what critics and readers of Momaday's work have been most interested in.

I gratefully acknowledge the help of the professional staff of the J.E. and L.E. Mabee Library at the University of the Incarnate Word, Mendell Morgan, Basil Aivaliotis, Robert Allen and Tammy Hernandez who helped with this and past projects. I am also grateful to Cynthia Guzman for typing my interview with N. Scott Momaday, and the work study students, Leslie Rodriguez, Robert Loera and Lee Northard, for transcribing the audiotape of Kay Bonetti's interview with Momaday. I would like to thank my friend and colleague, Kenneth Roemer at the University of Texas at Arlington, for asking me to take on this project and for supporting me along the way. Thanks, too, to all the individuals who helped secure the permissions to reprint the material in this collection. I am grateful to N. Scott Momaday who, once again, graciously lent his support and encouragement to this undertaking. Finally, I want to thank my children, Alexander and Claire, for their patience when my work on this book impinged on their playtime on the computer.

Chronology

1934   Born N(avarre) Scott Momaday, 27 February 1934, in Lawton, Oklahoma, to Kiowa artist Al Momaday and writer-artist Natachee Scott

1946   Attends Franciscan Mission School at Jemez

1947   Attends Leah Harvey Junior High School in Santa Fe

1948–51   Attends Our Lady of Sorrow School in Bernalillo, Saint Mary's in Albuquerque and Bernalillo Public High School

1951–52   Attends Augustus Military Academy, Fort Defiance, Virginia

1952–56   Undergraduate studies in political science with minors in English and speech at the University of New Mexico in Albuquerque

1956–57   Studies law at the University of Virginia in Charlottesville

1958–59   Graduates with B.A. from the University of New Mexico; Teaches at the Dulce Independent School on the Jicarilla Apache Reservation

1959   Awarded Wallace Stegner Creative Writing Fellowship at Stanford University; Marries Gaye Mangold

1959–63   Graduate and doctoral studies in English at Stanford University M.A. (1960) Ph.D. (1963) Thesis: *The Complete Poems of Frederick Goddard Tuckerman.*

1962   Academy of American Poets prize for "The Bear"

1963–69   Assistant/Associate Professor of English, University of California, Santa Barbara

1965   *The Complete Poems of Frederick Goddard Tuckerman,* published by Oxford University Press

1966   Guggenheim Fellowship; studies Emily Dickinson and transcendental literature in Amherst, Massachusetts

1967   *The Journey of Tai-me*

1968   *House Made of Dawn*

1969   Pulitzer Prize for Fiction for *House Made of Dawn; The Way to Rainy Mountain*; Initiation into Gourd Dance Society

1969–72 Associate professor of English and Comparative Literature University of California, Berkeley

1970   National Institute of Letters grant

1972   Distinguished Visiting Professor of Humanities at New Mexico State University, Las Cruces

1973–81 Professor of English, Stanford University

1973   *Colorado: Summer, Fall, Winter, Spring*

1974   *Angle of Geese and Other Poems;* Shares Western Heritage Award with David Muench for *Colorado: Summer, Fall, Winter, Spring;* Visiting professor at the University of Moscow

1976   *The Gourd Dancer* and *The Names: A Memoir;* art classes with Leonard Baskin

1978   Marries Regina Heitzer

1979   First one-man show of drawings and paintings at the University of North Dakota; Premio Letterario Internazionale Mondelo, Italy's highest literary award

1981   Father dies

1981–89 Professor of English, University of Arizona, Tucson; *The Ancient Child; Ancestral Voice: Conversations with N. Scott Momaday,* by Charles L. Woodard, with 23 illustrations by N. Scott Momaday; Native American Literature Prize

1992   *In the Presence of the Sun: A Gathering of Shields;* Returning the Gift Lifetime Achievement Award

1993   *In the Presence of the Sun: Stories and Poems, 1961–1991;* Twenty-year retrospective of drawings and paintings at Santa Fe's Wheelwright Museum

1994   Premiere of *The Indolent Boys,* Momaday's first play, at the Syracuse Stage, New York

Conversations with N. Scott Momaday

Discussion: The Man Made of Words

Rupert Costo / 1970

From *Indian Voices: The First Convocation of American Indian Scholars*. Ed. Rupert Costo. San Francisco: Indian Historian Press, 1970. 62–75. © The Indian Historian Press.

A Speaker: Would you deal more with the oral tradition?

Scott Momaday: The tendency is to regard things in the oral tradition as dead, but they are not. They are very much alive, and it's important to see the way in which they are alive, the way in which they are relevant to what we are doing. And what is being done to us.

A Speaker: What difficulties were there to try to get Kiowa translated?

Scott Momaday: Many difficulties. And I had to rely to a great extent on people who were much more conversant with the language than I am. My father speaks it very well. He did some of the interpreting for me.

A Speaker: I am interested in terminology. Such terms are being used, as "literature, American Indian, oral tradition, or oral history." There is this differentiation made between literature and history. We do have a literature, you know. What do you consider the definition of the word "literature" to be?

Scott Momaday: These terms, I think are only useful as conveniences. People talk about oral literature, but sometimes it's convenient to distinguish between the tradition that is created by word of mouth and one that is set down in writing. If you consider literature, we ought to take that word to indicate writing.

A Speaker: But what you have described is literature, if even oral literature. You would not object to the term?

Scott Momaday: Not at all.

A Speaker: The body of literature of the American Indian.

Scott Momaday: I use that term, yes. It is important to realize that there is a great body of oral literature among the various tribes. It constitutes an incredible wealth of material, and it is being lost at a very great rate. It should be preserved, I think, as much as we can, for its own sake. It is eminently worth preservation. And I became convinced of that several years ago, and since that time, have done something about it. I hope that those of you who have access to oral traditions and bodies of literature will try to preserve them. The time is now. A great deal remains and I hope I can interest the people in preserving it.

A Speaker: I have listened to a lot of people from various parts of the country. One of the things that I have noted, both in your talk and others, is the topic of ecology. I think that what we are talking about in ecology does not really describe the concept of what our Indian people are talking about when they use similar words. Particularly now, many of our people from different parts of the country have said that the end of the world is now in sight. It could be sometime within the next thousand years or sooner. So, I then tried to explain that American people are becoming aware of ecology, and the things of which you are speaking. But we have difficulty separating that which is truth, and that which is just words. I think what they are saying is that the word ecology is being used in a monetary or political sense, just like so many other words in the white society. And they say, you know, that the end of the world is imminent. I was wondering if you have any further insight into this, which I haven't been able to gain.

Scott Momaday: I do firmly believe that the extinction of life as we know it on this planet is threatened. I don't know about the word "imminent." I am not sure what that means, but I think we have polluted our atmosphere and spoiled our land to the extent that survival itself is necessarily brought into question. And unless we become aware of that danger, unless we change our style of life, we are on a disaster course.

A Speaker: My understanding is that it's too late.

Scott Momaday: I have heard that too. And I am in no position to judge. I certainly want to believe that it isn't so. The thing that I wanted to stress was that I think one begins to change his style of life by changing his frame of mind, to begin with. And this is one way in which I think the Indian has set an example that the rest of the world can benefit from. The Indian has always lived on the best of terms with the natural world. Western man and Western European civilization have always been at odds with nature. We are reaping now the consequences of that tradition, if that's what it is. We have to change our attitude towards the land. We have to develop, I think, an ethic—a land ethic.

A Speaker: One of the main hang-ups that most of us have is the restriction that the English language places on the attempt of native authors to translate. To a certain extent, each individual author will have to make his own decisions on how to overcome this. But I wonder if you had this difficulty.

Scott Momaday: Well, I think the question you are asking is a very complicated one. If you mean that there are intrinsic difficulties in the English language, I am not sure whether I would agree. Or to put it another way, I am sure there are limitations, but I don't think we have begun to exhaust the possibilities. If you mean that a man who has grown up speaking a native language, the use of English as the language which he's using to write a book certainly presents grave problems. Not only do you have to change languages, but you have to change the mentality which brought each language into being. And that, of course, is a difficulty which depends upon the nature of the two languages . . . English on the one hand, and whatever the other language may be. That's a complicated question. There is no ready answer.

A Speaker: Scott, there has been, I think many of us know, a program instituted by Navajo where they have taped and gathered together all their old historians, and I think Carl was one who did a lot in taping much of this oral history. I believe that Mr. Cassadore, who is here, has also worked among the Papago, and some of the Sioux also, and other people. There has been some work done among our people, and we still have our ceremonies at certain times of the year, when the history of our people is still being told. Sometimes it takes all of it and parts of another language to tell the whole story of creation, and it's still available. It is being worked upon in many areas. We are not losing, as a matter of fact, we are reactivating it, which is good. Because in answer to the gentlemen here on the question of translation, we may lose some of our story in translation. But the main body of what we wish to express is still available.

A Speaker: In your book, *The Way to Rainy Mountain,* and in relation to the destroying of the insects, and pesticides and insecti-

cides, you wrote a very beautiful passage where you relate how the
moon appeared in the night and the insect came towards your vision.
Would you recall that to mind and talk a little bit about that?

Scott Momaday: That happened when I retraced the migration
route. My grandmother, who lived just outside of Mountainview,
Oklahoma, near Rainy Mountain, had just died. She had died in the
Spring, on my trip. And when I visited her grave at Rainy Mountain,
it was quite a touching experience for me. The first time I went back
to the house in which she lived, was at night. I remember sitting on
the porch outside the house, and it was a beautiful moon-lit night. The
moon was full. And it was casting that moonlight upon the whole
landscape. And I sat there full of mourning, and memory. I was sitting
on the steps of the porch and there was a handrail to my left, and I
happened to glance in that direction, and there was a cricket perched
up, as it happened, in my angle of vision. The cricket was perfectly
framed by the full moon. And I wrote about that in the introduction
to Rainy Mountain.

Harold Driver: I am from Indiana University, and I want to tell you
about certain archives we have there that may be of interest to some
of you. We have the largest archives of tradition, one of the largest in
the world, and the largest of music. It's accessible to any scholar, and
if you are looking for a safe place to store a copy of anything you
have, whether it's analyzed or not, we will take it.

Scott Momaday: To resume our discussion about oral tradition and
its relevancy to our time and place, I would repeat that I think there
is a certain urgency to our consideration of preserving American
Indian literature. I know for a fact that very few young Kiowas, to
name but one tribe, are learning to speak Kiowa. It is a language that
is dying very quickly. And it's very sad to contemplate that, because
so much will be lost in terms of human imagination, as it is brought to
bear upon a long history, and a very rich experience.

The only way that this experience has been reported is in terms of
an oral tradition. And when the language goes, a lot of the experience
itself will have been lost to us. I can't help thinking that the more time
we can spend in convincing young people, particularly, that they have
access to this material, and they had better make the most of that, the
better off we will be, not only as Indians, but as human beings. I
know that the oral literature of the Kiowas is very valuable in terms

of human wisdom, the passing on of enlightening wisdom, the benefit of experience to future generations. I am sure that what is true of the Kiowas, is true of other tribes as well. And so we stand to benefit a great deal by looking into the oral tradition, into the various literatures and preserving as much of that as we can.

There are ways in which to go about it. It costs very little in terms of resources. Any one of you can arm yourself with a tape recorder and a box of tapes and do an inestimable amount in preserving tradition. If the Indian is to be defined in terms of his tradition, then it becomes a matter of asserting one's self and preserving one's identity. And that, I think, particularly now in this technological society, is worth doing.

Charles Loloma: Since you brought up the question of convincing the youth of our people that it is necessary to preserve our oral traditions, and to learn their language, can you give us an idea of *how* to convince young people of this? I really think that we just have to do it, and immediately. Because youth is demanding to know just what are we talking about in oral literature. I really appreciate that a person like yourself is here to discuss this. Not because I am in the arts. Because you too are in the arts, if you please. There are many art forms that can say a lot. We need to find different ways of communicating. For instance, your words ring a lot of bells, and I can't help thinking, when you said that a person who tells a story is not much in white society. But he is to me, a dignified person in his own native society.

These things touched you inside. And also, you mention that if in a story you brought forth the sorrow, and if it is projected effectively, the storyteller can really make you see it. And if a story is told in laughter, then, of course, you can laugh. And other forces are used effectively. All this is done in a verbal sense, not written. Which to me is very related to life itself, and how I think and feel and react. It is a whole system of profound and effective communication. And, also, if the storyteller gets stuck at times and some part of his story is weak, in a long storytelling, and if he catches himself doing it (mind you, he's not a trained professional man in this society), he acts this one out. How marvelous that is! He is acting in such a way that he could make you see it and feel it and taste it. Behold, he now tones down his voice; now he makes a hollow sound; now he makes whatever sound that animals may perhaps make. And if you are an intelligent listener, you know he's using the art of pantomime.

I cannot help but recollect and compare with the Kiowa situation, also experiencing somebody whom I greatly appreciated meeting. And he is really good. He was portraying a mask scene, and that ties into our discussion of myths. I heard about this man, and saw him in his own home, his own theater. His name is Marcelle Marceaux. This was in Paris, France. Seeing him doing what he did, you say to yourself, ha ha, he's a perfect clown. Saying nothing, but using his hands to make you laugh, to make you cry, to make you mad. I thought this is a great indication that we Indians have done as well, and that this, our native art, is not dead.

Scott Momaday: No, it is not dead.

Charles Loloma: The clowns perform. In this case, it is not necessarily the mask, but this guy is doing it with his hands. When they perform, they portray everything as to what the people in reality might be. Having met this man, I realized this is *communication* that really could be colorful to a fellow. In the pantomime, I sometimes do it in the Kiva, because I was chosen to do it; it's something that we Hopi take pride in.

Many forces are alive today for us to use in our Indian way. We have not analyzed all parts of it, certainly. I am sure the youth could develop ideas and techniques in this part of the art area. I know that the force of words, communication, is enormous. I believe a young Indian could possibly with this rich heritage become so great, beyond other people in this art. Because the source is very rich. At least where I come from this is alive.

Scott Momaday: I think that's true. I think that it is alive in more places than we realize. The native traditions are very widespread, and they are vital. We think of them as being lost. And there is no doubt that a great part of that wealth has been lost, but so much remains that it really is an inconceivable kind of wealth. I sometimes think that everybody is required at some point in his life to manifest his spirit, to express his spirit as he understands it. And for the Indian, I think that's one thing, as opposed to what it is for other people. He does that by keeping alive his traditions, by returning to them, by continually expressing them over and over again. He works within the verbal dimension, but there are other ways, which you have touched upon, Charles. He does it by dancing, painting.

Charles Loloma: This is what I'm getting at.

Scott Momaday: And certainly, all of those expressions are valid, and I wouldn't put one above the other, so long as you know you express the spirit.

Charles Loloma: What you get back to then are the forces of communication that you could examine and use in such a way that you don't lose your tradition. Really you can't talk to anybody. How can you communicate? I maintain that we act all the time, because whether we like it or not, whether we know it or not, it is a matter of how well you express yourself.

Scott Momaday: The question you asked about young people, about how you convince the young people of the necessity or action at this point is a difficult one to answer. I think there are many aspects to that. In my experience, I would say that a great many young Indian people now as never before are becoming aware of their native tradition, and they're seeing it for what it is. They are recognizing the value of it. And I think it's fair to say that there is a growing kind of tribalism. A sense of tribalism that we have not had before. There are many implications in this. It would seem that there is a real chance for unification now.

Charles Loloma: Do you know of an immediate way of convincing young Indians to think in such a way that they would choose sort of immediately; because if they don't, we are going to have young kids crying. And they are already.

Scott Momaday: I think you have to tell them. I think that each of us who realizes that the native traditional values are important has a great obligation to convince the young of that, who may be wavering with alternatives. I think that a number of young people are coming to that realization on their own. They simply see what's going on around them, and they look at the world and look at the dominant society which is destroying the world in which it lives. I think it doesn't take a great deal of experience or intelligence to see that, as an alternative, it's a very bad one. Surely there is a better destiny available to man. I don't think they have to look much further than that to see that they have one at their fingertips, and it's the one in which they've grown up and have a blood interest. But beyond that, I think it's really up to the older people. Those on the reservations, and those who are not on the reservations. You know, there is, of course, an intrinsic and primary obligation on the part of the parents for their children. I think that this business of becoming aware of this, the danger of superficial existence in the modern world, is not lost upon the older people, even the elders on the reservation, who have had relatively very little experience with the outside world. I think they have a sense of the kind of dangers that exist out there in that smog-filled horizon. They have a primary obligation to tell their children and grandchildren about the traditional world, and try to show them by example and tell them explicitly that there is an option available to them, and that they're damn fools if they don't avail themselves of it.

For a long time, the Indian culture, the traditional values in the Indian world, have not been valued in the terms of the modern dominant society. We've always, I think, thought of acculturation as a kind of one-way process in which the Indian ceases to be an Indian and becomes a white man. That's been an objective, whether we want to admit it or not, in historical diplomacy. I think, for the first time, that it is not a one-way process at all. Acculturation means a two-way, a reciprocal kind of thing in which there is a realization of one world that is composed of both elements, or many for that matter. I think many young people are aware of this. I think certain others are completely lost, because there are so many alternatives on the horizon. But I think more and more we ought to educate the white man. We ought to reconstruct the institutions within the dominant society, so that the Indian values are available to the dominant society. This could be done in many ways.

I teach at the University of California on the Berkeley campus, and I am working now on the institution of a program in American Indian literature within the Department of Comparative Literature there. This has not been done before, as far as I know. It's the only program of its kind. The only one that has this kind of literary focus which is very, very tight, very narrow, if you will. To deal with literature, and the oral tradition and the way in which it works in the academic framework. The more that can be done in this way, the more we can include within the existing academic framework things that are peculiarly native, and unique, the more we are making the horizon of opportunity for young Indian people wider, and all others as well.

At the University of California, the academic world stands to gain in this venture, just as much as the Indian does. The contribution accrues to both sides, and that's exactly the way it should be. But I would like to see many more programs of this kind. Not only in literature, but in art, history, sociology, economics, philosophy, religion. There is room for all kinds of experiments in education. They ought to be made. I sat in a panel yesterday in which the whole business of Indian studies programs came under discussion. But, you know, we talked about what could an Indian studies program be, and I think there is no single answer. I think there are a great many alternatives. We have a terrific opportunity at this point. And I think the more directions we can take, the better off we are.

A Speaker: There seems to me to be a small contradiction here. It may be I do not understand. One of the problems is mainly between making traditional ways more available; as opposed to going to school with, say, white college kids. Education, for what? It is a big problem. If you have that problem, that's one thing. But then you just said a very interesting thing about the Indian's teaching the more dominant culture; and if they stay in Oklahoma, how are they really going to do that. I think that white kids now are really open to that.

A Speaker: Two days ago I said I wanted to hear about Indian philosophy. And someone pointed out to me that people have been explaining about Indian philosophy for a long time, for example, Red Jacket. But now, some people are actually listening among the whites. San Francisco is a good example of that; Berkeley, too, I would think. But I would be deeply saddened to think that you have to lose who you are to become educated, because I don't think that needs to be true at all.

A Speaker: I don't think you have to stop being who you are. Your talk today was very beautiful. I thought it really got to the question of becoming a man, becoming who you are by birthright. And I don't really think that when you leave a place you have been in all your life, that you have to 'become' the place you're going to. If you can recognize that there are certain bad elements say in Princeton or Columbia or Radcliffe, that doesn't mean you have to "become" that bad element. As a matter of fact, you must be strong enough not to do that. Actually, you have the advantage over people. I would be insulted to think that getting a college education now means that a person simply takes what is offered, without giving what is *in* him. I think it would be an advantage to go to school, but you have to know who you are before you leave for school. I don't know about art. But you see the kind of contradiction I am worried about. How are you going to get this learning without giving up who you really are?

Scott Momaday: Well, I think that it is good to go into the enemies' camp. I think that's part of the educational process.

A Speaker: It is an educational process?

Scott Momaday: Yes, I don't think this is necessarily a contradiction. The Indian, in order to discover who he is, must do that on a comparative basis. It does him no good to know who he is, so long as that knowledge isolates him . . . alienates and shuts him off from the possibilities that are available to him in the world. No. He must take advantage of the possibilities, recognizing the opportunities and taking advantage of them, retain his identity. We don't want to "freeze" the Indian in time, to cut him off at a certain point in his development. We don't want to end up with a 19th century man in the 20th century. He doesn't want that, and neither do any of us. It's just simply not among the available and desirable possibilities. He has to venture out, I think, beyond his traditional world, because there is another very real world. And there are more worlds coming, in rapid succession. But it is possible for him to make that adventure without sacrificing his being and identity.

A very good point was made about the fact that the world at large is ready to listen to what the Indian has to say. It is ready to appreciate the traditions and the values, as it has never been before. Berkeley is a prime example of that. I have students in my classes who would give their left arm to be Indians. To be an Indian on the Berkeley campus now, is to be *somebody*. Everybody listens to you. They are curious about you, and they look at you with a great deal of respect. That's not necessarily good, in the long run, but it is an opportunity of which the Indian should avail himself. And I think that's not limited to Berkeley. Alcatraz is good as an example. I had very little hope for it at first. I was very skeptical about it, because I thought it was going to be terminated very quickly, and that the Indian would be left holding the bag, and simply the scapegoat in that whole venture. It turned into something rather more serious than that, and there is no way at this point to realize just what it's going to be. But *symbolically,* it's very important at this moment, and the kind of sympathy for the Indian that has been generated in the Bay Area is really quite remarkable and quite impressive. It's a sign of the times.

Mr. Lyons: I am a member of one of the Six Nations Confederacy. The question that arose here about how do you teach your children is very real to us. We are very traditional people. And yet, at the same time, we have managed to coexist. We go out and we come back. The thing that we have had to be very careful of was the dominance of this larger society which has a great deal of pressure and power so that it can bring to bear the way of the dollar bill and its values: Material values as opposed to what you said earlier this morning about the value of your land; your heritage is in the land. It's always the land.

We base our whole Confederacy, our whole religion around this. And how we teach is by example: You set an example and they will learn. You can't tell somebody what to do. If you don't do it yourself, they are not going to listen to you. So you teach by example.

A Speaker: And they believe in it?

Mr. Lyons: They believe in it. How many times do you do it a day? After awhile they don't think. They do it along with you. And you bring *this* up, and you bring *this* through. Simple things really. For example, you just don't interrupt other people. Yet we do operate in the outside world very well. I myself have been working in New York for ten years, and yet, I am a Chief of the Confederacy. I believe in it whole-heartedly, and I find that all the things that I have learned are nothing but fictions. I know we are right. Now, the people are turning back, as you might say, and looking for somebody to tell them what to do. Show us the way, they say. They don't know particularly if it is going to be an Indian. It could be anybody. But it so happens that we *do* have the way, and we should show them. It's for the benefit of mankind. There are two hundred million people here and we are very small in comparison. Yet, we have maintained our identity up to this point. And it's really because our basis is the land. I mean, if the economic values of this United States should disappear, how many people are going to disappear with it? What else do they have? That's why they are searching for something stronger and more lasting. We have it. You have the land under your feet. And it's your duty to subsist on this land. If something is going to happen, and you can raise your own food, then you are not going to have to worry about

that supermarket down on the corner with the empty shelves. And
then the dollar bill does not rank supreme. I am very happy to hear
the way you spoke this morning.

Scott Momaday: I think you have the responsibility not only to
teach your children, but to reach the rest of us who have not had the
same experience. You know you have been able to retain your
traditional values in the most urbanized society of all in this country.
And that the knowledge of how to do that and the conviction that can
be developed is worth a great deal, because most Indian people in this
country don't face the conflict in the same way that obviously you
have. To realize that you can maintain your own identity in New York
City—it ought to be terribly revealing to the rest of us, and we ought
to be informed about how you do it. I wonder if you would tell the
story that you told me earlier.

Mr. Lyons: I will go to the story Dr. Momaday asked me to tell.
About the question of "who are you?" What is an Indian? I went
fishing with my uncle, he's an old chief from home, and we are out
there in a boat in the middle of the lake and talking about this and
that. I had just graduated from college at that point, you know. And I
was kind of feeling my oats a little bit. And we were talking and he
said, "My, you are pretty smart, you know. You learned a lot of
things." I said, "Yeah." I was surprised. And he said, "Good. Then
you ought to know who you are then." "Sure," I said. "I am Farland
Lyons." He said, "Yeah. That's who you are, I guess. Is that all?"
So I started to suspect right away something is going on here. Here I
am in a boat, and I can't get out. And we were out in the middle of
the water. He said, "That's your name alright. We know that. Is that
all you are?"

Well, then I started thinking. I started to feel a little track already,
and I went to my father's line, my mother's line, my clan. I searched,
and he chased me all over that boat for two hours. He wouldn't let me
out. I was ready to swim. I was getting mad. Then I said, "Well, who
the hell am I then?" And he said, "Well, I think you know, but I will
tell you. If you sit here, and look out right over there; look at that.
The rocks: the way they are. The trees and the hills all around you.
Right where you're on, it's water." And he said, "You're just like
that rock." And I listened. He said, "You're the same as the water,
this water." I waited and listened again, as he said, "You are the

ridge, that ridge. You were here in the beginning. You're as strong as
they are. As long as you believe in that," he said, "that's who you
are. That's your mother, and that's you. Don't forget." I never have.

Charles Loloma: Not long ago, the power people from the electric
company were coming in on our land and they put the poles in by
force. Somehow something happened, and the people came out and
pulled the poles all back out. These people don't want the electricity.
I mean, it's not really clear why a lot of people who are termed
progressives want electricity and stuff. I think what the older people
are pointing out is they would—if they could afford it—welcome
electricity. Their point is, if they want it, they will buy it. And it
comes from you yourself and you will respect it.

Mr. North: University of Arizona. It's precisely because of this
split among adults that we are not learning our oral history, and it's
their responsibility. I have uncles who will not teach me our history.
And they are the conservatives. I would like to learn from them. Our
own people will go out of the community rather than communicate
with me about our oral history; they will go out and tell the white man
about our history. But they won't tell me.

Scott Momaday: Why do you suppose that's true? And I think
you're right. That's been my experience too. I know of cases like
that. I wonder if you have any idea of why they shut up at a certain
point like that, why they won't talk to you.

Mr. North: Well, this is because of factionalism. I don't want to go
into heavy history, but it's precisely the fact that we are living in
close communities; families are close, but as a unit it works in reverse.
As a result, we the young aren't learning our history. There are so
many factors that enter into this. This is a proposal that I would like
to make—talking about Indian Studies Programs yesterday. Why
couldn't we have something like an Indian Studies program within our
reservations, and particularly, in the communities where we have the
opportunity to do so? We have a Navajo girl, who is at the University
of Arizona. She's an anthropologist, and she's tired of reading books
in anthropology, and what they have to say about the Navajo. I mean,
I am an anthropologist, myself. Why couldn't we go out and collect
our history ourselves and tell it from our viewpoint? This is her point,
too. She's hiring youth, and she will have these kids go out to the
hogans and interview older people. They are transcribing the tapes.

This is really a great idea, because we have the need to teach oral history to our own youth.

A Speaker: You see, I work in a museum, and they said to me, you catalog this. It's a Hopi dress. I said yeah, okay, I can. This is my first reaction: They say, it's named such and such, and this is the description. But they are also telling me how it's made, and it is not wholly correct. And, of course, I disagree. I look at the old catalog system, and see how they describe it. I use the same terms. Then, I think, well, that's not right. I am going home, and ask someone what this was for. Then it begins to make a lot of sense. With a project like the Hopi history, you have also to consider ceremonies and a cultural center. At this center, I would like to see something done like this. Have an anthropologist ask for research, and try development, hire Indian youth in the summers to do a project in language. I am interested in language and collect oral history. There are a lot of other possibilities, and there are kids in geology, biology and anthropology, now. This would be done by the Hopi people themselves.

Scott Momaday: There is no reason this can't be done. I mean, there ought to be, I think, from people like you, a lot of agitation for that. It certainly is desirable. In a cultural sense, it's absolutely necessary. I would love to see that done by the Hopi, and every-where else.

A Speaker: But we are fighting among ourselves. Whether electricity is going to come into our communities or not. You say something like that is desirable? Something like this? It would probably threaten the community more than electricity does. So, you mean—

Scott Momaday: You mean with devious methods?

A Speaker: Right.

Scott Momaday: I suppose there is that risk. And I think maybe that risk is always going to have to be run. But I think it's time to run those risks. The alternative is that we are going to lose a lot of that tradition, and we cannot afford the loss of it. I am just talking off the top of my head, now. Some of you have a much better sense of this, as regards your own communities, but I think it may be worth it. If you are going to run the risk of alienating a certain section within the community, that's just the way it has to be. We're thinking of some-thing in longer terms of time, and of greater importance, as far as posterity is concerned. Some of you may have different ideas.

Ben Barney: We have been talking about convincing students or
young Indian people, just as well as younger people across the
country. I am Navajo, and my training is sort of different from other
Navajos. My background is that up to about the age of eight I had a
teacher who taught me Navajo tradition, and it ended because he
died. It was my grandfather, and ever since then, I have been going
around at a loss. He sent me out to a school, because that was the
only possible way I could go. So I have been going around all over,
trying to find Indians, older people especially, who can take a position
that he had, and it's really hard for youth to be able to figure this out,
to be able to find people. I don't mean to throw this whole thing back
on the older people, but in a way, I guess I am doing that. I think, you
know, this is the first time the whole picture could be seen. We come
out here to this Convocation and hear not only from Navajo, but from
other tribes too.

A Speaker: We say that it's hard to find old people who will talk to
you, and it's also hard to get them to give you the oral literature or
old tradition. Well, my grandfather died, and he was one of the last
men in the village who knew the whole ritual cycle of songs. He died
without letting me or my father, or any of us record any of it. I think
he felt that this thing that he had was too precious to just give out,
and have it exposed to someone whom he never knew well. And he'd
rather die with it than have that happen to it. It seems to me that he
was saying, you're not going to live it. You're one of these people
that's fighting for the electricity. (I am not, in fact.) But he was saying,
you're one of these people who are fighting for this. My people never
had electricity. We never lived that way. And if I give you my lifeway,
if I tell you my lifeway, you're going to sit and laugh at me, because
you're laughing anyhow just by your behavior. Naturally, they are
not going to tell you. I mean, they can't. I can see why he felt there is
no way to communicate experience; the essence of it, the reality of it.
I believe he was saying: I could give you words, and you could put
them down, but that wouldn't mean the same thing. It's an entirely
different thing.

Scott Momaday: I think there is no doubt that we had some very
valuable contributions to this discussion, and I am very pleased that
some of you have shed some very important light upon the business

of oral tradition, and other kinds of tradition that are beyond any question worth our very careful scrutiny and preservation.

[The discussion ends here with a description of a program at Navajo Community College in Chinle, Arizona.]

An Interview with N. Scott Momaday

Lee Abbott / 1972

From *Puerto Del Sol*, 12, no. 2 (1973), 21–38. Reprinted by permission of *Puerto Del Sol* magazine.

N. Scott Momaday was born in 1934, the son of Indian artist Al Momaday and writer Natachee Scott. He grew up on Indian reservations of the Southwest, including the Navajo, the Apache (San Carlos and Jicarilla), and the Pueblo (Jemez). Among other publications, he is the author of the 1969 Pulitzer Prize winning novel *House Made of Dawn,* and *The Way to Rainy Mountain.* Presently, he is New Mexico State University's first Visiting Distinguished Professor of Humanities.

Interviews are awkward experiences. However well-intentioned they begin, they invariably result in distortion. What began as synthesis ends as fragmentation. The questions tend to exaggerate, they become self-important. An interview becomes, as Momaday noted in a lighter moment, "Heap Big Medicine, to put it in indigenous terms." And yet, it is this medicine-like quality which makes an interview so important, ultimately. It seems, somehow, like Tai-Me itself.

"Tai-Me is the Sun Dance fetish of the Kiowas," Momaday explains. "It's a fetish which is medicine. And it was the most powerful medicine in the tribe. The only time it was exhibited to view was during the Sun Dance."

Unfortunately, for the Kiowas, the Sun Dance was prohibited as an act of barbarism in 1887 by the U.S. government because in most of the Sun Dance ceremonies, there was some display of self-torture. "Ironically," Momaday points out, "the Kiowas didn't practice that aspect of the Sun Dance. Their Sun Dance didn't involve the piercing of flesh."

At the time of the last Sun Dance, there was an official Tai-Me keeper, "a very important man in the tribe," whose responsibility it was to care for the Tai-Me bundle. He was the only one who had the right to open the bundle.

"In 1963," Momaday relates, "when I was visiting my grandmother, I had known about Tai-Me, but I had no idea that it still existed. And so I was talking to her one day and the business of Tai-Me came up. I said something to her about it and she said, 'Oh, Yes. So-and-so has it.' And I thought, 'My God, that's fantastic. It's really still around.' And I said, 'Do you suppose I could see it,' and she said 'Well, I don't see why not, if you go to this person and ask.' So I did. I went with my father, and the Tai-Me bundle was in the possession of a Kiowa woman in Oklahoma. She was the daughter of the last official Tai-Me Keeper."

As only the daughter, however, the woman had no authority to open the bundle.

"Anyway, I told her that I was very much interested in seeing the bundle, and so she let me see it. She was very formal about it. There was a certain way to do it. You have to make an offering and I didn't know anything about it. I said, 'Well, you tell me what to do,' and she said, 'A customary offering is a piece of yardage, some material, the kind of material the Kiowa women make dresses from.' So I went down to a department store, and I bought several yards of material, and I brought it back."

After a kind of story-telling session, during which the woman told Momaday and his father about the Tai-Me, its significance and history, she led them into a room in which there was a closet-like recess without a door.

"There was a tree about four feet high and from the tree there hung the Tai-Me bundle. It was a strange feeling, one of the most intensely religious experiences I've ever had, because I really felt I was in the presence of something sacred."

Momaday draped the material over the bundle and stepped back. "My grandmother, who was behind me, and my father prayed to the bundle for a long time in Kiowa."

But Tai-Me is not merely a symbol. "It is something in which power is inherent. Tai-Me is the source of power. If you told a Kiowa to open the Tai-Me bundle, that would be the height of sacrilege for him. He would be afraid to open it."

Another source of power for Momaday is the land, "the repository of heritage." As he says, "the more you depart from a given landscape, the greater the risk you run in losing your heritage. I am

fortunate in this respect: I have a heritage I can look back to, and it
has substantial character to it, and I can identify things about it. Most
Americans, at this point in time, can't do that, and I think they're
beginning to feel the need to do it, now more than ever." In fact, for
his book *The Journey of Tai-Me* (originally a hand-printed limited-
edition collection of Kiowa legends and tales which later became,
with the addition of his commentaries, *The Way to Rainy Mountain*),
Momaday retraced the migration route of the Kiowas from Yellowstone to Oklahoma—"looking at the landscape first hand, travelling
over it, taking pictures of it, interviewing people, thinking about it."

Besides the land, of course, there is his family. "My parents are
very special people. And though that's not really an event in my life,
I somehow always think of that as being very important in my wanting
to write and having written. My mother is a writer, and my father is
an artist, a painter."

Still another source of power for Momaday is the Jemez Pueblo in
northern New Mexico. "I lived at Jemez for five or six years before I
had to go away to school. I had never seen a landscape like that, and
I'd never had an opportunity to get into a landscape of that kind." As
a Kiowa, however, he was not eligible to participate in the ceremonial
life of the Jemez. Yet he became very close to that society. "I went
there for Feast Day, this November 12th, a few days ago and it was
like going home. I was embracing people and crying. I really feel
deeply about Jemez. I went out and planted the cacique's fields."

Yet, it is Momaday the writer who speaks in this interview, and it
is doubtless unavoidable that some of what follows is in a certain
sense incomplete. Still, as Momaday says when speaking about witchcraft, "It's natural, but it's part of the unexplained, and therefore not
logical. It is, it exists, everybody knows it exists, everybody has a
deep conviction that it exists. It is an expectation, and it is an
expectation that is not disappointed among Indian peoples."

Puerto: When did you start writing?

Momaday: I first started writing seriously when I was an undergraduate in college at the University of New Mexico.

Puerto: Did you always conceive of yourself as a writer?

Momaday: Yes. Well, no. There were times when I wanted to be

things other than a writer. When I first started college, for example, I
thought I wanted to be a lawyer. And as a matter of fact, I went to
law school for a year, well before I had graduated, and decided that I
didn't like law. And so I came back to college, really without knowing
what I wanted to do. It was about that time that I really got seriously
interested in writing. I started writing poetry.

Puerto: How did you decide your direction?

Momaday: I really didn't have any direction. When I had decided
that I had prepared for a certain amount of time going to law school,
and then decided that I didn't want to be a lawyer, I didn't know what
to do, so I went back to college just with the idea of graduating, and I
wrote some at that time—entered some writing contests—and it just
happened after that. I wasn't working to be a writer then, but I
was writing.

Puerto: Do you remember your first publication?

Momaday: Yes. I published a poem in the *New Mexico Quarterly*
in 1959.

Puerto: If you started as a poet, how then do you account for your
success in the prose realm?

Momaday: After writing poetry for several years, I went to Stanford
as a creative writing fellow in poetry, and I wrote poetry all the time
I was there. About the time I got out of Stanford, I just decided that I
wanted to work in something other than poetry for a while. I needed
a little more freedom of expression, a little more elbow room than
poetry was giving me, so I started writing prose.

Puerto: How do you mean "giving you more elbow room" when
making the transition from poetry to prose?

Momaday: Well, I didn't have any idea what poetry was. I was
writing something that I thought was poetry, but I didn't have any
basic understanding of English verse, and so I spent virtually all of
my time studying traditional forms, and becoming more and more
narrow in my expression, which I think is something that happens to
you when you write poetry. You train yourself very narrowly to focus
upon precise things and to make as precise a statement as you can.
That's what poetry is about. Yet I got tired of that. I found myself
getting restless after a while. I didn't like the idea of becoming

narrower and narrower in my expression. That's basically when I started to write prose, fiction.

Puerto: Did you find the "narrowness" just because you were working with the traditional form, or with poetry in general?

Momaday: Both things. Largely because I was working with traditional poems and trying very hard to limit myself to standard patterns. But even if I had been writing a freer kind of verse, if I hadn't been as much concerned with traditional forms as I was at that time, I still would have gone into prose, simply because it represents a different kind of intellectual exercise which I felt the need for. Maybe, in time, I'll feel the same way about prose, in which case I'll probably move back to poetry.

Puerto: You said that when you were at Stanford, you spent time relearning traditional forms and that is where one should start in writing poetry. Do you feel that this is for everyone, or something for yourself, and do you feel that you will grow from this?

Momaday: I think it's pretty much true for everybody. It is very necessary. I don't think you can ignore the traditions in poetry and expect to write good poetry. But once you've learned what there is to know about traditional forms, then I think you are, in a sense, free to depart from those forms. But I don't think you have any business expecting to depart from them without knowing what they are. Because if nothing else, the forms provide you with something to depart from, with a tradition, with a norm of some kind. I think a lot of people are writing poetry today, without really knowing what poetry is. Some of them are successful at it, in some ways, but in the long run, they're selling themselves short.

Puerto: Is it important whether you consider yourself one or the other—a prose writer or a poet?

Momaday: No, I don't think it's especially important to me to think of myself in one of those categories, as opposed to others. I don't feel that I'm one thing or the other now. I hope to keep writing both prose and poetry. I'd like to write a play sometime.

Puerto: Are you working on anything now?

Momaday: Yes, an autobiographical narrative. I've been working on it for a long time, off and on, and I'd like to get it out of the way, so I think that I'm about to make one great effort that will take me through it. I've got about five chapters in a book, which I think will run to about eight chapters.

Puerto: Where does it begin?

Momaday: With my birth. It's not in any sense complete, though. I'm not in any way trying to make a full account. I'm just writing about things that I have experienced and people I've known. As I see it now, it's going to end in time in about 1965.

Puerto: Do you have a particular process when it comes to writing? For instance, do you have to have yellow paper or white paper, or that kind of thing?

Momaday: I don't feel superstitious about those things, but I write in two ways. I write at the typewriter, which I do most of the time. And I can also scribble things out in longhand. When I work at the typewriter, I always have a scratchpad with me, and I do a lot of feeling out with a pencil, but I can compose pretty well on a type-writer.

Puerto: Could you give us an example of a typical Momaday story—how it begins? The pattern it follows from idea to execution?

Momaday: My subjects come from ideas in my mind. I'm not sure where they originate. I don't, as many writers do, take notes, carry a pad around with me and jot down things which might later become germs for a story. Sometimes I should. It's a good idea in principle, but it's not the way I have ever worked. I think in terms of writing. I'm always thinking about what it is that I am writing or going to write. And I spend a lot of time working things out in my mind. For example, when I go to bed at night, I'll turn off the lights and close my eyes and will immediately start thinking what I might write, and sometimes I'll work out fairly elaborate scenes in my mind. I keep a journal, but as far as I know, it hasn't been especially useful to me in providing material for writing. I hope it will someday, which is more than anything else, why I keep a journal. But I haven't found myself using it in that way.

Puerto: What kind of work habits do you have?

Momaday: Lousy.

Puerto: No schedule?

Momaday: No, I did have, at one time in my life, a terrific schedule. But I seem to have lost the knack for that. I had a ritual: I'd get up at five, shave and dress, and I would go out to a restaurant, and would have coffee and maybe something to eat, and I would read the paper. By that time, I had built myself up to a state where I was just dying to work. I would go home, and at about seven o'clock, I would get to work and would work non-stop until one or two. That was a great schedule. I was very productive when I was doing that. And felt very good about it. But now I write in the mornings, but I don't write nearly as rigidly.

Puerto: You don't have a quota, then. Two pages a day, perhaps?
Momaday: No.

Puerto: Do you think a schedule is a valuable tool?
Momaday: Yes, a certain amount of routine is necessary to writing. When I sit down now, it's very rarely at seven o'clock in the morning. I can't get going at that hour at this point in my life. But when I sit down to write, I maintain a kind of routine, I won't let myself get out of it. I stay at the typewriter, and more often than not, I will write somewhere between three and five pages of typescript before I consider that I have any right to get up or do anything else.

Puerto: Do you rewrite a lot?
Momaday: Yes. In fact, that's a problem with me. I do so much of the really important work in the rewriting that it's very hard for me to get very far with the first draft. Right now, in this book that I'm working on, I said that I was about five chapters through it. The first of those chapters I spent a great deal of time on; I rewrote it several times. It's highly polished now. But I decided, having spent so much time on the first chapter, that what I should do is simply write my way through the book, in a draft, and then go back, which I'm trying to do, so that the next four chapters are extremely rough. I find it frustrating sometimes to go from chapter four to chapter five, because my inclination is to go back and polish, but I'm trying to convince myself that it will be better in the long run if I get all of the material down, so that I don't have to worry about completing the draft, and then go back and polish.

Puerto: Is rewriting for you a matter of simply changing words and sentences, or is it wholesale cutting and reshaping of parts, and a retelling of the narrative?

Momaday: It works both ways. If I write a page, and I see that it isn't going to work, I will do away with it right on the spot. But if I keep it, the chances are pretty good that it's going to show up in the final product, though it will be reworked considerably. When I rewrite, I delete very little. Because that's all been done in the first process, but I rework a great deal, and I almost inevitably add a great deal when I rewrite.

Puerto: Do you find it easy to add?

Momaday: I find it easy to add at that point because I have the raw material and then I'm constantly thinking as I'm going over it of things that can work in addition to it, things that I can add to it. So the revision, in a general way, is reworking what I have and adding to it, rather than deleting things.

Puerto: Did you find *House Made of Dawn* easy to write?

Momaday: No. I find writing of any kind very difficult. It was difficult to do, but I enjoyed it immensely. I got a great satisfaction out of writing that book.

Puerto: Capote says that scarcely anybody he knows "enjoys" writing; they'd rather be doing something else.

Momaday: That's certainly not true in my case. When I'm writing, and I have the sense of writing well, I can't think of a more satisfying thing. I have the sense that I'm doing exactly what I ought to be doing, and that's a great feeling. It's hard, it's difficult work, but I'd rather be doing that than anything else I can think of.

Puerto: You consider it work, then?

Momaday: Oh, it's drudgery. It's backbreaking work, but there is, against that, the satisfaction of it. Maybe someone else would say, "because it's so satisfying you don't think of it as work," but I do. Nonetheless, it's terribly satisfying.

Puerto: Do you believe in inspiration?

Momaday: Oh, yes. Writing is the logical product of inspiration. And a person who is writing without being inspired is really working without satisfaction. Inspiration is essential to writing. The best inspiration I know of is to pick up something, to look at it, and admire it and say, "God, I wish I'd written that."

Puerto: As a consequence of that idea, have you ever felt yourself in competition in terms of your writing, either with your contemporaries, or with writers of the past?

Momaday: Yes.

Puerto: Has it been healthy?

Momaday: Oh, it's been extremely healthy. When I first began to write, I was competing with other people, who were writers, all aspiring to write. When I went to Stanford, the way that poetry was taught was based upon a type of competition. The "Writing of Poetry" class was limited to about four or five people and we all submitted things and we all talked about them and that makes for a pretty competitive atmosphere. And I think I benefitted from it.

Puerto: Do you still conceive of competition in terms of writing—now that you're established as a writer?

Momaday: Not as much as I did at one time. I find myself now, when I write, not in competition with people, but with things.

Puerto: Such as?

Momaday: Well, when I write now, I usually write with a book in mind that I admire very much. In a sense, I am competing with what I'm holding up as a model.

Puerto: Do you have any favorite authors?

Momaday: Again, not authors, so much as books. There are things that I admire in English literature very much, and they cover a wide range of things. They don't represent writers so much as writings. I admire James Joyce, in certain things that he's written. I think his story "The Dead" is one of the great stories of the language. I admire the writings of Isak Dinesen, particularly a book entitled *Out of Africa*. I think more of that book than I do of anything else in recent English literature. I read it over and over.

Puerto: Are you aware of any recognizable influences on your own style?

Momaday: No. I'm sure there are some, but I'm not aware of them as such. I can tell you writers that I read and admire, and I'm sure that I have been influenced by them. I like Faulkner, and I've read a lot of Faulkner, and I've wanted to write like Faulkner; I take a passage from Faulkner, and I say, "Gee, I'd like to write that sort of thing," and I'm sure that I have tried to, but to what extent Faulkner is an influence on me, I really don't know. I have no idea. There are things in Hemingway that I admire, not nearly as many as there are in Faulkner, but I would certainly be willing to believe that Hemingway might be an influence on me, and any number of other writers. But as to choosing one as against others, I really don't know.

Puerto: How would you characterize your writing?

Momaday: Well, I hope that my writing can't be pinned down. I think that my writing is characterized by a number of things which reflect my temperament and my interests. I like to write descriptions, and a lot of my writing is descriptive in kind. I'm also a kind of amateur naturalist, and I deal with nature in my writing—landscapes, creatures, wild creatures, things of the kind. If I had to pick one word to characterize my prose, it would be "descriptive." But that's not the whole story by any means.

Puerto: Do you think the whole question of style is important? Do you think a writer should develop his own unique expression?

Momaday: Style is terribly important in writing. I'm not sure I could define style, but what is remarkable or extraordinary about prose is a kind of individual expression that I guess would be called style. I'm not sure that one needs necessarily to formulate a unique style, but a style of some kind is important to every writer. A person can emulate Hemingway, can write in the style of Hemingway, and succeed perfectly well as a writer. I don't think you need to be unique in that respect. It's a good thing to be unique, but I'm saying that I don't know that it's absolutely necessary. If I were starting out to be a writer, I don't think that that would be one of my chief objectives, to formulate a unique style.

Puerto: Should a writer have a mission? Should he write for something or against something, or just write, period?

Momaday: I've never thought about it in those terms. Yet if I were pressed on the point, I'd say "yes, a writer has to have a mission," though I'm not sure I'd call it that. He has to have an objective. He has to be writing for a purpose. In my case, I never did think of myself as writing for the purposes of reform, or I was never addressing myself to a particular group of people, and I was never writing against any specific thing. My objective in writing is simply to write what it is in me to write, and I realize that's about as vague as you can get. For me it works. I've talked to some people about this, who are writers and painters, and I feel the way a friend of mine feels about it, who is a painter. He has been lauded and criticized and identified with particular movements, and he said, "I just don't give a damn what anybody thinks I'm doing, so long as I'm satisfying my own needs. I paint because I want to paint, and I paint particular things because I want to paint those things, and if I never sold a painting, that would be somehow beside the point, because I would nonetheless be doing what I wanted to do. And I think that's really all that matters in the business of painting." I feel pretty much the same way about writing.

Puerto: Do you consider yourself as an Indian writer, or do you think those labels apply, in the sense that we have black writers, Chicano writers?

Momaday: No, I don't think of myself as an Indian writer, and I'm not sure why I don't, because what I've written to date, with the exception of some poems, has been very much an evocation of the Indian world. The book that I'm writing now is less so. It will turn out to be less an evocation of the Indian world than something else, and I'm not sure I know what it will be. But no, I don't think of myself in that line.

Puerto: What do you think of the critics?

Momaday: I've been treated very well by the critics. I don't have any great prejudices against them. There are an awful lot of silly critics around.

Puerto: Can the critics in their function be helpful?

Momaday: Yes, they can be. They should be, but very few of them are. When I think back over the things that have been written about my writing, by reviewers and critics—most of it is very imperceptive—I have the impression that a lot of that stuff is written by people who never bother to read the books. On the other hand, I've been

fortunate in being reviewed by a few people who really were perceptive and I learned something from their reviews. They gave me
insights into my own writing that were valuable to me. That's what
should happen in criticism.

When a man is writing, he is operating on two levels: he writes out
of his consciousness and out of his subconscious. And very many
times he will not, after the fact, know all about his writing. Sometimes, a reader who is very perceptive, can indicate to the writer that
he was doing things that he was not aware he was doing. It's not that
he was doing them accidentally, but he was doing them without being
conscious of doing them. It's a strange feeling. I'm sure that happens
all the time.

Puerto: For example?

Momaday: I don't think I could give you a precise example, but in
connection with *House Made of Dawn,* I have read things that people
have written about it and they've been, in some cases, very perceptive
things, and I find myself saying, "Yeah, I'll be darned. He's right
about that. That's what I was doing." It came as a kind of revelation
to me, until, thinking about it long enough, I realized that that's what
was really going on in my mind, but it wasn't at the conscious level
when I was doing it. It just came out of me, and it had to have a
source within me, and this man has identified something about the
source.

Puerto: Do you write short stories?

Momaday: No. But I think they're among the most interesting and
intricate and valuable things in literature.

Puerto: As Faulkner says, second to the poem it's the toughest?

Momaday: I would be willing to believe that. I don't have enough
experience with the short story to know really how tough it is, but
I'm sure it's a hard thing to write. For one thing, just the length of a
short story, and the way in which you have to bring things off within
limits, makes it seem to me a difficult form. I've only written a couple
of stories in my life.

Puerto: How important do you consider technique in writing? To
me, this seems separate from style.

Momaday: Well, explain the difference.

Puerto: I'm talking about the way of the telling, in the sense of the design, the purpose, the overall structure and form, the overriding idea of the way this story *must* be told.

Momaday: Technique is crucial. I find it almost impossible to write without an idea of the shape of the finished thing. And I'm very conscious of such things as symmetry in writing and balance. I try very hard to incorporate design in my writing.

Puerto: How do you see that design in *House Made of Dawn?*

Momaday: Oh, *House Made of Dawn* is very symmetrical. I see it as a circle. It ends where it begins and it's informed with a kind of thread that runs through it and holds everything together. The book itself is a race. It focuses upon the race, that's the thing that does hold it all together. But it's constantly a repetition of things, too. At the beginning, you have Abel in his relationship with Angela, and that is picked up again in the relationship with Milly. I see it as a kind of circle, which finally closes upon itself. Abel, at the end of the book for example, goes back and becomes in effect a kind of reflection of Francisco. Counterparts of that kind run all the way through it.

Puerto: Do you feel a camaraderie with any modern writers?

Momaday: In the business of writing, I'm pretty much on my own. I don't keep up with what other people are writing. I know some other writers, but I don't make it a point to keep up with what they're writing. I don't exchange writings with other people.

Puerto: Do you have any words about the contemporary scene? Any way you'd like to characterize it.

Momaday: I really don't know what's going on at the present time in the novel, say.

Puerto: How about the whole idea of the death of the novel? Do you think that's true?

Momaday: The novel is a long way from dying. I think it's changing. Our ideas of the novel are changing, and that's probably a good thing. The novel has become more flexible as a form in recent years. It's hard to say now just what the expectation of the novel is. The form, right now, is in a state of flux. We're not sure what it is. And you get all kinds of things now that are called novels, which simply would not have been thought of as novels fifty years ago.

Puerto: Would you say that something like *Catch-22* would fall into that category?

Momaday: Yes, that may be an example of what I have in mind. But I'm not familiar enough with *Catch-22* really to talk about it in those terms. I was trying to think of a fairly recent novel that was thought of as such, but . . .

Puerto: Is there a consideration of length? James had pretty strict notions as to what he thought of as a novel, as opposed to a novella, as opposed to a short story.

Momaday: I don't have any strong feelings about that one way or the other. I have read in E. M. Forster, that a novel is, I think, at least 50,000 words in length and I've always just assumed that as my own idea of the length of a novel.

Puerto: What would characterize a novel for you?

Momaday: A novel should tell a story of some length; it should involve characters to whom something happens in the course of the action, and who are themselves affected in one way or another by the action, and who change in some way, or who react in some essential way, some way in which the meaning of their lives is significantly influenced.

Puerto: I suspect that the emphasis for you is on character, *life,* as opposed to action.

Momaday: Yes. The crucial action in *House Made of Dawn* is subjective, and that basically what happens to Abel in an interior way is the real action of the book.

Puerto: How much of the book is autobiographical?

Momaday: Well, that's a question that I never really know how to answer, because all writing is autobiographical in certain ways, and certainly *House Made of Dawn* is autobiographical in the sense that all comes out of my own experience. When I was writing Tosamah's sermon, for example, I was in effect writing about my grandmother. But as far as Abel is concerned, I knew people of whom Abel is a composite. Abel is based upon real people and people that I knew. Angela is pretty much a figment of my imagination, though I would have liked to know somebody like Angela. So is Milly, for that matter, a figment of my imagination.

Puerto: I was thinking in terms of the war scene. Were you in the service?

Momaday: No, no, all the business about the war in *House Made of Dawn* is purely imaginary.

Puerto: Has your writing improved?

Momaday: I would like to think that it is improving. I don't know. It ought to improve. But I just don't know. When I get this next book, the book I'm working on now, out and can see it as a whole thing, I'll have a much better idea of whether or not it is an improvement over the former writings.

Puerto: What kind of a measure do you set for yourself? What kind of goal in terms of your writing?

Momaday: I have to be convinced that it does what I want it to do. I'm not trying to be evasive here. It's just that your raising the question puts me on the spot, because I'm not sure I've thought about the criteria. But when I have looked at my writing and been pleased with it, it has been because I have realized what it was I wanted to do. I accomplished what I set out to accomplish. And that involves a great many things. I'm interested in description and when I describe something in writing I always ask myself if I have described what it is I set out to describe; of course, you can write beautiful description which is inaccurate but still beautiful. But my idea of writing good description is writing something accurately. So this is one of the criteria. And there must be any number of other questions that I ask myself, but at a subconscious level.

Puerto: Do you conceive of an indispensable ingredient in a work? Is there an element without which it absolutely will not succeed?

Momaday: Well, to answer that offhand, I would say honesty. You have to be true to yourself as a writer. You can't write something that is untrue to your experience and get away with it very easily. You'd have to be awfully devious to do that. And I don't think you have any business being devious as a writer. Still what I mean by honesty is really a very complicated thing. It's not simply a matter of telling the truth; it is simply a matter of being honest about the way you feel about something. If you delineate a character, for example, you have to be true to your feelings about the character, however you conceive of the character. And you have to be consistently true to that idea. If you lie to yourself anywhere along the line about that, it's going to come out false.

Puerto: How about the whole idea of experience? Can you talk to that as James talked about it? Experience as the atmosphere of the mind.

Momaday: The kind of experience which is most valuable to me is an experience of the imagination. That's what seems crucial to me in the business of writing. I rely a great deal on my imagination, like the business about the tank in *House Made of Dawn*. I had no practical experience of that. I've never been in that situation, nor have I seen anybody in that situation, but I could imagine it, and I could write out of that imaginary experience. So I don't hold with that business of overt experience as being necessary. And yet, of course, experience of some kind is all you've got. You can't write out of anything else.

Puerto: Is there any particular person that you review your material with? For instance, before you start sending to publishers, a friend, or another writer, or your wife?

Momaday: Yes. I like to read things that I've written to people. Most often it's my wife, sometimes it's Bobby Nelson, sometimes it's somebody else. Not to get another person's impression so much as to hear myself read it and formulate impressions of my own on that basis. I hear everything that I write. When you asked me how I evaluate my writing, I should have said before, I have to hear it, and so I babble a great deal at the typewriter. I read things to myself, and even when I don't articulate them, I hear them in my mind, and this is one of the·ways in which I can tell whether or not something I've written really satisfies me or not. It has to sound right to me.

Puerto: What would you tell a beginning writer? The student, for example?

Momaday: I would tell him to write a lot, to exercise himself as a writer, and to write regularly and often. Just to keep in practice. You needn't write seriously all the time, but I think it's important that you keep the juices moving. I think the principle of "write little and write well" is particularly appropriate to poetry. If you were writing poetry, I might very well give you that advice, as a mentor gave it to me. And

I would say write about what you know. Do write out of your experience, whatever the experience may be, whether imaginary or not. Write out of something that you have definite ideas and feelings about and be true to those feelings.

Puerto: Would you say the whole value then of a creative writing course is essentially discipline and nothing else? Or do you think the real learning of how to write and how to affect people can be taught?

Momaday: I think it can be taught to an extent, and it's largely a superficial thing. You can learn in a creative writing class a lot about technique and you can learn maybe more about criticism than about anything else, but I don't think you can be taught to write well. I don't think you can be taught to write a novel in a creative writing class. If you have the talent to begin with, the genius and the gift of God, or whatever it is to be a writer, then you can develop that ability within certain limits, under direction, within a classroom situation. But if you haven't got it to begin with, then I don't think a creative writing class is especially useful.

Puerto: How do you see your teaching in relation to your writing?

Momaday: I find the two things quite compatible. I find that the classes that I teach provide me with a certain kind of incentive. Being around people in a learning situation, talking to them, exchanging ideas, and so on, gives me a certain incentive to write and a certain material. From a practical point of view I find that teaching gives a lot of time in which to write.

Puerto: As opposed to being a longshoreman?

Momaday: Right. To this point in my life, the two things have not been in conflict. The business of writing generally has to proceed out of a tremendous urge. Either you have it or you don't, and if you have it, you're going to write, whether well or not. If you've got the basic incentive, or the desire, the impulse, then you're going to do it, and you can use direction at that point; but if you don't write, and aren't motivated to write, I don't think any amount of urging is going to be useful.

A Conversation with N. Scott Momaday

Lawrence J. Evers / 1974

From *Sun Tracks: An American Indian Literary Magazine*, 2, no. 2 (Spring 1976), 18–21. Reprinted by permission of Lawrence J. Evers.

On November 1, 1974, N. Scott Momaday met with Dr. Larry Evers and students in his American Indian literature class in the studios of KUAT-TV, Tucson, Arizona. The following conversation was transcribed from a videotape of that session. The videotape itself is one in a series of instructional aids in American Indian literature, traditional and contemporary, currently being produced by KUAT-TV. Professor Momaday was at the University of Arizona as a guest of the Poetry Center, the Amerind Club, and the American Indian Studies Program.

Q: You teach a course in American Indian oral tradition at Stanford University. Would you describe how you approach the material in that course?

M: Yes. The course is as you say a course in American Indian oral tradition. And it has been very well received. I have been offering it now for several years. First at Berkeley, now at Stanford. I teach it once a year, and I have about one hundred and twenty people in the class as a rule. So it's very large and difficult to manage at times. It becomes a lecture course necessarily, and the subject doesn't lend itself so easily to a lecture situation. But nonetheless, it's extremely interesting.

We try to determine what the nature of oral tradition is. We talk about the man who lives in an oral situation and has no recourse to writing. There is a lot to be said about that. Very few of us, I think, know very much about oral literature, and we're finding out more and more all the time. So the class focuses on the nature of oral tradition, man as he thinks of himself within the dimension of language. We talk about the relationship between the oral tradition and the written tradition. Again, there is a lot to be said about the relationship.

Q: Rather than a single, homogenous Native American oral tradition, aren't there many oral traditions, oral literatures?

M: I think there are many oral traditions. As a matter of fact, I've said on occasion in the class that I think each of us, each individual, has a private oral tradition in which he deals in his daily life. We, all of us, do that and very few of us know it or stop to think about it. There are, however, certain common denominators. You can generalize about oral tradition to a certain extent, and you can generalize very profitably. Talking about attitudes to language, there are certain attitudes toward language which inform all oral traditions.

Q: One of the most intriguing things for me about the oral tradition is the relationship between the storyteller and his audience. It's a dynamic kind of relationship. Have you thought about that relationship? I think of your reading last night and the way you interacted with the audience. Is that a reflection of traditional storytelling procedure?

M: I think it is. I've thought a lot about that relationship between the storyteller and the listener. And, of course, I write, and I have compared that relationship to the relationship between the writer and the reader. They're very different things. I think that in a sense the storyteller creates the situation, and in a sense creates his audience. If I'm sitting here telling you a story, the role is very specialized. We have entered into a very particular kind of relationship, and I think of it in many ways. I think of my self as appropriating your experience to my own. We become very closely united at the level of language. I am creating you in a sense. I am determining certain reactions in you. And you, if you are interested in or excited by the story I'm telling, you have entered into that relationship willingly and have allowed yourself to be created in a sense. I think that is the basic function of the storyteller.

Q: You also talk about the storyteller and, by extension, the man who tries to imagine his way into the storyteller's mind, as having a particular relation to the land. In several places you say that once in his life a man should try to imagine his way into a particular landscape and the way it has been—I think you say—"in the long turn of seasons and of years." From there you move to talk about an American land ethic. I wonder if you might comment on that concept, and how it constitutes an act of the imagination.

M: One of the things that distinguishes the American Indian oral tradition, and I suspect this is true of many—if not all—oral traditions, is the understanding of the landscape. Man's understanding, man both as a race and as an individual, his understanding of the physical world in which he lives. I think that's very important in an oral tradition especially. Man understands himself in relation to the tree over here and the mountain over here and the river and naturally operates out of that environment, operates immediately out of it. It qualifies his language in innumerable ways. And I think that this is basically a moral kind of relationship. In the Indian world it is almost irrefutably. Man understands that he is obligated in certain ways to the landscape, that he is responsible for it, that he shares in the spirit of place. That's a very important concept, I think. It has been important to me personally. I have written out of that understanding.

Q: Is this sense of place, this spirit of place, tied to genetics, tied to Indianness?

M: I don't think it's bound to it. I don't think that this sense of place is unavailable to people who have no aboriginal experience of landscape. But it certainly makes a difference that the Indian has lived in the landscape of North America for perhaps thirty thousand years. That means something. It has to qualify his understanding of himself. He thinks of the land in that way, according to that tenure somehow. And it's more difficult for people whose experience is not so deep to relate closely to understand that dimension, that relationship between man and the landscape. I talk to any number of my students at Stanford, for example, and they are deeply interested in that, in finding out about their investment in the landscape. It becomes a very exciting prospect for them.

Q: I take it that gaining that relation that you talk of requires an act, an active act, of the imagination which is expressed in language.
M: Yes, it does.

Q: Which leads me to wonder about Abel in your novel *House Made of Dawn*. Could you talk about his dilemma in this context?
M: One of the most tragic things about Abel, as I think of him, is

his inability to express himself. He is in some ways a man without a voice. And in his situation—in the context of the Indian world—that is a particular tragedy. He has been uprooted. He has been physically dislocated. He has lost his place in the world, and he's desperate; therefore, he's a man who's trying to fit himself back into his natural world. And he can't do it. One of the reasons he can't is that he's lost his voice. So I think of him as having been removed from oral tradition. That characterizes his dilemma.

Q: You say in the novel, I believe, that he comes back not dumb but inarticulate. At the end of the novel—in the last sentence, in fact—Abel does have words. And the words are "house made of pollen, house made of dawn." Are you suggesting there that as Abel does have words he has found a way to re-imagine himself in that land-scape?

M: I am suggesting that as a possibility, yes. It seems to me that Abel at the very end of the novel stands that chance. He is there face to face with the possibility of re-entry, to use a space age word. The words that he does come up with are as you know from the Night Chant, the Navajo ceremony. And one of the crucial concepts within that prayer, "house made of dawn," is the idea that the man who makes the prayer should be restored. And he says, among other things, "restore my voice for me." And that seems particularly appropriate to Abel to me.

Q: Would you say something about the circumstances surrounding the composition of *The Way to Rainy Mountain?* I have the impression as I read that book that you went on a journey, that you went up into Montana and followed the path of the Kiowas down into the southern plains. Is that the case?

M: Yes, I did that literally, and, of course, the journey had many dimensions. It was a great spiritual experience for me too. I had become interested in the recent migration of the Kiowas from eastern Montana to what is now southwestern Oklahoma, and I made that journey. I did it so that I could see for myself the landscape and take possession of it in my mind. And I put myself into that migration, as it were. I tried to think of myself making it in the way the Kiowas did three hundred years ago. It was a great experience for me. I modeled *The Way to Rainy Mountain,* the book, upon that experience. The book has the shape of a journey. I wanted to reflect in the stories as closely as I could the basic nature of the journey, which was I think in many ways a journey of the imagination.

Q: The journey in *The Way to Rainy Mountain* has an end. It ends in a cemetery. At the end of the book, I was very conscious of the passing of the Kiowa People, the Kiowa culture. I'd like you to comment on this: many people say that Native American oral traditions are last whispers, that they're dying or altogether gone. Do you think that is a valid statement?

M: I think that it is not a valid statement. And I think the oral tradition is much more vital than most of us realize, though it is easy to realize if you stop to think about it. It goes on and on. There is a great persistence in it. I don't understand it yet. I can't account for the persistence of it. I know of incredible things where great intricate stories appear to stop, appear to die out with a given generation, only to emerge after the passing of one or more generations. And I don't know how to account for that when you're talking about an oral tradition, but it happens. It's almost as if the traditions of the people are recorded somehow in blood. And in a racial memory that leaps across generations. No, it is not a dying thing. It is remarkably vital. It goes on and on and on. In *Rainy Mountain* one of the things I remember having said in the preface is that there are many journeys in one. In a sense, the Kiowa migration ends at the cemetery at Rainy Mountain, but in another sense it goes on and on and on. It's unending.

Q: In the passage you just read ("An American Land Ethic," *Sierra Club Bulletin* 12, pp. 8–10) you use the terms magic and conjuring. There is a rather romantic quality to it that is unusual in your style. In your other writing there is a toughness and a sparseness that stays away from that sense of romance which sometimes creeps into an interest in the landscape in other artists.

M: Magic, and the idea of magic, is very highly developed in oral tradition as you probably know. It is everywhere. One of the things which distinguishes oral tradition from writing is the fact that the storyteller tends to be much more consistently aware of the magic in language. He is aware of its power. He understands that by exerting the force of language on the physical world, he can bring about actual change. And that's a marvelous attitude. It insures that people use language responsibly, that he will get much farther with it than the man who does not understand it in the same terms. I think that I think about that so much that I have a lot of reflections of it in my work.

Storytellers are magicians, among other things. That is how the storyteller must think of himself. He deals in magic.

Q: How durable is oral tradition?

M: I think that in many ways oral tradition is as durable as writing. In the long run it may be more so. It has survived, obviously, over a much longer period of time. We've only had writing for about six thousand years, and that's a small period in terms of man's tenure on the planet. The oral tradition has been from the beginning, and it is here now. It is as strong, I think, as it ever was. Over half the population of the world at the present time does without writing. When you think of statistics of that kind you have a real sense of the power of oral tradition. You realize how pervasive it really is. I think of the human voice as being virtually indestructible, one of our greatest forces. And the oral tradition is a vehicle for the human voice.

Q: You talk about the living aspect of oral tradition, and it sounds like a lot of the energy that's involved in that is involved with just carrying on the older traditions. Do you see new mythologies being born now? New traditions that will be passed on orally?

M: It's very hard to get a perspective on the contemporary scene. It's very difficult to know what is happening at this moment in oral tradition, but I think there's no reason to believe that myths are not being constructed every day. I think that one of the things that happens within the oral tradition is the matter of appropriation. That's a word that I have come to think about a lot in relation to the oral tradition. It seems to me a key word in many ways. In the oral tradition one appropriates things to his experience. This is the business of being a human being. And the only way we can express that idea of appropriation, of course, is through language. So that it's a key word in talking about the oral tradition itself. I think myths are appropriated to our experience, myths from the long distant past, but we also appropriate things that happen to us in our daily lives, very immediate things. In the oral tradition these recent appropriations have a way of becoming merged with the whole of our experience. It is a process of renewal as I was trying to suggest a few minutes ago; I think that space age terminology, for example, will become a diction in mythology and in a hundred or two years or even two hundred generations will constitute a valid part of oral tradition. I see no reason to think otherwise.

Q: Are you saying that the language of oral tradition must be archaic?

M: I don't think that an expression in oral tradition has to be archaic. But I think it's important to understand that the oral tradition itself is very old. We don't know how old. It is there. It is original, originative. And that's an important aspect of it. I think the storyteller in Indian tradition understands that he is dealing in something that is timeless. He has a sense of its projection into the past. And it's an unlimited kind of projection. I am speaking, I am telling a story, I am doing something that my father's father's father's father's father's father's father did. That kind of understanding of the past and of a continuity in the human voice is a real element in the oral tradition. And it goes forward in the same way. I am here and what I am doing is back here and it will be here. My children's children will follow me in this path.

Q: What about the rhythms in oral literature? Can they be carried over into writing?

M: Too infrequently, I think. It is something that should be carried over into writing. I think you see in what we customarily think of as our best literature precisely those things which characterize oral tradition. I look at the people whose writing I admire most—people like Herman Melville and Emily Dickinson and Isak Dinesen, who is one of my favorite writers; and it seems to me that their attitude toward language is virtually the attitude which informs oral tradition. It is the storyteller's attitude. Too few writers have developed that understanding of literature, but it's possible that the things which separate oral tradition and written tradition are more apparent than real, and that they can be virtually one and the same thing. That is, they can be informed by the same principles, and they should be. I hope that's one of the things that will happen in time. We should be working to bring those traditions closer together than they are.

Q: Last evening you read a poem called "Plainview II" which struck me as having a very deep and conscious debt to the patterns of Navajo song. The poem emphasizes to me again the strong relations of your work to American Indian oral materials. Does that kind of relationship carry with it any responsibilities? Do you need to worry about the kinds of sanctions that controlled what a traditional story-teller said within his community? Are you accountable for what you say in the same way?

M: I think so. I think that happens in the course of things. We are controlled by language in the sense that we all belong to language communities. And there are sanctions which are imposed by the community. So the first thing I want to say in answer to that question is there are sanctions and one must be aware of them. But so it is in all language situations. The most important sanctions are those imposed by the nature of the language itself. The community matters are a consideration, but I think that they are not as important finally as the sanctions which are imposed simply in the nature of language and man's understanding of language. Anytime that a man takes it upon himself to speak or to write he runs risks. He encounters dangers. He runs the risk of being misunderstood for one thing, that's an obvious kind of risk. But one uses language at his peril. He assumes a responsibility that is intrinsic in the nature of language. And we could go on all day talking about the kinds of risks for they are many. I think this attitude, again, is more highly developed in an oral situation. You know we have a stereotype of the Indian who speaks the truth, the white man who speaks with the forked tongue. I think that grows out of this; there is a basis to it. Not that the stereotype is true, but there is a basis for the association that in an oral tradition one deals in the truth. One has a higher regard for language; one tends to take it more seriously. One tends to have a better understanding of what can happen to him if he uses it carelessly, if he abuses it. And so you have attitudes of that kind, and I think they are valid within limits.

Q: What about the role of imagination in all this?

M: The imagination is one of the most powerful forces in the human being. And language is the vehicle of the imagination. The imagination is worth very little in itself as far as I can see; it is what happens to it when you bring language to bear upon it. Then it becomes viable in a sense it wasn't before. If we did not have language, we would have no thoughts, as we understand that term, we would have no way of organizing things that go on in our minds. I think that it is possible for us to function intellectually without language but only in a very limited way. That is, we can put our hand to a flame and experience pain. And our mind registers some kind of perception of what has happened, but until it becomes language in the mind it is of no use. It is not something we can deal with in ourselves, and it is not something we can communicate. So there's no getting away from it, we are imprisoned in language. We cannot function without it. We express ourselves in language because that's all we have. And when you think about it in those terms you see how really all inclusive it is. Language is an element in which we live. This is something I am fond of saying to my students. It is like the air we breathe. It's like water to fishes. We exist in that element, and it is impossible for us to exist beyond that element.

Landscapes: N. Scott Momaday

Wm. T. Morgan, Jr. / 1975

From *Sequoia,* 19, no. 2 (Winter 1975), 39–49. Reprinted by permission of *Sequoia* © Board of Trustees of the Leland Stanford University

Once in his life a man ought to concentrate his mind upon the remembered earth, I believe. He ought to give himself up to a particular landscape in his experience, to look at it from as many angles as he can, to wonder about it, to dwell upon it. He ought to imagine that he touches it with his hands at every season and listens to the sounds that are made upon it. He ought to imagine the creatures there and all the faintest motions of the wind. He ought to recollect the glare of noon and all the colors of the dawn and dusk.

The Way to Rainy Mountain

I feel deeply about the landscape and I mean that literally. I think it is important for a person to come to terms with landscape. I think that's important; it is a means to knowing oneself. I think one's idea of the self involves the environment. You can't really know who you are until you know where you are in a physical sense. You need to know what the things in you are, how they feel, how they change in various lights.

A young girl awoke one night and looked out into the moonlit meadow. There appeared to be a tree, but it was only an appearance; there was a shape of smoke; but it was only an appearance; there was a tree.

"The Colors of Night"

I think that there are kinds of landscape. One understands first of all the physical landscape, what the country is there around him. But beyond that, once you have possession of the landscape at that level, it is possible to understand it in other terms too—it becomes a landscape that has finally to be imagined; and then it is different in some sense. One imagines the landscape beyond seeing it with the natural eye: one sees it with the eye of the mind. In "The Colors of

Night'' for example I was trying to deal with an imagination of the landscape proceeding really from that. I think that's largely true of writing in general. When you write descriptive passages it is not a matter of taking a notebook out and looking at the sunset. What you are really doing is remembering and imagining landscapes you've seen, places you've been. You are developing in the course of the writing a sense of place.

In *The Way to Rainy Mountain* it is a grand landscape. I had in mind all the time I was thinking about that book and writing it the migration route of the Kiowas from the Yellowstone to the Southern Plains. I retraced that route myself. It is an incomparable landscape; that's one of the things I say about it in that book—it has to be seen to be believed. It is grand and I wanted to evoke the grandness of it. There was the fact also that I was dealing with the racial memory—the landscape not only as I know it, but as my parents and grandparents knew it. That long possession of the landscape means something too in terms of writing, can be understood in those terms as something that has come down in the blood for generations.

Natural settings are extremely important to me; those experiences which are closely related to a landscape, a particular landscape, are the experiences that mean most to me. I tend to look for such experiences when I think about writing, and such experiences suggest themselves to me when I write.

> A word has power in and of itself. It comes from nothing into sound and meaning; it gives origin to all things. By means of words can a man deal with the world on equal terms. And the word is sacred. A man's name is his own; he can keep it or give it away as he likes. Until recent times, the Kiowas would not speak the name of a dead man. To do so would have been disrespectful and dishonest. The dead take their names with them out of the world.
>
> *The Way to Rainy Mountain*

I think that language is sacred. I have been for a long time interested in the power of language. I think we don't know nearly enough about the power of language. We don't understand how powerful words are or can be. In our daily lives we tend, I think, to disregard language in that sense, we don't try to understand it in terms of the sacred. We

think of it as communication rather than spiritual expression or a
vehicle for the sacred.

I think that writers in general are forced to deal with language in a
way that other people in general are not. That's what really sets them
apart as I see it and I have a fascination . . . language fascinates me,
words are endlessly mysterious to me. And I think by and large that's
good. A writer should have that sense of wonder in the presence
of words.

*Do you think the writer has a responsibility to the people of his
society? To keep alive that sense of wonder in the power of words?*

I think so. I think so. He is a story teller and there is nothing more
important, I think, no function more important than that of story
telling within a given society. That really is the life's blood of the
society. It consists in language. I think of language as an element in
which we exist. We all share in it; we really have no existence apart
from it. Therefore the story teller, the man whose function it is to
deal primarily with language, has an enormous responsibility. It is his
job to keep language alive to his fellow men; he must always demonstrate the possibilities of language—and that's a big job; that's a heavy
responsibility. But it is a necessary one.

*I understand the Kiowas retain today a vital oral tradition, that in
fact the written word is a somewhat recent and subordinate form of
social discourse. Do you detect the influence of verbal rhythms, of
the heritage of oral narrative on the style of your written works?*

I think it has influenced my writing to a great extent. That's a large
question. I mean, I could talk for a long time about it. I think that
there were real differences between oral tradition and the written
tradition. The man who exists within an oral tradition, who doesn't
have writing, tends, I think, to take language more seriously. He can't
afford to take it for granted. He doesn't have the kind of security that
writing represents. He has in some ways a better understanding of
language and its possibilities. I have been, I suppose all of my life,
aware of the oral tradition of the Indian people and I think that my
awareness of it has been a very positive thing in my life as a writer.
It's good to understand the nature of the oral tradition. One can
understand that to the benefit of his expression, written and otherwise.

Do you see certain similarities between the oral and written traditions?

Yes. There are many similarities, and I think that the writers whom I admire most are precisely those who have the kind of understanding of language that informs the oral tradition. I'm thinking of Isak Dinesen, for example, who really has an unusual understanding of language. I think she deals with language more completely than most other writers of my experience. She thinks about it all the time. She is fascinated by words. They represent to her wonderful things and she has a great capacity for wonder; she uses languages to that effect. And she's very good; her talent is very great. You see the oral tradition in her writing, and that's very exciting. It also proves that the two traditions can merge, and should at some point in art.

Would you say the visual element plays a prominent role in the composition of one of your stories?

I can say this, that I have always been concerned to *see* what I'm writing, and I have a real image of the subject I am treating. I deal a lot in descriptive writing. I write descriptions of things. I try to render them to the mind's eye accurately. To that extent I would say that my writing tends to be pictorial. I really want to see things in my writing, literally, and I want the reader to see what I'm talking about, to have a visual impression.

Does that imply a particular intended meaning for those images?

There is a meaning to it, but there is a meaning inherent in the image, most images, and I wouldn't know how to separate those things. It isn't that I'm concentrating more on one than the other as far as I know. But I believe that both things are there. When I was writing "The Colors of Night" (I wrote that in Russia by the way) I was recalling things from my ethnic experience. There is an Indian flavor to those stories (if that's what they are—I think of them as being very small stories). I was recalling these things across a great distance, an actual distance, which may have been worth something in itself. I was seeing a landscape very far away—I was thinking of the landscape of the Southern Plains when I was writing that and trying to evoke the spirit of that landscape in those colors. So I think there are various levels of meaning in those things. The meanings somehow consist in the visual reality of the stories.

Tai-me is to my mind a striking figure, not only as a legendary object but as a form of symbolic representation of an aboriginal articulate utterance. How would you describe the significance of Tai-me to you?

Tai-me is the sun dance fetish of the Kiowas. And as such, it has been very important to me. It was, when the sun dance was alive, the most powerful medicine of the Kiowa tribe and has a long history. It is said that the Kiowas were given the Tai-me bundle (this is essentially a medicine bundle) by the Crows when the Kiowas first entered upon the Great Plain. They took it with them on their migration, they kept it, and still have it in their possession. So it has been for me an object of great mystery with religious significance; it continues to be, and I will no doubt write about it again.

What role do you think personal experience does, or ought to play, in fiction?

In a sense personal experience is all you've got to work with. It is terribly important; it is indispensable. The question is how do you deal with personal experience. It seems to me that you have many possibilities, and it becomes a difficult choice. I am teaching a course in the autobiographical narrative, and I have been thinking a lot lately about this problem. Why does a man choose to write about himself at that level in the first person, dealing with his experience, dealing with it very closely? It seems to me that it is difficult to do, that is, there must be a difficult choice to be made. But personal experience is all you have. You can think of it perhaps in different ways, you can see it as history, actual history, you can write what is *essentially* history. You can imagine your personal experience—you have it there, you know what it is objectively; you can translate it into some other kind of reality; you can imagine it; you can write fiction out of it. But it is where you must begin.

Why, in House Made of Dawn, *did you choose to have Tosamah, the Priest of the Sun, speak from out of what was essentially your own personal history?*

The character of Tosamah appeals to me in many ways. I enjoyed writing his part into the novel. He became a character who interested me immediately, and I still wonder a lot about him. He is intriguing to me. There are many facets to his character. He is intelligent. He is

cynical. He plays games. He likes to misrepresent himself in certain
ways . . . he is interesting on various levels. He gave me though in
that section of the book a chance to say some things that I wanted to
say about language and so on. This section is of course also the
introduction to *The Way to Rainy Mountain,* which is as you say
autobiographical. I had wanted to say some things about the Indian
world, and he became the logical vehicle for it. I could talk about my
grandmother and put the words into his mouth. Those things were
more appropriate for Tosamah, than, I think, for other characters in
the book simply because he was what he was—he became himself a
kind of oracle in the book; he thought of himself in those terms. He
was fascinated by language, took it upon himself to deal in language,
to be a spokesman of a kind; to represent his culture in language. And
so I took advantage of him in that way.

*Would you ever identify yourself, as a writer, with the role of a
spokesman of some kind?*
No, and it's something I don't think about very often. I don't
identify with any group of writers, and I don't think of myself as being
a spokesman for the Indian people. That would be presumptuous, it
seems to me. I don't . . . when I write I find it a very private kind of
thing, and I like to keep it that way. You know, I would be uncomfort-
able I think if I were trying to express the views of other people.
When I write I write out of my own experience, and out of my own
ideas of that experience, and I'm not concerned to write the history
of a people except as that history bears upon me directly. When I was
writing *The Way to Rainy Mountain,* for example, I was dealing with
something that belongs to the Indian world, and the Kiowa people as
a whole, but I wasn't concerned with that so much as I was concerned
with the fact that it meant this to me—this is how I as a person felt
about it. And I want my writing to reflect myself in certain ways—that
is my first concern.

*You write both poetry and prose fiction, and I think even your prose
has lyrical qualities. In what ways do you think prose and poetry are
different; by what qualities or expressive potencies would you distinguish the two?*
I think of them as two different things, but I also think that they are
closer together than we realize. It is hard to define poetry and prose.

You can say that poetry is an expression, a measured expression; talk about it as verse, and say that which is verse is poetry, that which is not written in verse is not poetry. But that's about as far as you can go. Prose should be lyrical. It can certainly be lyrical. Some prose in my experience, and this is true in yours too—you've seen prose things which are more lyrical than certain poems. I strive for a lyrical expression. I am very conscious of the sound of language. When I like something I have to sound it out to myself, it has to appeal to me at that level, perhaps first at that level. I am extremely conscious of sound, the rhythms of language. I think of poetry as being more precise generally. If I want to express something as precisely as I can, then I think of writing a poem. But prose, too, can be precise, and should be.

You tend, it seems to me, to write often in traditional forms of verse. Do you find these forms to be particularly fertile in mastering poetic expression?

I think I have until recently written in traditional forms for the reason that those forms are worth something in themselves. I want to master traditional forms, I want to write in iambic pentameter for example, because there is a good reason for writing in iambic pentameter. It is an extremely flexible line, and there are many things you can do with it once you have established that as your unit.

You are working on a collection of poems now, are you not?

I have a couple of things going on right now. I have completed a collection of poetry that will be, I think, the next published book. I am also working on a nonfiction account of something that is essentially autobiographical. I'm writing about certain parts of my life, certain people I've known.

That collection of poems is growing all the time. I'm pleased to say that I've been writing a lot of poetry lately. Interesting things are happening it seems to me in my life as a poet right now, because I am dealing with it in a way that I haven't before. I have been moving away from the traditional forms that we were talking about a moment ago, and I find that my poetry is becoming much more flexible and free in a certain way. I don't know what that means just now but I feel good about it. The book, the collection of poems, is entitled *The Gourd Dancer*. There are four parts to it. The first is called "The

Gourd Dancer,'' and it deals with poems of an Indian character. The
second part is called "The Strange and True Story of My Life with
Billy the Kid,'' and it is autobiographical. Billy the Kid—he means a
lot to me. He's a figure in my past, as they say. I grew up with Billy
the Kid. I lived much of my life in New Mexico, which was his part
of the world, and so I had heard stories about him all my life, and he
excited my imagination. I appropriated him to my experience when I
was growing up; I spent a lot of time riding horses out in the open
country, and always out there I would encounter Billy the Kid in one
way or another. So this is a group of poems that bears upon his life,
and upon my life, and the way in which those two things come
together in my imagination. The third part of the collection is entitled
"Anywhere Is a Street into the Night" (these are all tentative titles—
I'm pretty sure about the first two. I'm not so sure about that one;
that's the working title for that section). It consists of poems that I
wrote for the most part in Russia. Then the last part is "Angle of
Geese," which has been published, as a matter of fact, as a Chap
Book. So that's the whole collection. And as I say, I've been very
active writing poetry lately, and keep adding things to it, so I'm not
sure how many poems it's going to end up having—somewhere in the
neighborhood of fifty or sixty, I think.

*Last spring you lectured in the Soviet Union as part of a program
sponsored by the Fulbright Foundation. How would you describe the
response you received?*
   I found the Russians very receptive to all of us who were there as
representatives of American culture. Two of us were there in American Literature specifically, and they are extremely curious about
America, about American literature, and I thought they were especially curious about American Indians. They have, I think, a highly
developed appreciation of native traditions. One of the things that
impressed me most was the folklore of Russia, which is very great,
and very rich. Everywhere I travelled in the Soviet Union I found
evidence of that interest. So that when I talked to them about the oral
tradition of the American Indian they were very receptive, they were
with me, they knew what I was talking about, in a sense, because it
was very close to their own experience. This was true not only of the
Russian people proper but also true of the Soviet people in Central

Asia. I spent some time in Tadzhikistan, and again I saw a great deal of evidence in support of the fact that those people deal in folklore all the time. It is very meaningful; they are story tellers. And so we could get very close together at that level.

I understand the Soviet government is taking steps to record much of that folklore.

They are taking a very active interest in the preservation of folklore. I visited institutes in Central Asia where they were going about the business of collecting ancient manuscripts and taping stories in remote villages. They are compiling great reserves of these things—it is very impressive. I think that they are doing very good things in that area.

The most exciting lecture I gave, I gave in collaboration with another fellow in Moscow. I lectured the whole team on American Literature of the twentieth century, and I decided that it would be a good thing to talk at some point about folk music, the literature of American folk music. I thought that it was something they probably didn't have much access to. I can tell them something about that and it will be perhaps more meaningful than William Faulkner or John Steinbeck or what have you. So as my final lecture I did talk about American folk music. I was very fortunate to run across a fellow there who knows a lot about folk music, Christopher Wren, a correspondent of the *New York Times* in Moscow, who has been actively interested in folk music for a long time. Somebody tipped me off that he was there, and I called him and told him what I wanted to do, and asked him if he could help me, and he said yes, certainly, he would be happy to come along and bring a guitar. Well, as it turned out, he brought two guitars and a banjo, and he knew all of the folk songs that I wanted to talk about, he knew them by heart, and he could play them. So it turned out to be a wonderful Saturday afternoon. The Russians were enthralled, and it was a great time. I would pick a number of folk songs that came from different parts of the country. I think we moved geographically from east to west and touched many bases along the way. I would talk about a song, and then Chris would play it and sing it, and it just couldn't have worked out better.

Do you detect an influence in the last 10 or 15 years of Indian writers on "mainstream" American literature?

I think I do. I wouldn't be able to point to it specifically off the top

of my head, but I have a real sense that this great interest that
Americans in general have taken in the traditions of the Indian world
in the last few years is showing up everywhere, in literature certainly,
as well as in other arts. I think that contemporary writers are aware
of that; their own perceptions have been sharpened in view of that
general interest, that growing interest. I think that they are thinking
about the landscape, for example, in the light of the Indian experience,
and this is surely showing up in contemporary poetry and fiction. I
think there will turn out to be a very great influence. It is a little
difficult to get a perspective on it now. But I think that in twenty-five
years' time we will see that there has been a considerable influence.

*What would you consider to be the major literary influences on
your own writing?*

One is influenced of course by what one reads. I have a special
interest in American literature. I have a professional interest in
American literature. There are writers I admire very much and would
like to think that they have played a part in the development of my
style, but I can't point specifically to anyone. I admire Wallace
Stevens and Emily Dickinson a great deal. I think I have tried here
and there to emulate them in certain ways, because I think that's what
a writer should do. If he sees something he likes, he should try to
benefit from being in its presence. Isak Dinesen, whom I mentioned,
is a great figure I think in English literature—she wrote *Out of Africa*
in English. So I don't know . . . as I say, I like to think that such
writers have influenced me to the good. I hope that is the case.

*A translation from a verbal to a written medium has great interest,
as does that from a written to a kinesthetic medium. I understand a
film was made of* House Made of Dawn. *What is your impression of
that translation?*

It has never been distributed but the film was made and I don't
know what's happening to it now. That is to say, I don't know if it is
being edited again or not. I think it is. I liked the film; my impressions
of it were good across the board. I saw it twice, and the first time I
saw it I had very mixed feelings, and some grave reservations about
it. I was trying to analyze that business because after I had seen it the
second time I liked it a good deal and had not nearly the same
reservations, and I wondered why. That may be because I didn't

really see it the first time around; I was in some ways keeping myself
from seeing it, withdrawing from it, holding it off because I was so
close to it. But my impression is finally that it was well done. The
photography was very impressive. I think the film dealt honestly with
the novel. It isn't a representation of the whole novel, but it deals
fairly with a part of the novel. The producer once said to me that he
could make eight different films of the book, and I think that's true.
He made one of them.

There are problems I suppose in the sense that there are time
confusions in the novel—distortions of time, which belong there
because they reflect Abel's mind in certain ways, valid ways. There
are things which at the level of film I suppose represent flashbacks,
and as a matter of fact, in the film that *was* made of the book there
are a number of flashbacks, and there is a thread running through
them. They have Abel running. The film opens with Abel running and
it becomes a thread which runs through the whole film. There are
many flashbacks of Abel running. It ends that way, too. It is a race.
The film itself is in one sense the visual impression of Abel running
through the landscape.

How would you evaluate your career, as both student and teacher,
at Stanford?

There's a lot to say about that. I have very fond recollections of my
graduate student days at Stanford . . . it was a different place then, in
certain ways. I came from New Mexico. I had graduated from the
University of New Mexico and had taken a job teaching on the
Jicarilla Apache Reservation, and was there in '58–'59. Then I won a
Creative Writing Fellowship at Stanford. I had never been here before.
I came here really for the first time in 1959. My advisor was Yvor
Winters, one of the first people I met here on the faculty, and we
became very close friends. I knew him throughout my graduate career
and admired him very much. He was a very important man in my
life—he taught me a great deal. I was very naive with respect to
literature, I think, when I came here, and under his direction I learned
a great deal about, for example, traditional forms of English poetry.
When I graduated from Stanford I went to Santa Barbara, where I
joined the faculty of the University of California. After six or seven
years I went to teach at the Berkeley campus, and all that time I had

remained in touch with the Stanford community in one way or another. I had visited the campus several times. Of course, I was on the mailing lists, so I kept getting magazines and newspapers telling me how life was going at Stanford. When I had the opportunity to return, I did so with great pleasure, because Stanford means a great deal to me. I feel good about being at Stanford.

How do you conceive your role as teacher at Stanford (to ask the usual question)?

Now that's a big question too. I have a lot of ideas about that, but let me see if I can condense them in some way. When I am in the classroom (of course, it depends to a certain extent on the size of the class), I most often see myself as a leader, a discussion leader. I don't like the idea of doing all the talking. I think that the classroom is a place where an exchange should take place. The student should contribute something to the ideas that are being defined. So I think of myself as being in a position to encourage students to think and to express their thoughts. It is exciting to me to think that I may be encouraging someone else to think. There is a marvelous electricity to that business, and you can sometimes sense it in a classroom when a class of mine has read an exciting book, and we are together, responding to that book, to the excitement of it. That's very gratifying. I like that.

Those are the things that occur to me immediately . . . I also think of myself as a storyteller, I try to keep that in mind. That's what teachers should be, in one sense . . . one learns from stories. We invest ourselves and all of our experience in stories. A class can be taught as if it were a story, and that's good.

We've covered a lot of territory!

An Interview with N. Scott Momaday

Gretchen Bataille / 1977

From *Iowa English Bulletin*, 29, no. 1 (1979), 28–32. Reprinted by permission of Gretchen Bataille.

N. Scott Momaday first gained national recognition in 1969 by winning the Pulitzer Prize for his novel *House Made of Dawn*. In his first publications, *The Journey of Tai-me,* and later *The Way to Rainy Mountain,* Momaday had brought Kiowa myth and legend together with historical and personal experience. In his most recent book, *The Names,* he traces the genealogy of his family. His skills as a teacher, however, are far less well-known, although anyone who has sat spellbound during one of his lectures or poetry readings must certainly recognize that his presentations demonstrate an awe of and respect for language. In all of Momaday's writing and in his speaking there is a control and a precision in his language and so it should be, for as he says, ''a word has power in and of itself . . . the word is sacred.''

N. Scott Momaday, writer and teacher, remarks in this interview that he has never taught his own novel *House Made of Dawn*. But here he responds to some of the questions that students have repeatedly asked about the book. He stresses the emphasis that must be placed on the oral tradition if one is to understand the contemporary literature of the Native American, and he uses examples from *The Way to Rainy Mountain* to demonstrate his own use of Kiowa oral materials.

House Made of Dawn is one of the most complex Native American novels. It is a difficult book for high school students; indeed, even college students find it a challenge. Momaday's collection *The Way to Rainy Mountain* is somewhat easier once the three-part pattern of myth, history, and contemporary statement is discerned, and it is a book which could be taught in junior high as well as high school.

Q: In my own teaching I have come to believe that one must begin a course in American Indian literature by giving students a firm foundation in the oral tradition, spending time on the idea of ceremony and the songs and the stories which make up ceremony. I think part of that idea came from reading some of your things, and I suspect you would agree with that. Is that where one should begin teaching Indian literature?

M: I agree with that completely. In the first place, it is very difficult to understand the oral tradition and difficult for most of us to imagine what the oral tradition really is. We're so used to the written tradition that it's hard, maybe impossible for us, to conceive of what it means to deal only in the spoken word, but there are obviously really great differences between the two traditions. They may be more apparent than real, but so much more emphasis is put on listening and remembering in the oral tradition and so much more emphasis is put on the *word*. When someone in the oral tradition takes it upon himself to speak, I think he does it much more seriously and is much more aware of the responsibility involved.

Q: As you grew up you experienced the tales in a natural context, learning them within the family, within the home. Indian people often have suggested that because of this, one should not teach the oral tales in the classroom. Do you think it's possible to teach the oral tradition in the classroom?

M: I think it is. Last term I taught a course called "The Storyteller and His Art" and we ended up with too many people, about twenty-five. I wanted simply to talk about what it means to tell a story, who the storyteller is, what his relationship is to his listeners and we ended up by telling stories for the most part. I thought there was great value to that kind of course; taught over a period of time it ends up by being something very, very important.

Q: What is your attitude toward the changes that translators have made in the oral materials? Some critics have spent their lives seeking the "correct" versions and others, such as Rothenberg or Brandon, have attempted to get at the sounds of the literature and have, in the process, perhaps changed some of the stories and songs. You used a version of "Falling Star" in *The Way to Rainy Mountain*. How do you deal with this in the classroom?

M: I think we overemphasize the problems of translation. There are many kinds of translation. You can put the emphasis of translation on many different aspects. I happen to believe that that is not really important in the long run, and I'm skeptical of the prevailing attitude that something is inevitably lost in translation. Of course something is lost in the translation. But there is such a thing as a good translation. It is really, after all, the spirit of the story that I'm most interested in. The translation poses no real problem in that regard. Looking back on one of those early prayers that Washington Matthews translated, as far as I can tell (and I've talked to a number of Navajos about it—native speakers who have looked carefully at the translation), it's a good one. It brings across the principal ingredients of that prayer and the concepts within it. When I was writing down the tales in *Rainy Mountain,* for example, I was initially worried about that. What happens? What am I doing to these wonderful things in the oral tradition by freezing them into print? I still don't know the whole answer to that, but I think that in getting the *spirit* of the stories across and being as true as possible to the expression as it was given to me, it ended up by being eminently worthwhile.

Q: In *The Way to Rainy Mountain* Grandmother spider has difficulty recognizing the sun's child as either a boy or a girl. It turns out to be a boy and then the twins emerge. Would you comment on the story of the twins?

M: I love that story of the twins. I have an idea that there at one time must have been a kind of epic story, and I have an idea that many tales of the twins have been lost or at least haven't come down to me. I think several of the stories in the collection in *The Way to Rainy Mountain* have a part in that first story about the child who is carried up to marry the sun and gives birth to the boy who divides himself in two. There are several stories about brothers, and I have an idea that they are the twins, though connections get lost.

Q: One of the problems I have in teaching Indian literature is confronting the "wholeness." Students need to understand something about anthropology, comparative religion, history, and psychology. How much do you feel one must know in order to teach American Indian literature and how much can we expect students to know?

M: The more you know the better, of course, but I think it's also possible to teach Indian tradition simply by pointing out that there is a difference in viewpoints. We're talking after all about a specific world view, and it's a very complicated world view. It's intricate in many ways. That's the initial realization—once you understand that you're talking about fundamental differences in ways of thinking, then you've made a big step and you can go a long way on that basis. If you understand that, it's possible to teach without understanding all the intricacies of the particular world view.

Q: There's always the question of whether or not non-Indians can teach Indian literature. What is your feeling on that?

M: I think they can. I think, that is, within limits. I've talked to a lot of people who seem to have been entirely successful teaching Indian world view who are themselves not Indian. I know several people in that category. Peter Nabokov, who's a friend of mine and whom I call a Russian Crow because he spent some time on a Crow reservation and wrote a book called *Two Leggings: The Making of a Crow Warrior,* has a very keen understanding and many fine perceptions of the Crow way of life and is perfectly qualified as far as I can see to teach courses in Indian world view.

Q: When *House Made of Dawn* first came out, one reviewer in *Commonweal* called Abel a "muddled" character and generally seemed not to understand the book, feeling the hero didn't come through and wasn't a hero at all. Do you find a greater understanding now of the things you're doing and others are doing than existed five or six years ago?

M: Yes, I think so. I think there's a growing understanding of the Indian in our society and, of course, that's all to the good. I think the situation is changing.

Q: I would also like to ask you some questions on symbolism in the novel. Most of these are questions that have come up in classes. In an interview that was published in *Puerto del Sol* you said people sometimes come up with things you weren't sure were there but you discover they are indeed there. Do you see the Albino as a real person or do you see him as an imaginary figure?

M: I think that I see him in both ways and maybe more emphatically in the second way. He is a kind of spiritual realization to me. Of course we're talking about the whole concept of witchcraft in Pueblo society and that's a very, very large subject. I had many things in mind when I was dealing with the Albino. I think I thought of him primarily though as a kind of symbolic and spiritual reality—rather than as an individual man.

Q: The Albino's attraction to Abel appears to be much like Angela's in that both see Abel in sexual and sensual ways. Both scenes (key scenes with the Albino and with Angela) stress an animalistic attraction, and both the Albino and Angela seek a vision of the land that other whites (perhaps represented by Millie and her father) have spent their lives denying. Angela seems to achieve it, but the Albino is evil and is destroyed. How much did you intend Angela and the Albino to be alike?

M: I had, to some extent, a kind of comparison in mind when I was writing the book. They both test Abel in certain ways—not in the same way. But they are alike in that they demand certain difficult responses from Abel. Yes, I think there is a parallel there.

Q: Many critics have assumed that the "Cain" of the novel is white society. I guess my own interpretation is that Cain is just another side of Abel. What did you have in mind when you named your character Abel? Were you thinking in terms of twins or brothers?

M: Yes, but perhaps to a lesser extent than most people realize. I didn't want to make too much of the Abel-Cain story in the novel. Of course it was there in my mind, but I think at a fairly low level. I knew someone at Jemez whose name was Abel, and I had that character very much in mind through part of the writing anyway. So the name is more suggestive than I meant it to be.

Q: This is a very naive question about *House Made of Dawn.* Why do the people keep an eagle in the cage in the town?

M: I don't know clearly *why* they do it. I suspect that it's simply to keep the spirit of the eagle close by. They hunt eagles still and there is an Eagle Society at Jemez. They go out at least once a year and they are gone until they come back with eagles—one or two at least. I have very fine memories of that Golden Eagle in the cage at Jemez. I used to go by and look at it and in *The Names* I wrote a little piece about the confrontation—looking through the wire at the eagle who glowered at me. I suspect they keep it just to have the spirit close by.

Q: In reading Paul Horgan's *The Heroic Triad,* I came across a section where he talked about the initiation into the kiva and that the

masked kachinas would beat the initiate prior to initiation. I was
wondering if in your mind you were thinking of the beating scene in
terms of the initiation into a kiva society?

M: Yes, that figured into my writing that particular passage. It is an
initiation of some kind.

Q: Would you tell me something about the symbolism of the
running?

M: The running has to do with harvests. The race which is run at
Jemez is an imitation, I understand, of the water flowing in the
channels in the spring—the irrigation ditches. The running is in
connection with the ceremony of clearing the ditches—making the
ditch ready for the water. That is essential symbolism—the water
being so important to the culture and to that part of the world. The
man running is fitting himself into the basic motion of the universe—
the water running through the channel. That is simply a symbolism
which prevails in the southwestern Indian world.

Q: What were the ashes then? How would that fit in?

M: I can't tell you exactly. I suspect that the ashes represent a kind
of purification—another basic element. The man covers himself with
the evidence of fire.

Q: Do they burn the ditches out when they clear them?

M: No, they don't, as far as I know. It's just a matter of raking the
ditches clean of debris and stones and so on. Maybe they do in some
cases burn the ditches out. I don't think I've seen that.

Q: Going back full circle from the oral tradition and *House Made of
Dawn,* do you think it's possible to teach *House Made of Dawn,*
without students understanding the oral tradition?

M: No, I'm just guessing about this. I've never taught *House Made
of Dawn.* I've talked to people who have, and I suspect that the
answer is no; one really must imagine at least what the oral tradition
is in order to understand certain parts of the book. Tosamah in his
sermon instructs the reader in the oral tradition to an extent. If you
fail to understand that instruction, then you risk losing a part of
the book.

Q: There's the sense of overlapping symbolism when Francisco
dies and Abel lives that the old generation passes on and in the

process of dying gives life to the new generation. Did the fish fit in with Francisco's death?

M: Yes, I think so. Probably not at a very conscious level in the writing, but just as I have said on a number of occasions, and as you commented a while ago with reference to the *Puerto del Sol* article, so much goes on in the writing. I have been asked questions by people, "Is it true that you meant this?" I have on a number of occasions had the perfectly wonderful experience of realizing that, yes, of course I meant that, though I wasn't necessarily consciously aware of it at the time. But you write out of the subconscious to such a degree that you're not always aware of what the implications and consequent meanings of your expression are. That's one of the most exciting things about writing. I know other writers have had that experience of understanding something they've written long after the fact. There are probably things in *House Made of Dawn* and in my other writings that I understood at the time at one level and have come to understand on a different level and will again in the future understand on yet another level.

Interview with N. Scott Momaday
Gretchen Bataille / 1979

From *Studies in American Indian Literatures: A Journal of Literary Art, Criticism and Reviews, / ASAIL Newsletter*, N.S. 4.1 (Winter 1980), 1–3. Reprinted by permission of John Purdy, editor.

In the following interview N. Scott Momaday briefly discusses his reaction to and participation in the preparation of *House Made of Dawn* as a film. Because Momaday is the only Native American whose primary work has been presented in both the written and visual media, it is useful to examine the relationship between the two forms. There have been other novels made into film and the usual debate about "what has been changed" and the characters not appearing "real" are of course always there. Hollywood has not, however, dealt with the presentation of a major film from a novel by an American Indian with a decidedly Native American world-view. Because Momaday's novel was filmed by a company made of Native Americans and because many American Indian actors participated in the project, the film becomes a unique presentation.

Q: Can the visual media communicate the essence of your novel?

M: I would suspect so. I think that it is possible to make a film that does express the essential character of the novel. It is possible for a film to express the essential character of any novel. The problem is that you can take a novel such as *House Made of Dawn* and make eight or ten films of it, all valid. It is a matter of picking and choosing.

Q: What were your initial expectations for the film?

M: I had no expectations. Of course, I had hopes. I wanted very much for a good film to be made, and I was happy with the film that was made. The external photography was good; the way the race and the man running worked as a thread throughout was well done. There were things that disappointed me. The acting was not particularly distinguished, but I'm not sure that distinguished acting was called for in the parts.

Q: Were you disturbed by the change in time period?

M: Not really. In order to reflect the time span and the convolutions of time in the film one would have had to make a very long and complicated film. Probably such a film would be tedious.

Q: In what areas did you make suggestions about the film?

M: I had something to do with determining where the filming should be done. I was familiar with the landscape of the novel and could be helpful in pointing out various locales. I found out that the writer of a work which is made into a film had very little to do with the filming. It is a mistake to think that the author continues his creative function and carries over his creative work into the film. It is a different thing altogether. I want to be remembered as the man who wrote the novel. I willingly admit that I had very little to do with the film. It is a new creation.

Q: The only negative comment I have heard about the film *House Made of Dawn* was about the peyote ceremony. Some felt many in a movie audience wouldn't understand the ceremony and it shouldn't be shown. Those same people were not upset about it in the novel. What can and cannot be communicated in terms of audience?

M: I would disagree to the extent that the viewing public is more intelligent than Hollywood has ever given it credit for being. Much more important is whether or not it is done imaginatively because the peyote ceremony itself is highly imaginative and very dramatic. It is an artistic consideration more than anything else. There is, however, an area of experience that isn't available to literature. There are ineffable qualities of Indian religious experience; there are sacred areas that are sacred because they are private, and those are unavailable to us. There are always questions of that kind, whether you are making films or writing books.

Q: Do you see a future for American Indian filmmakers or companies or is it too difficult to compete with Hollywood studios?

M: I certainly think there is a future. I think it's more difficult for a company because the competition on that level must be prohibitive. I certainly think that individuals are going to excel. There are a good many Indian people who have talent as filmmakers, who have the kind of imagination and pictorial vision that one needs in order to make a good film.

Q: Do you believe that if more American Indian people get involved in filmmaking, the traditional Hollywood Indian image will change?

M: I think that is inevitable. I think it's already changed to a remarkable extent and it will continue to change.

Q: Have recent images of Indians on the screen (*A Man Called Horse, Little Big Man, Soldier Blue*) been any improvement over the past?

M: Those you mentioned are probably less an improvement than some others—such as *One Flew Over the Cuckoo's Nest.* The part that Will Sampson played was a good remove from the traditional stereotyped image. The days of the befeathered Indian chasing John Wayne across the screen are gone, and it's good that they are.

Q: Did it bother you that in the film version of *One Flew Over the Cuckoo's Nest* it was not clear that the story had been narrated by Chief Bromden?

M: No, it didn't bother me because I thought the film worked. It wasn't the question of giving adequate representation to the Indian voice; it worked the way they did it. Sampson's part was substantial and real.

Q: There really haven't been many major Indian films in the past few years. Do you feel there is now a reluctance and perhaps a fear about how to portray Indians?

M: I don't think there is any organizational prejudice by people in Hollywood against Indian films. Their judgment is shaky here and there, but given the right material they'd make the most of it.

Q: Do you see any potential for *Winter in the Blood* or *Ceremony*?

M: I think there's potential. I don't know if Jim Welch or Leslie Silko have prospects; I think the subject matter is very rich. I think wonderful films can and ought to be made which focus upon the Indian world and Indian experiences. I'm not terribly knowledgeable about filmmaking, but it is a medium which interests me and I think it has great potential. I think we ought to make some good films about Indians. We shouldn't worry about the representation of the cultural realities; that should be secondary to the idea of making an exciting, creative and inspirational film.

An Interview with N. Scott Momaday
Matthias Schubnell / 1981

From a previously unpublished manuscript. Reprinted by permission of N. Scott Momaday.

Schubnell: Yvor Winters has been a central figure in your personal and artistic development. How would you briefly describe his influence?

Momaday: Winters praised me highly in his last book in which he listed me among some of the very good poets of our time; and he cited one poem or two in that book. I'm not sure what effect that has had upon my reputation. But knowing Winters, the other side of that question interests me more, and that is did Winters have any influence on me, and was it good? The answer to that is a flat yes. I did not know Winters when he selected me as a fellow. It was a Stegner Fellowship, and at the time I got my fellowship to Stanford there were four fellowships in fiction and two in poetry each year. And Winters was entirely responsible for selecting the poetry fellows. So in 1958, I applied, and Winters read my prospectus and looked at some of my poems and awarded me the fellowship. I had a letter from him when I was teaching in Dulce; it was a wonderful letter. He said, and I can quote a little bit from that letter: "Well, by this time you have probably heard that you are the poetry fellow this year. There was only one, and you got it. If you haven't heard, I made the selection and the matter is settled." A startling kind of statement from a man you have never known. But it turned out to be exactly Winters. That was exactly his attitude in the way he spoke. And I knew very little about poetry. I thought I knew a lot, and I was writing things that I thought of as poetry. The fact of the matter is I knew very little about traditional English poems; I didn't know a trochee from an iamb. So I had a great deal to learn, and he was exactly the man to teach me. So when I got to Stanford, I got in touch with him, and we liked each other from the very beginning. He was a great help to me not only

67

because he could teach me a lot but because he encouraged me a lot; and I needed encouragement at that time in my life, more, really, than learning. And, I think, he realized that he gave it to me. He encouraged me all along the line until he died. Long after I graduated, we kept in close touch; he was my great counselor.

S: What was Winters's influence on your academic development?

M: On my academic career, very great. When I went to Stanford, I intended to stay there a year, and I had no intention of working for an advanced degree. I had graduated from the University of New Mexico with a BA, and I was teaching on an Indian reservation in New Mexico when I was awarded the fellowship to Stanford. And I took a year's leave of absence, fully intending to come back at the end of the academic year and resume my job of teaching. But when I went to Stanford, Winters talked me into going on through the doctoral program. He said, "Look, you have been accepted at this high-powered institution and we are going to pay your way for a year at least; why don't you work for a master's degree?" And so I did. I took a full load of course work, and I took the master's degree in three quarters and by that time Winters had seen to it that I was welcomed to stay and given funds to continue my graduate work; so I went through the mill. I took my Ph.D. in four years, and that's how I got into the business of teaching at the college and university level. And I think it was a wonderful thing, an advantage that came my way, and I had the sense to make the most of it, with his help.

S: Academically, you seem to share many of Yvor Winters's own preferences, such as an interest in anti-romantic writers, Tuckerman, Dickinson, Melville; appreciation of Wallace Stevens. Some critics of Winters have argued that, in his absolutist and rigid stance on literature, he, at times, was putting blinders on his students. Do you feel that Winters could be limiting by the sheer power of his conviction?

M: In one sense, yes, and I tell you what that is. He taught me so much about poetry and the writing of poetry, it was such a concentrated dose that when I left Stanford in 1963, I had been stifled in a way. I wanted more elbow room, and so I turned to prose. If I had received as much inspiration and instruction over a longer period of time in a less concentrated way, I'm not sure I would have felt that need to expand myself into extra-poetic form. But as far as the

teaching of literature is concerned, I don't think I felt that. I listened
to Winters on many occasions lecture on Hawthorne and Melville and
the chief American poets, including Wallace Stevens. Yes, Winters
was big on two or three of Stevens's poems and taught me a lot about
"Sunday Morning" in the course of a particular seminar, introduced
me to the subject of my dissertation—Frederick Goddard Tuckerman
was one of Winters's great glories—and he wrote the best explication
of it that I have ever read in *In Defense of Reason.*

S: Winters seems to have regretted your move from poetry to prose.
Did you find it difficult to take this step? Did it involve a sense of
disloyalty to your mentor?
M: No. I think he thought of me as a poet. But I don't think he
regretted my venturing into prose. In one of his letters to me, and I'll
show it to you, he told me that I had both gifts, and hoped that I
would pursue both. But he certainly would not have wanted me to
abandon poetry.

S: The thing that made me bring this up was a footnote in *Forms of
Discovery.* There, Winters says that "Scott Momaday has, to my
regret, concentrated on prose in the last few years but I am glad to
say that it is distinguished."
M: I think that his statement is based on his conviction that poetry
is a much greater activity than the writing of prose, and I agree with
him on that point. I'd rather be a poet than a novelist. But if you can
do two things, he would have approved. When I won the Pulitzer
Prize, he was dead, but I had a note from Janet [Winters, his wife]
that said Arthur [Winters's first names were Arthur Yvor] would have
been proud.

S: Winters was well acquainted not only with the Southwestern
geography, but also with native cultures. He was deeply impressed by
native American Art. In his early poetry, particularly in "The Mag-
pie's Shadow," this interest becomes part of his own art. To what
extent was your own native heritage of interest to Winters?
M: I think it was of great interest. He didn't know as much about
the Plains tribes and the Kiowa tribe in particular as he did about the
Pueblo tribes. He had suffered tuberculosis as a young man, and he
had gone to Santa Fe to a sanatorium there. So he knew the country

around Jemez and Santa Fe, and we could talk a lot about that. He remembered Cerillos where he taught for a while just outside Santa Fe. He had a great love for the Southwest and so that was one bond between us. And, as you say, in his early poetry he has been influenced by oral traditions in the Indian world. Some of these very short one- and two-line things were based squarely upon Indian expressions. So that meant a lot to him. I have the impression that he always wanted to know more about that, and frankly I think that was what appealed to him in my samples that I sent him first. They were clearly Indian in character, and I think he had an appreciation for what I was doing that very few other people would have had.

S: Do you remember what poems they were? "Earth and I Gave You Turquoise"?

M: Yes, I think it was. The truth is, I don't remember what I sent him, but I do remember that when I applied for the fellowship I had in mind a collection of poems based upon and held together by some narrative thread. Seems to me that I might have called it "House Made of Dawn," if you can believe that; but I forgot what the poems were. I'm sure that many of them no longer exist.

S: Did he encourage you to write in this native vein?

M: No, as far as I remember, he did not encourage me to do that. But when I did it, he seemed to approve of what I was doing. I don't remember him ever saying to me, "Good, you put your finger on the Indian idiom, do that more often"; but I did it a number of times in class, and I showed him these things, and he very often approved. And in his writing, when he wrote of such a poem as "Buteo Regalis" or "Pit Viper," he said something to the effect that there is a native element in it that is a kind of absolute economy, something he very obviously approved of and thought of as coming out of my Indian background. But he never told me to write in that vein.

S: Did you have any plans to research an Indian subject?

M: No, as much as Winters appreciated American Indian songs and prayers and expressions, I don't think he thought he knew much about that. He did mention to me one time to try a long poem, a long didactic poem on some phase or chapter of Indian history. He thought that would be a good exercise to do something long and didactic, and

I suppose he thought of the migration of the Kiowas or the battle at Wounded Knee, but he never was more explicit than that about it.

For a time I've been fascinated by Indian migrations. Once I got the migration of the Kiowa under my belt, I began thinking about the migrations across the Bering Straits; and at one time I was seriously thinking about trying to write some sort of poem which dealt with it. Nothing came of that. I did begin it once or twice but never got very far.

Of the poems that I want to keep, and you can use *The Gourd Dancer* as a catalogue of those I chose for publication, there are very few which antedate my time at Stanford. "Earth and I Gave You Turquoise" is one; it may be the only one.

S: What about "Los Alamos"?

M: I think I had lost it once it was published in the *New Mexico Quarterly*. Everything else that is in *The Gourd Dancer,* it seems to me, was written after I had gone to Stanford. Several of the poems in the early part of the book were written at Stanford, and then, of course, I included a number that I wrote thereafter.

S: While we were talking about early poems, "Los Alamos" is your first, I believe, explicit statement about the clash between technology and nature, between a realm of organic wholeness and the potentially destructive force of modern civilization. The bridge in the poem, as I have learned, connects Los Alamos with the scientific laboratories. Apart from this realistic aspect, did you have Hart Crane's "The Bridge" in mind?

M: Yes! I don't remember now how I happened upon Crane. It was probably an English course in my undergraduate years at the University of New Mexico, but I had discovered that Winters and Crane were very close. It's strange, I don't remember the poem "Los Alamos" very well, but I do remember that I had Crane in mind when I was doing it. He served as a sort of model not only for that poem but for several others that I wrote at the time. They are probably gone now. I admired Crane very much; in fact, I still do. When I was scouting around for a dissertation at Stanford I thought of Crane, and I intended, for some weeks at least, to write my dissertation on Crane. When I went in to talk to Winters about it, I had the sense that I was being manipulated. I think he said something like "Well, that's very

good, Scott, oh yes, that ought to be done, but you know this man
Tuckerman?'' "Of course I know him, I listened to your lectures.''
''You know, his complete poems have never been edited.'' So I agreed
to the project, and that's how it happened.

S: What was so fascinating about Crane? Crane was trying to fit the
primitive, instinctual, mythic aspects of the American continent and
the modern, scientific and artistic achievements of America into an
organic whole. Do you see such a possibility for reconciliation?

M: Absolutely! I have always been interested in that dichotomy and
in that great paradox in our history. The clash between the pastoral
and the technological, and Crane wrote about that, as did Whitman,
as did Leo Marx, as have a lot of people. And certainly that has been
one of the themes in my writing; that appeals to me a great deal; and
Crane did a very good job with it in his poems, especially in the
conception of ''The Bridge'' itself as a narrative. I like that very
much. So he was a very important figure to me at the time and, though
he is not as important to me now, he remains important. I think he
was an important writer, and I felt about him at one time as I feel
about Emily Dickinson now.

S: Are you as optimistic as Crane regarding this kind of reconciliation?

M: He made the reconciliation, as did Whitman, as did several
painters, American artists, who were painting pictures of the pastoral
scene as it was being rended by trains and industrial plants. ''The
Lackawanna Valley'' by George Inness. And a lot of things like that
which seem to me central and very important statements, and I think
Crane was mindful of that. He wanted to record it and did it brilliantly.
Of course, writing as much as he did . . . Winters always said that the
output of any poet was always going to be small; there were only
going to be a few great poems in the lot. And that's certainly true of
Crane; he wrote a lot, a good many poetic lines, and of that lot a small
percentage, maybe five or six, are great lines.

S: Winters seems to have had a love/hate relationship with Crane;
he offered praise, but also made accusations of obscurity.

M: Who knows? Yes, he knew Crane, wrote to him at least. There
was a correspondence between them, and I think one of the great
literary discoveries of future times is what that relationship was.

S: In "The Morality of Poetry," Winters writes that "through the study of other poets" a poet is striving toward an ideal of poetic form and a perfection of "a moral attitude toward that range of experience of which he is aware." Could you give a brief outline of how, in your own development as a poet, this process occurred, if indeed it is relevant?

M: The poem is a moral judgment. That's, I believe, what Winters believed. A poem is a poet's judgment of his subject that is necessarily moral, because our lives are moral. The poem as an institution raises the moral judgment to the highest level possible. So that a great poem on a great subject, as Winters might say, such as George Herbert's "Church Monument," is about the highest expression of morality that one can get. Or better yet, Ben Jonson's "To Heaven," which is a deeply religious poem. If you accept that as a fact and as a standard of poetry, then every poem becomes a moral consideration. So the best poem is by the poet who understands that fact. I believe that is a fair way of looking at a poem; everything in Winters's view then can be evaluated according to a moral standard, poetry most of all. Poetry, being the highest expression, is therefore the most moral expression. One can get so easily into trouble carrying that along, but that's the basic idea, and I think it's a fair one.

S: One of Winters's key statements, one that you have quoted in a *Viva* column, has been this: "Unless we understand the history which produced us, we are determined by that history; we may be determined in any event, but the understanding gives us a chance." Did this notion have any significance for your own restoration of your racial heritage?

M: He wrote that in *Forms of Discovery,* in the early chapters, and I have never forgotten that statement. I have often thought of using it as a kind of epigraph to begin a book of some kind. Certainly it has had a significance, I agree with that. Winters was a cynic in a certain way; he didn't believe in an afterlife, and he had very little patience with people who did subscribe to the Christian answers to death. In an important way I believe Winters's statement. My interest in Kiowa history can be justified in that way. There is something important about it, important about understanding it. If you don't understand it, you forsake your humanity in a way. Let me put it on a more personal basis. If I don't understand my Kiowa background, I forsake a lot of my human potential. By understanding it as far as I can, I fulfill my capacity for being alive as a human being. I'm talking about a very narrow frame of experience; and everybody can say the same thing about a narrow frame of experience. And yet it is important because if you don't say it, you miss a lot.

S: Allow me to ask you about your encounters with William Faulkner and Georgia O'Keeffe. You met Faulkner in Charlottesville in 1956. Why did you go to the University of Virginia?

M: I thought I wanted to go to law school, and I had heard the University of Virginia was an excellent law school. I had graduated from a military school in Virginia, and that's where I decided to go, and I did.

I belonged to a debating society, called the Jefferson Society, at the University of Virginia. Faulkner had a son-in-law, if I remember that rightly, in the law school at Virginia, and so his daughter prevailed upon him to come at our invitation. The Jefferson Society invited Faulkner to come and speak, or give a reading. And he accepted. Curiously, we had at the same time a guest on campus, John Dos Passos, and Faulkner and John Dos Passos had met something like thirty-five years before and hadn't seen each other again; so this was an historic occasion, bringing those two giant figures in American literature together. I met Faulkner at that time. And there is a very funny story about that. I had seen photographs of William Faulkner, this very distinguished looking man with grey hair and a mustache. He looked like an RAF pilot, and somehow I had assumed he was tall, but when he came into the room, he turned out to be this very small person; and I was sitting in the front row and the lectern obliterated him. I could not see him; all I could see was this column of smoke going up behind it, from his pipe. One other footnote to this little story. At the end of his reading he entertained questions from the floor, and I asked: "Mr. Faulkner, I know that you write a great deal, and I am very curious about your reading. How much do you read? What do you read?" He considered that for a moment. Then he said: "I don't read."

S: When Faulkner was asked what contributions he was hoping to make during his stay at Charlottesville, he replied: "I think the contribution would come out of my experience as a writer, as a craftsman, in contact with the desire of young people to be writers, to be craftsmen, that maybe out of a hundred there may be one that will get something of value from the fact that I was in Charlottesville for a while." Did your encounter with Faulkner affect your own aspiration to become a writer in any way?

M: I think that Faulkner's writing has been an inspiration to me, perhaps an influence; but I'm not sure what that means. But the meeting with him, I can't imagine that made any difference. But I can say this: he was an inspirational man, even to talk to. He had a bearing, and he had a confidence, I think that's the word, that was pretty remarkable. When he answered a question, he did it with a kind of authority that is very rare and remarkable. You don't doubt what he was saying.

S: Many critics have commented on parallels between Faulkner's and your own writings, both technically and thematically. I am thinking of the use of multiple narrative perspectives, stream of consciousness technique, the use of the diary in *House Made of Dawn,* which is reminiscent of the ledger in *Go Down, Moses,* the use of italics; and thematically, your indictment of the desecration of the land, the prevalence of the past in its bearing on the present, the communion of man and his land. Would you like to comment on your reading of Faulkner?

M: I can't spell out a possible influence. I admire certain writings by Faulkner, and I can mention *The Sound and the Fury. As I Lay Dying* is one of the great masterpieces of our time. I like "The Bear," and in fact my poem, "The Bear," which is one of the first I wrote at Stanford, is based on Faulkner's description of Old Ben. Partly, anyway. I suppose to some extent I had Faulkner in mind when I was writing "The Bear and the Colt." I know not much else of Faulkner's work. I mentioned those books and whatever influence there might be comes from them, I'm sure. I like Faulkner a great deal, I admire him, I find him exasperating. I can read him and become aware of his gimmicks. He has tricks as, I suppose, most writers do. One of the things I noticed about him is that he writes in negatives for a long time. Like, this is not so and it was not that and well it wasn't this, but it was this. So by process of elimination, he makes his point, and this gets tiring to me after a while. But at the same time when he's describing certain elements in the landscape or creatures like Old Ben or people like Benjy or Caddy, he can do it very very . . . [smacks his lips]. He's an enigma. You wouldn't know how to assess his talent. But he was very good.

S: The notion of identity in *House Made of Dawn* and *Light in August* intrigues me in particular. Faulkner had this to say about Joe Christmas: "I think this was his tragedy—he didn't know what he was, and so he was nothing. He deliberately evicted himself from the human race because he didn't know which he was. That was his tragedy, that to me was the tragic, central idea of the story—that he did not know what he was, and there was no way possible in life for him to find out. Which to me is the most tragic condition a man could find himself in—not to know what he is and to know that he will never know." It seems to me that much of this is true of Abel, as well; only he eventually has a chance to find out who he is.

M: The similarities sound close, but I don't know *Light in August*. I've never read it.

S: You have said at one point that *House Made of Dawn* is about an Indian who is running. Now there are a lot of alienated characters in American Literature who are on the run. Huck Finn may be the first one who wants to "light out," and he is followed by Ralph Ellison's *Invisible Man,* Faulkner's Joe Christmas, Updike's Rabbit Angstrom, to name only a few. What I think makes Abel special is that his running is not only, as with the other figures, a symbol of alienation, of wanting to run away from something without a viable alternative, but that Abel has something to run to, namely his native culture; in fact, his final running manifests, in ritual terms, a return to his roots. How do you feel about this?

M: That sounds perfectly sensible to me, and I would subscribe to that in a way. A lot of contemporary and modern American literature, maybe modern world literature, has to do with people who are running from something. It's an escape motif that is widely prevalent. That sounds very good to me. I would like to think more about that. That strikes me as a kernel that one could develop into something very large and true.

S: It just struck me that the running motif is really all negative in most modern novels. It's maybe positive in a sense that the person has realized that something's wrong and wants to put a distance between it and him or her; but in your novel it is almost a stroke of genius that this turns into something wholly productive, whereas in most other works it's open ended.

M: That's something that I want to think about; it's provocative to me. Why do people run? You might even relate that to joggers today. It may be an attempt to outrun themselves, to outrun ill-health, or muggers, some negative elements in the background. Abel . . . there is a great paradox there, too, because I think he is running from something and certainly he is running towards something, and where do you strike the balance? I don't know. I was interested though in the various pieces you read, like Huck Finn. Joe Christmas I don't know, because I don't know *Light in August*. But I know *Light in August* as Irving Howe discusses that novel in his book on Faulkner. I can't speak to it directly, but I kind of wish I knew it on the basis of what he says about it.

S: Faulkner seems to have arrived at a rather pessimistic view of the human-land relationship, namely that with the destruction of the wilderness humans have deprived themselves of the possibility to sustain their humanity through nature. You seem to be much more optimistic in this respect. How come?

M: I think our environment is threatened even more than it was in Faulkner's times, and I can understand his pessimism. It's true that I don't share it. I am very optimistic. I think the earth is yet greater than all we have devised, and we can destroy ourselves, but I don't think we can destroy the earth or the wilderness. You can sometimes see grass growing up through the freeways, and that to me is evidence that nature is finally greater, and it will pop up out of the concrete despite everything, given enough time. A friend of mine lived in Brooklyn for quite a while and brought up his children there. He was telling me one day that he came home from work, and he saw his children and a number of others from the neighborhood all gathered round a part of the sidewalk across the street, and he went over to investigate. Some roadworkers were digging up the sidewalk with jackhammers in order to repair a pipeline or something, and the kids had all gathered round because it had not occurred to them that there was earth under the sidewalk. And they were all enchanted to see dirt there, earth. I think the earth finally emerges through the sidewalk in spite of everything. So that's reason to be optimistic, I think.

S: The other important artist I want to ask you about is Georgia O'Keeffe.

M: I met with her three or four times in all. There is a very funny story which I'm sure you know about the first meeting with her when she offered me a drink. I had written to her asking if I might call upon her to pay my respect, because I admired her paintings. And she wrote back and said yes, indeed, please come on such and such a date. So my then wife Gaye and I drove up to Abiquiu, and I knocked upon her door and she met me in a tuxedo. She affects the wearing of little black suits and starched white collars and her hair was drawn severely back, very beautiful. She asked us in and showed us the living room of her house. There were very nice window boxes full of stone which she had picked up in river beds. As I say in the poem, there were skeletons around, wonderful things, and we chatted, and we got along very well, but after twenty or thirty minutes it occurred to Georgia O'Keeffe, who was already in her eighties, that she had not offered us refreshment. So very apologetically she said: "Oh, please, I'll pour you something to drink, what would you like?" We asked for Scotch and sodas. So she excused herself and went out into the kitchen, and she did not return. And we got very uneasy, because 15 minutes went by. What's wrong? And then we began to hear this din from the kitchen, like the rattling of pots and pans, some kind of commotion, which didn't make us feel any better; and then at last Georgia O'Keeffe returned, and she was all a flutter. She said, "Oh, you know, it's my maid's day off, and I don't know what she did with the key to the liquor pantry; I can't find it." And we, Gaye and I, were very understanding. "Oh please," we said, "don't give it another thought; we are perfectly alright; don't trouble yourself." But Georgia O'Keeffe, that eighty-odd-year-old woman, had got it into her head that we would have a drink, and so, much to our chagrin, she excused herself again and went back to the kitchen, and again this long wait, again the rattle of pots and pans, and we were sweating with discomfort. And then she appeared again with our drinks. It turned out that she had taken the pantry door off at the hinges with a screw driver to get to the liquor. And then we found out about her great love for goat cheese, and we had wonderful lunches, and she showed me her studio and we talked about the features of that house at Abiquiu. She bought it because of a door in the patio; one of the great doors. We talked a lot about that. When was that? 1971 or 1972 was the first time I met her. And then I saw her all those four or five times in the space of a year or two. So it's been a long time since I've seen Georgia O'Keeffe. She's in her nineties. And surely she isn't painting much, I think her sight was very weak several years ago, so it's almost gone by now.

S: The Georgia O'Keeffe poem is one of my favorite ones, particularly read aloud. Reading her comments on painting, the American landscape, and life in the Southwest, I came across this passage which highlights the meaning of your poem: "I have picked flowers where I found them—have picked up seashells and rocks and pieces of wood where there were seashells and rocks and pieces of wood that I liked . . . When I found the beautiful white bones on the desert I picked them up and took them home too . . . I have used these things to say what is to me the wideness and wonder of the world as I live in it." Your spiritual kinship to Georgia O'Keeffe must be founded on perceptions like these.

M: You have probably seen, as I have, those early photos, nude photos, of her [taken by her husband, Alfred Stieglitz]. She's so beautiful and delicate. But in her old age, she's become gnarled and strong. And her hands, huge hands, you wouldn't think of them as a woman's hands. When I first saw her, I marveled because her hands were huge and very bony and gnarled and rough, you know, beautiful, but not feminine. Not in the way those early photographs are. And I thought she has been somehow conditioned by the land. This is rough country, canyon country, full of gnarled growth, and look at those hands.

S: Did you talk about your writings or about painting with her? About Alfred Stieglitz?

M: Lots of talk about painting and rocks. She was painting rocks when I first met her. I took her a little stone that I had, and she very much admired it, and we talked a lot about it.

S: On what occasion did you write "Forms of the Earth at Abiquiu" for her?

M: I wrote the poem in commemoration of our meeting. I think maybe I wrote that poem in Russia. One of the things about Russia that I could not have anticipated was the amount of time I would spend in my mind in the Southwest when I was in Russia. My mind, at odd moments, when I was alone, harkened back to the Southwest. There seemed to be some kind of urgency to project myself back to my native landscape. So some of the poems I wrote, and I think that was among them, were about the Southwest. So I remembered those meetings, and I wanted to commemorate the first time we met.

S: Let me ask a few more questions about your painting. Your mother told me that one of the reasons why you have published very little since *The Names* in 1976 is the fact that you have concentrated a great deal on painting. Can you tell me something about this aspect of your creative work?

M: I still have trouble seeing it, have trouble figuring out how to see painting. But it is important to me. I have an idea that in all the time I was growing up and watching my father at work on his knees or at his drafting board, I was learning certain things about art, but I didn't put that together at first, and when I went to Russia in 1974, something clicked inside me, and I started sketching things there. I was writing poetry mostly. But I also began sketching and drawing. It became very important to me from that moment. And when I returned to the US, I kept it up, and in 1976, two years later, there was a great burst of energy in me, and I audited a drawing class at Stanford. Somewhere I met Leonard Baskin whose work I had always admired, and we became friendly, and he taught me generously a couple of things about drawing. I started drawing on large sheets and painted in acrylics on canvas and on paper, and I've been very active in the last few years. I had my first show in 1979 and have had six or eight exhibits since then, and some are coming up. I have sold some work, have been awarded prizes. I think of that as being a whole new expression of my spirit, and one that I want to keep up and develop as far as I can.

Even when I wasn't painting, my publications were very sparse. I'm not a prolific writer. I write little; I may be more productive as a painter than a writer, I don't know. We just have to wait and see. I'm not bothered by such comparisons at the moment.

S: You have written and lectured on Native American art. You have pointed out that the aesthetic perception of the Indian world is a result of a "native intelligence." Could you explain this notion a little further?

M: I believe that from the time the paleo-Indians, to use an anthropological term, set foot on the North American continent, they began developing an aesthetics that is in keeping with and somehow related directly to the American landscape. This accounts for the fact that Native American people have a highly developed artistic sense. Navajo children, Pueblo children, Plains Indian children, can draw better than their white counterparts. I think that could be proved, across the board; that has been my experience. I have never known an Indian child that had not some sort of demonstrable artistic talent, and you account for it that way; it's kind of a genetic experience of the landscape, a way of seeing that has been developed over a long period of time.

S: Much of your writing is concerned with the human relationship to the earth, with the formulation of an appropriate land ethic. Have you been involved in the conservation movement?

M: I wasn't actively involved in conservation; still, my spirit was there. Now I think of myself as a conservationist. I have great sympathy for the Sierra Club and such organizations.

S: You have in many public speeches drawn attention to the Indian's particular investment in the American land. Do you see a danger of creating or reinforcing an Indian-as-ecologist image through this portrayal?

M: In "A First American Views His Land," I noted that the paleo-Indian who came across the Bering Strait was hunting animals to extinction, and had no sense of conservation at all. But over a period of thousands of years, maybe twenty, thirty thousand, he developed a sense of conservation so that the Indian of the Great Lakes region in, say, the middle nineteenth century, was what we call a multiple use conservationist. And that's important to me; I think that great knowledge gained over thousands of years was very important. We all ought to be conservationists in that sense, especially in our time.

S: Your concept of an American land ethic has grown mainly out of your knowledge of Native American attitudes to the environment. To what extent have people like John Muir, Aldo Leopold, Wallace Stegner, and Stewart Udall contributed to your formulation of a new American land ethic?

M: I think not much. I wish I could say that they contributed more because I respect them all, but the fact of the matter is I came to them very late, and though I've read Leopold and Stegner and others, I wrote what I wrote really before I knew them.

S: Let me move on to another crucial aspect of your work. Much of your writing reflects your preoccupation with language and the imagination. I would like to ask you a few questions regarding these two central issues. You have said that "we are what we imagine ourselves to be," and that "we have our best existence in the element of language." These statements and a direct reference in one of the *Viva* columns to Berkeley's proposition of "esse est percipi"—to be is to be perceived—suggest a strongly idealist position. In the same *Viva* column you wrote: "Existence itself is illusory; we inhabit a dream in the mind of God." Would you like to comment on this idealist position, and how you arrived at it?

M: I arrived at it by simply thinking about it for a long time. What is it to exist? You know I wrote that one piece that I am fond of reciting about Koh-sahn stepping out of the page and confronting me, and she ends up by saying: "Be careful of your pronouncements, grandson. If I am not here in this room, grandson, then surely neither are you." At this point I was thinking very much and deeply about existence. And I think existence *is* illusory. I don't know what it is to be, and I sometimes think that being and existence is simply a dream that we have, as in that case.

S: The single most significant piece on this subject is your essay, "The Man Made of Words." The title brings to mind Wallace Stevens's poem, "Men Made Out of Words." To what extent do you share Stevens's belief in the supremacy of the life of the imagination, which finds expression in such statements as "The final belief is the belief in a fiction, which you know to be a fiction, there being nothing else," or "The magnificent cause of being, the imagination, [is] the one reality in this imagined world"?

M: All of that seems very seductive to me. I don't know Stevens's writings beyond his poems that well, but certainly with these things that you have just quoted I can go along. I believe in a supremacy of the imagination. And I believe that fiction is a superior kind of reality. What we imagine is the best of us.

S: In the oral tradition, language, memory, and the imagination are crucial for the survival of culture. It seems to me that much of your imaginative effort is directed toward the reconstruction of your Kiowa heritage and thus toward the affirmation of an Indian identity. Do you see this as the only way in which a tribal identity can be perpetuated in a modern world?

M: I think so; I have understood much more about my Indian heritage and much more about myself by virtue of having written things down. *The Names* is a great case in point. I can't tell you how much more you know about yourself if you go through the business of writing an autobiographical narrative, recalling your childhood, trying to project yourself even into your ancestral antecedents. You end up knowing an awful lot about yourself, more than would otherwise be possible. Depending on what sort of things you write you inevitably learn a lot in the process. Yvor Winters once made a statement that I will never forget; it was almost off hand, but it rang true. He said, "If you write enough poems you become educated." And I know exactly what he means. Writing is, among other things, a way of learning.

S: Is it fair to say that your theory of literature and the imagination is rooted both in the oral tradition and in modern literary concepts?

M: Absolutely. Oral tradition, the stories that I know from oral tradition, seems such a big part of my life, when I stop to think about it. My father told me stories when I was little; and at a certain point I realized that they were very special, that they had never been written down, they came from a real experience of people in touch with the land and with each other, and that blew my mind. That's big in my life, and also the books that I have been privileged to read. I think I take my imaginative life from both of those sources.

S: You said about Emily Dickinson that "she taught [you] a good deal about language—and in the process a good deal about the art of intellectual survival." Can you tell me what exactly you mean by that?

M: Emily Dickinson is nearly infinite in her expression. She wrote seventeen hundred and seventy-five poems, and they constitute a very rich literature certainly. And she was, God knows, highly imaginative, highly intelligent, highly perceptive, and she had a kind of regard for language that a great writer must have. It was a mystery, a miracle to her. I learned a little something about the mystery and miracle of language by reading her. I think her survival was largely intellectual. She was a curious lady, as you know. I don't suppose we know exactly what her life was. But it must have been painful to her in many ways, and I suspect she wrote in order to make it endurable.

S: And you see that function of creative work as a way to accommodate life in your own case?

M: Yes, and more and more so. I don't want to make pronouncements, but I believe that I fashion my own life out of words and images, and that's how I get by. If I didn't do those things, I think that I would find my existence a problem of some sort. Writing, giving expression to my spirit and to my mind, that's a way of surviving, of ordering one's life. That's a way of living, of making life acceptable to oneself.

S: Marcel Proust suggests that life can be restored, illumined, realized within the confines of a book. Through a work of art, a book, we defy oblivion and the inevitability of death. You, too, have written in praise of books, and about the power of language to deflect the force of time. Are these issues central to your own creative work?

M: When I hear you articulate those ideas, I say to myself, yes. What comes into my mind are instances that bear that out. Going to the Yeibechei, when we were talking about Shiprock Fair, and when I hear those singers and catch the smoke of the bonfires in my nostrils, it is involuntary memory, that's right. I am suddenly eight years old at a Squaw Dance near Lukachukai. It brings the memory back to me like that, you know. And if I tried it without that stimulus, if I merely tried to remember the Squaw Dance at Lukachukai, it would not be nearly as valid a recollection.

S: How about your encounter with Koh-sahn? You said you had finished writing *The Way to Rainy Mountain,* and you felt exhausted. You felt that there was something missing, and you tried to get back into the creative act. That seems to have been a conscious attempt, and yet you get this almost mystical experience afterwards.

M: Both things are true. I sensed that it wasn't finished, and so consciously I took it up again, but what happened after that was beyond consciousness. I didn't really bring Koh-sahn to my mind so much as she came upon me, involuntarily.

S: You have written "the name was that of the seed from which the man issued into the world as well as that of the memory into which man dissolves." Could you explain your own theory of names? Does the power of names reach beyond your own life time into the past and future?

M: I believe that a man is his name. The name and the existence are indivisible. One has to live up to his name. I think names are terribly important. Somewhere in the Indian mentality there is that idea that when someone is given a name, and by the way, it transcends Indian cultures, certainly, when a man is given a name, existence is given to him, too. And what could be worse than not having a name. I used to think a lot about that, and I wrote that story about the boy who came into the camp. No one could understand his language. He spoke, and his language, as the story has it, was pleasant enough, but no one could understand it. And the next morning he was gone. Everyone was troubled until an old man pointed out that the boy never was, as it were. How can we believe in that child if he gave us not one word of sense to hold on to. What we saw, if we saw anything at all, must have been a dog from a neighboring camp or a bear that wandered down from the high country. So that the whole existence of the child was negated easily, and on that basis, and it should have been. I, for one, would hold that yes, the old man was right, the boy never was. He was a figment of our imagination. But if he had spoken something that we could understand, if he'd given himself a name or could have named something within our frame of reference, then one could not have doubted his existence.

S: In *The Names* you wrote, "Had I known it, even then language bore all the names of my being." Are you suggesting that the mode of reality which is language has preexistence to individual personal existence?

M: Yes. You grow up into an understanding of language and through that to an understanding of yourself. That's how it has to happen. We are determined by our language; it holds the limits of our development. We cannot supersede it. We can exist within the development of language and not without. The more deeply you can become involved in language, the more fully we can exist.

A *MELUS* Interview: N. Scott Momaday—A Slant of Light

Bettye Givens / 1982

From *MELUS*, 12, no. 1 (Spring 1985), 79–87. © 1985 The Society for the Study of the Multi-Ethnic Literature of the United States. Reprinted by permission.

On March 26, 1982, Pulitzer prize-winning novelist Dr. N. Scott Momaday visited Texas Tech University to take part in the Kiowa Symposium, an investigation into historical and contemporary issues relating to the Kiowa nation. Momaday is a novelist, poet, historian, and artist. His works include *The Gourd Dancer* (poems), *The Way to Rainy Mountain* (Kiowa folktales), memoir called *The Names*, and *House Made of Dawn*, a novel for which he won a Pulitzer Prize in 1969. His art hangs in galleries in Texas, New Mexico and Oklahoma, and he teaches at the University of Arizona.

Our talk took place in the college museum where he had spoken the evening before. Now he is waiting to watch the Indians dancing. The conversation is relaxed; Momaday speaks with a deep resonance using cultivated speech, for he cares as much about how language sounds as how his words look on the page. In the wide hallway where we sit we can see people gathering for the presentation of Kiowa painting, beadwork, featherwork, hidework, ritual, music and dancing.

Momaday: There's a Greek writer who once said that there are three amphora outside every door: one is full of good things and two are full of bad. But I don't ascribe to any such division of things.

Interviewer: Not even in your writing?

Momaday: I'm basically a poet, I think. Fiction is kind of a spinoff from my poetry. I started writing poetry first, and so I think virtually everything I write is lyrical. That's just the way I write. That's the way I deal in words. I'm very much aware of the sound of what I write. That's how I judge my own writing. I listen to it. I revise as I go, and I write rather slowly. And if I'm writing well, I might come up with three or four pages a day. When I wrote *House Made of*

Dawn, I wrote over a period of about two years, but sporadically. Maybe six months of actual writing time.

Interviewer: Does your teaching interfere with your writing, or do you build inspirations when you teach?

Momaday: I don't think teaching interferes with my writing. I have enough time in which to write. I can write at best only four to five hours a day. And then I'm exhausted. That's the end of my concentration for that sort of work. I find that teaching is a good occupation for a writer. It gives me the kind of change of pace that I like very much. And yet, teachers, after all, have a lot of time; so they can arrange their schedules. When I'm really writing I will arrange my classes so that I teach in the afternoon only. And I keep the morning completely free for writing. Teaching allows you that flexibility, which is very good. If I were a truck driver or an advertising executive, I'm sure that I would have much less time for writing than I have.

Interviewer: Do you enjoy speaking before groups?

Momaday: Yes, I find it a kind of artistic enterprise. It's like writing or painting. It's something that if you do well you realize a great satisfaction.

Interviewer: Do you write a completely new talk each time you speak?

Momaday: No. Absolutely not. The reason I prepared this one was that it was one of the conditions of the contract. When they invited me, I told them what my fee was. And it's an exorbitant fee. I would never pay me what they pay me to come speak. But they said okay. We'll pay you your standard fee if you will turn over to us a publishable text of the speech. Now that's very unusual. Most often, I don't have anything before me but notes. And I extemporize a great deal of what I say. They were very clever. So I had to get up at four o'clock yesterday morning in order to finish that piece. But I kept my end of the bargain. I did hand over a publishable text. And that was good for me because it demanded a kind of discipline that usually I don't have to muster.

Interviewer: You have an excellent speaking voice. Did you take speech lessons or did you teach yourself how to talk.

Momaday: I have what one of my professors described as a very

fine vocal mechanism. The voice box which God himself gave me is a
pretty good one, I guess. I did minor in Speech when I was an
undergraduate. I don't know that that accounts for my ability. I have
that to begin with. But I've had a lot of experience speaking. At one
time I was very nervous when I stood before an audience. Stage
fright. But now I've done it so many times that I'm perfectly at ease
when I'm talking to a group of people because I've had so much
experience. It becomes easier each time.

Interviewer: Your audience becomes fascinated with your ability in
the art of storytelling. What is it about?—this desire of people to sit
and listen to a story.

Momaday: It's a realization of oneself in language for the audience
and the speaker. That's one of the ancient traditions of language far
older than writing. The storyteller and his audience, that's a sacred
relationship. The storyteller creates his audience.

Interviewer: The storyteller creates his audience?

Momaday: That's right. Don't you forget it. Language is so creative
in itself, it is intrinsically so powerful that storytellers, people who
use language, are in possession of a great power. When the storyteller
tells his listener a story, he creates his listener, he creates a story. He
creates himself in the process. It's an entirely creative process.

Interviewer: So the storyteller does manipulate?

Momaday: At least the teller is in control of the situation. The
audience, in order to realize the experience to its fullest, must allow
itself to be determined by the storyteller. He creates the situation. He
creates the audience.

Interviewer: The attitude of the audience?

Momaday: The attitude among other things—it's not only attitude.
It's a whole state of mind and consists of attitudes, philosophies,
beliefs. The listener who comes into a storytelling situation must
allow himself to be created, changed. He must become another
personality for the sake of the experience itself. Same thing can be
said of the storyteller. Storyteller is a man who walks around like
another man, but when he begins to tell a story, he becomes someone
else. He becomes someone whose whole being is there for that
particular purpose and no other. It's like a spell. And when it's over,

he changes back. This is to say that the story, the storytelling situation, is unique. It's never the same thing twice. When I was speaking last night, there was a period of some minutes, almost an hour, in which I was at one with these people. It was a one-time thing. It will never be duplicated. I had an audience before me. And I could determine who and what they were, for that period of time. If I were to go say the same words, give the same talk tonight, it would be entirely different. That's what I mean. The audience was willing to have a spell cast. They did their part and that makes a successful story.

Interviewer: Back to your fiction; is your writing autobiographical?

Momaday: Every character that a writer creates is autobiographical in a sense. It is the writer's own experience that he must draw from. There is no other source. So all writing is autobiographical to that extent. But that's not a term that I would use to describe the character. Abel, for example, in *House Made of Dawn,* is a composite of several people that I knew when I was living in Jemez, New Mexico. I had models for him. So I took this aspect from one person and this from another and so on. And finally, I came up with my character, Abel.

Interviewer: You seem to identify with the Kiowa legend, the seven sisters and the brother?

Momaday: That's right. I've told a lot about the boy. The Kiowa legend has very little to say about him. You know, he turns into a bear. The seven sisters become the stars of the Big Dipper. In a sense, they are immortalized. But I'm serious about the bear. I want to know what happened to him. And I identify with the bear because I'm intimately connected with that story. And so I have this bear power. I turn into a bear every so often. I feel myself becoming a bear, and that's a struggle that I have to face now and then.

Interviewer: Do you mean every man?

Momaday: No, I don't know if any other people turn into bears. But I know that I do. And so that's a great fascination for me. I'm curious about that. I want to know more about that story. So I build upon that legend. I extended it in my own terms. The legend itself is very small. And it ends, the seven sisters were born into the sky, and they became the stars of the Big Dipper. I just go on from there. The boy becomes the bear.

Interviewer: Then you think of the bear as bad?

Momaday: No. If you think of the bear as being primitive. The boy who turns into a bear, what does that mean? What is the metaphor? What is the symbolism there? I suspect it is that part of man which is subhuman. Primitive. Most people cannot recover nature. At one time, we lived in nature. But somewhere along the way, we were severed from nature. And we cannot any longer comprehend the creatures of nature. We don't know about them as we once did. But this boy is an exception. He turns into a bear; that means that he reconstructs that link with nature. You could talk about the bear as being the underside of his existence.

Interviewer: What are bears?

Momaday: Bears are wonderful creatures. They are human-like, adventurous, powerful, curious, extremely confident in their elements. If you took a lion and you pitted him against the bear, I would bet on the bear. Bears are powerful. I was sitting by a man on the plane the other day who was a graduate student in wild life management; he was telling me about bears. He hunts bears with a bow. He's had a lot of experience tranquilizing bears with a dart gun. He said that he'd seen bears perform incredible feats of strength. Take a boulder that 20 men cannot budge. The bear can come along and just hurl it out of the way. He'd seen that. A lion can't do that. Yes. I'd bet on the bear. Grizzlies are ursus horribilis. They are the horrible. Polar bears. Tremendous creatures. Huge. Incredible strength.

Interviewer: Do you hunt?

Momaday: Only with a camera. I've gone hunting with my father when I was a boy. I went deer hunting one time. But I'm certainly not a hunter.

Interviewer: A critic said of *House Made of Dawn*: "This book is no *Uncle Tom's Cabin,* but its successor could be." How do you feel about that statement?

Momaday: I'm not interested in writing anything like *Uncle Tom's Cabin*. There has been an unfortunate chapter in American history where the Indian is concerned. But I don't care about changing attitudes. That's not the sort of writing I do. I don't make any sort of social comment. I'm not that sort of writer. I like to tell a story. My father told me stories when I was small. Told me something about the history of the Kiowa people. And then I got very much interested in it and wanted to write about it. Everybody who writes about the history of the Kiowas has to dwell on Mooney's calendar history of the Kiowa people. It's the most authoritative thing that was ever written on the Kiowas in the nineteenth century. I know the calendar history quite well. I read it thoroughly. And Mayhall's book, *The Kiowa;* Ney's book, *Carbine and Lance,* and *Bad Medicine and Good.* The Kiowas are fortunate people in the sense that a lot of people have written about them. You find out a good deal.

Interviewer: Do you have a secret place from which you write?

Momaday: A provocative question. Yes, I suppose every writer can say something like that, can think of writing in those terms. Sure. One writes out of a particular intelligence, and it is an intelligence that most people will never understand. So it's secret in that sense. Language is a risky business. Writing, speaking . . . you always stand to be misunderstood, misinterpreted. Language is powerful. You can make someone angry by saying things. And even if you don't say them, they can be taken the wrong way. Bad things become of it. Wars can be started at the level of language. Sure, language is very risky. That's what makes it wonderful.

Interviewer: And who are your favorite writers?

Momaday: Favorite writers? Herman Melville. Norman McClain, Emily Dickinson, and Wallace Stevens. That's enough.

Interviewer: What contemporary authors do you read?

Momaday: I'm reading a book by Jonathan Kenner right now. I've read a little of John Cheever. I've read a good deal of fiction this year because I'm on a jury for the awarding of a prize in fiction. So I've had to. I've had to read a lot of contemporary fiction. Most of which I found hard to read. But as a rule I'm too busy with other things. I'm teaching a course in Emily Dickinson and reread and reread things that I've read in the past in order to teach them well. And I write and I paint. So I don't spend much time at all reading my contemporaries. Not at all. That doesn't interest me either.

Interviewer How do you feel about teaching writing?

Momaday: I'm not very enthusiastic about it. I have taken creative writing courses. I did not find them very valuable. I have taught once or twice a creative writing course, and I was not happy about it. I think that writing is a very solitary business. It's something that one has to work out for oneself. But understand that I'm speaking only for myself and that other writers may find a community of writers inspiring. They might find creative writing courses helpful for them. But I don't. I don't like to take them, and I don't like to teach them. So I don't. Writing is so many things. It's satisfying sometimes. It's frustrating, it's agonizing. If I'm doing well, I can get very much involved in my writing and I am anxious to get back to it. Look forward to the morning when I can go back and pick up that current and carry on.

Interviewer: Do you discover your story as you write or do you make an outline?

Momaday: It works both ways. I have made outlines which very rarely turn out to be . . . what I write very rarely coincides with the outline. More often I think I just start writing without an outline. I develop it from page to page or scene to scene. I was reading a collection of interviews with Nabokov and somebody asked him how he wrote, what his method of writing was. And he said, "I don't write chronologically, that is, I don't proceed from page 1 to page 390. I take index cards, and I write scenes. And this scene may fall on page 44 and the next one might be on page 212. I just create the pieces of a jigsaw puzzle, and when I have them all together, when I have a collection of them, then I arrange them. I fit them to the pattern." And that seems to be eminently wise. That's a good way to go about it. And that's something of the way in which I write. When I start writing I always imagine, here's page one, this is how it begins. But it rarely happens that way. Write something and you find that it doesn't belong here in this space but belongs in another place.

Interviewer: What places in the world are important to you?

Momaday: There are several places. Rainy Mountain, Jemez Springs, Santa Fe, Samarkand in East Pakistan, Soviet Central Asia, and the old, old silk route. I was living in Moscow, and I was traveling through Central Asia. Samarkand is one of the magical cities in the world. A year or so before I went there, they celebrated officially their 2500 anniversary. But the ruins at the edge of the city, the ruins that are called Afrosiab are twice as old, 5000 years old.

Interviewer: Are you as good an artist as your father, Al Momaday?

Momaday: No, not yet. I won't ever be the same sort of artist. I feel that I have to develop; that's the challenge. I want to see how far I can take it. I want to be good at everything I try. I don't want to be bad at anything.

Interviewer: And a good poet?

Momaday: Oh, a great poet.

Interviewer: Richard Tilingast said, "If you've written one perfect poem, why do people keep asking what you're writing?"

Momaday: There's something to that. To have written one such an accomplishment, and it puts you in such a minority that it is almost a justification in itself. "After great pain, a formal feeling comes—"; "There's a certain slant of light." And there are, as I say, maybe two or three more that are up to that level. Beyond that, though they are very fine poems, they're nonetheless a cut below these.

Interviewer: In your opinion which poems do you think reach a certain perfection?

Momaday: "Sunday Morning" by Wallace Stevens, certainly. Then Jonson's "To Heaven," George Herbert's "Church Monuments," well, that's enough.

Interviewer: Which of your poems achieved the greatest perfection?

Momaday: "Angle of Geese," "Rainy Mountain Cemetery," and "Before an Old Painting of the Crucifixion." And one called "Nous avons vu la mer"; this one hasn't been published. It's a love poem; I don't write many love poems, and I like it very much.

Interviewer: How would you rate your novel, *House Made of Dawn*?

Momaday: I think it's a terrific novel. I like it a lot. Pleased to have written it.

Interviewer: Was it hard to write?

Momaday: Yes and no. All writing is hard. There are things that have been harder for me to write. What makes writing tolerable is inspiration. If you are inspired, then the writing goes—it flows, it happens. And if you're not inspired, then it's drudgery. And, of course, I have been in the position a number of times when I've had to write things about which I was not inspired at all. And that's the worst kind of writing. That's just work. But writing *House Made of Dawn,* I was inspired. And so it was much easier in that sense. Writing is never easy, but with inspiration it is easier.

Interviewer: So you have inspiration some days and some days you don't?

Momaday: Yes, that's a fair statement. Of course, it depends upon the subject too—what it is that you're writing about. Some things are of interest to you. And so you're inspired to write them; other things are not, so the inspiration is not there.

Interviewer: One writer said that he felt guilty because he was spending so much time at writing. How do you feel?

Momaday: I think we all have feelings of that kind. There's always a balance. There's always—what is the popular term?—a trade off. If you write through the morning, and work at home as I often do, there's a question that pops into your mind, well, shouldn't I be spending this half-hour with my two year old? Pangs like that. But they don't amount to anything. The answer, of course, is no. I should be writing. It is, after all, unusual that I am at home. And she's here. I can look at her playing on the patio. She knows where I am. She knows that she can come and cry on my shoulder if she needs to. Then, how many fathers can say that? So there's no reason to feel guilty. Because it's in me to write. It's like saying why do you climb the mountain?

Interviewer: Edward Hogland in his book of essays made an interesting statement, "To live is to see." What do you think?

Momaday: What you see is what you are. I have seen wonderful things.

The Magic of Words: An Interview with N. Scott Momaday

Joseph Bruchac / 1982

From *Survival This Way: Interviews with American Indian Poets,* Tucson: University of Arizona Press, 1987, 173–91. First published in *American Poetry Review.* Reprinted by permission of the University of Arizona Press.

This interview with N. Scott Momaday, the first Native American writer ever to win a national literary prize—a 1969 Pulitzer for his novel, *House Made of Dawn*—took place on December 7, 1982. The setting was his office at the University of Arizona in Tucson where he is a professor in the English Department. After many years of self-imposed "exile" in California, Momaday has returned to the Southwest which is the backdrop for so much of his important writing. Few people have described that landscape and its people with such love and precision.

With Momaday's deep awareness of details in mind, I made a conscious effort to observe the particulars of this place he had chosen for our meeting. It was not that easy to do, for N. Scott Momaday is an imposing man of dominating, though agreeable, presence. More than six feet tall and large of body in the way a buffalo or some other great animal is large, he seemed to fill the room. The voice with which he greeted me was warm and deep, the words spoken in a way which gave weight to each syllable. It was the voice one might expect from a man who wrote and continues to write of the magical nature and power of language, whose essay "The Man Made of Words" is one of the most important contemporary statements about the American Indian writer. Clean-shaven (unlike the photographs on the backs of his books in which he wears a full beard and looks vaguely Japanese), his hair cut short, and his clothing of the sort one might describe as "informal academic," there was little to distinguish his appearance from that of a thousand other men sitting at ease in their college offices and awaiting the arrival, perhaps, of a student for a conference about a term paper. Yet there *was* something different, beyond his seeming self-assurance and the Kiowa cast of his features, something reflected most clearly, perhaps, in his beautiful voice. Perhaps it was only my own flawed perception, but it seemed to me that I was in the presence of one who was aware of and most careful with *strength*.

He carefully lettered a sign: DO NOT DISTURB, TAPING SESSION. As he taped it to the outside of his door, I thought how much the contents of the room mirrored its principal occupant. A large desk was placed to face the door. A few papers were arranged on it neatly, but it was the two carvings placed there which drew my attention. One was a large, roughly shaped wooden bear. The other was a Plains Indian on horseback. Between the two of them was a big magnifying glass. There were only a few books in the case to the right of the desk, but there were two paintings on the wall, both signed by Momaday. One was a figure resembling a harlequin, the colors bright, the lines bold, almost idiosyncratic. The other was a man in late middle age with a dark face standing in the midst of a wide bare landscape which made one think of the plains of southwestern Oklahoma.

When Momaday was ready, the tape levels set, my questions in front of me, I asked him if he would begin by reading a poem. He reached out a hand to touch the carving of the bear and I thought I detected a faint smile.

JB: In a recent book entitled *Four American Indian Literary Masters,* Alan R. Velie links your poetry strongly with those whom he calls "the post-symbolists" and your former teacher, Yvor Winters. Do you think that really was correct?

Momaday: Well, to an extent, yes. I don't remember what Velie had to say, exactly. "Post-symbolist," by the way, is Yvor Winters's term, not Velie's. It is an important concept in Winters's critical canon, and I would not presume to say what it is or what it has to do with my work. Anyone interested in it ought to go directly to Winters's last work, *Forms of Discovery*. I didn't know much about the traditional aspects of poetry until I went to Stanford and studied under Winters. Winters was a very fine teacher, and no doubt he had a significant influence upon a good many of his students over the years. In 1959, when I went to Stanford, I was just ready to be educated in terms of prosody, and I owe a good deal of what I know about poetry to Yvor Winters. I think that my early poems, especially those that are structured according to traditional English forms, are in some respects the immediate result of his encouragement and of his teaching.

JB: Poems such as "Angle of Geese" or "The Bear" . . .

Momaday: "Angle of Geese" and "The Bear" are written in syllabics; that is, the number of syllables in each line is predetermined and invariable; it is therefore the number of syllables to the line, rather than the number of "feet," which constitutes the measure. I was just playing around a lot with syllabics at Stanford—I wasn't even aware of the term "syllabics" until I went to Winters's class in the writing of poetry. So, yes, those would be two examples. But I got tired of the traditional forms. When I left Stanford I had worked myself into such a confinement of form that I started writing fiction and didn't get back to poetry until much later—three years, perhaps—and when I did, I started writing a very different kind of poetry.

JB: I notice, before we talk about that different kind of poetry, that you chose the poem, "The Bear." What is it that made you choose that poem to read? What is important to you about that particular poem?

Momaday: It was pretty much a random choice, but I like the poem because it is early and it is one of my first really successful poems, as I think of it. It deals with nature, as much of my work does, and it is rhymed in syllabics, and so there are good, solid, controlling devices at work in the poem, and that, that aspect of control, is important to me. I wanted to see how closely I could control the statement, and it seems to me that I controlled it about as well as I could. "The Bear" won some sort of prize at Stanford—a prize awarded by the Academy of American Poets, I think. I was ecstatic.

JB: What forms do you think you're working in now in your poetry? I've heard them described as prose poems by Velie and other people. In some cases, I know some aren't.

Momaday: No. I continue working in syllabics. I have written what is called "free verse," though to my mind that is a contradiction in terms. I'm greatly interested in the so-called "prose poem," another contradiction in terms, but what I mean is, I like writing what is essentially a lyrical prose in which I'm not concerned with meter, but with rhythms and fluencies of sound, primarily. I wrote a piece, which no doubt you've seen in *The Gourd Dancer,* called "The Colors of Night," which is really a collection of quintessential novels, I suppose—very short, lyrical stories. I would like to continue working in that free form.

JB: As a matter of fact that particular poem is one of my favorites in *The Gourd Dancer.* I thought it interesting that in that book you combine both the earlier poems and the later poems, and they didn't seem to be combined in a chronological order but rather in terms of subject matter. When you put the book together, what was your structuring theory or device?

Momaday: I wanted, as you say, to group the several poems in certain ways. There is a chronological progression to it. The early poems, recognizably traditional forms, I think, are contained in the first section, then the second section is of a very different character, informed by a native voice, and the third section is, or was then, quite recent work. Much of it was written in the Soviet Union.

JB: Did it affect your writing when you worked in another country?

Momaday: I think it did. I'm not sure that I can say how, exactly. There was a great compulsion there to write, and that surprised me; I could not have anticipated that. But when I got there and had been there a while and had begun to understand a little bit about my isolation and my distance from my native land, this somehow became a creative impulse for me, and so I wrote much more than I thought I would. And I wrote about things I saw and felt in the Soviet Union. "Krasnopresnenskaya Station" is an example. The little poem called "Anywhere Is a Street into the Night" is a comment upon my understanding of that distance that I mentioned a moment ago. But I also found myself writing about my homeland, the Southwest—perhaps as a kind of therapy. I wrote the poem that I dedicated to Georgia O'Keeffe ("Forms of the Earth at Abiquiu") there, for example, and it is very much an evocation of the Southwest, isn't it?

JB: This southwestern landscape which turns up in your poems throughout your writing . . . how do you define that landscape? What are the important qualities of it for you? The qualities of life in the Southwest which are important . . .

Momaday: Well, I think it's a much more spiritual landscape than any other that I know personally. And it is beautiful, simply in physical terms. The colors in that landscape are very vivid, as you know, and I've always been greatly moved by the quality of light upon the colored landscape of New Mexico and Arizona.

JB: Yes, that's evident in your work.

Momaday: And I think of it as being inhabited by a people who are truly involved in it. The Indians of the Southwest, and the Pueblo people, for example, and the Navajos with whom I grew up, they don't live on the land; they live in it, in a real sense. And that is very important to me, and I like to evoke as best I can that sense of belonging to the earth.

JB: I think that idea of belonging is also of central importance. In *The Names* or even in some of your poems, you present us with situations where there is a possibility for distance, or a possibility for alienation. But I don't see that alienation coming about. I see, rather, a motion in a different direction—toward a kind of resolution. Am I correct in seeing this?

Momaday: I think that's a fair statement.

JB: Why is that so? Why are you not an existentialist, for example, a "modern" man looking at the world as separate from the person?

Momaday: Well, I'm a product of my experience, surely, of what I have seen and known of the world. I've had, by the way, what I think of as a very fortunate growing up. On the basis of my experience, trusting my own perceptions, I don't see any validity in the separation of man and the landscape. Oh, I know that the notion of alienation is very widespread, in a sense very popular. But I think it's an unfortunate point of view and a false one, where the relationship between man and the earth is concerned. Certainly it is one of the great afflictions of our time, this conviction of alienation, separation, isolation. And it is certainly an affliction in the Indian world. But there it has the least chance of taking hold, I believe, for there it is opposed by very strong forces. The whole world view of the Indian is predicated upon the principle of harmony in the universe. You can't tinker much with that; it has the look of an absolute.

JB: Do you differentiate between prose and poetry in a strict sense?

Momaday: When I talk about definitions, yes. Prose and poetry are opposed in a certain way. It's hard to define poetry. Poetry is a statement concerning the human condition, composed in verse. I did not invent this definition, skeletal as it is. I think I may be repeating something I heard in class years ago. In that refinement, in that reservation, "composed in verse," is really, finally, the matter that establishes the idea of poetry and sets it apart.

JB: I wonder, because I see in the work of a number of American Indian writers, for example, Leslie Silko, places where prose suddenly breaks into what appears to be verse in parts of *Ceremony.* There the stories that are told are in a form I would describe as verse. I see, also, in a number of other writers who are American Indians, if not a blurring of that distinction, a passing back and forth, rather freely, between verse and prose. I see it, also, in your work . . . your prose in such books as *House Made of Dawn,* and especially *The Way to Rainy Mountain.* There are sections which one could read as poems. Is this observation a good one? Why do you think it's like this, with yourself and other American Indian prose writers?

Momaday: That's a large question, and I've thought about it before. The prose pieces in *The Way to Rainy Mountain* are illustrations of the very thing that I was talking about before, the lyrical prose, the thing that is called the prose poem. The oral tradition of the American Indian is intrinsically poetic in certain, obvious ways. I believe that a good many Indian writers rely upon a kind of poetic expression out of necessity, a necessary homage to the native tradition, and they have every right and reason to do so. It is much harder, I suspect, for an Indian to write a novel than to write a poem. The novel, as a form, is more unfamiliar to him in his native context. That he does it at all is a kind of tour de force. I am thinking of Jim Welch's *Winter in the Blood,* for example, a fine novel, to my mind. Again, I have to quibble with the word "verse." Verse, after all, strictly speaking, is a very precise meter of measure. My "Plainview: 1," for example, is composed in verse. If you look at it closely you see that it is a sonnet, composed in heroic couplets, rhymed iambic pentameter. "The Colors of Night," on the other hand, is not verse. Meter, as such, is simply not a consideration in that piece. You can make the same distinction between, say, "Abstract: Old Woman in a Room" and "Forms of the Earth at Abiquiu." I will indeed quibble over terms

here, for they are important. Verse greatly matters, though too few
contemporary poets take it seriously, I'm afraid. Verse enables you
to sharpen your expression considerably, to explore and realize more
closely the possibilities of language. A given prose poem, so-called,
may be superior to a given Shakespearean sonnet, but we are talking
about an exception; the odds are against it. Sometimes, of course, it
is worthwhile to go against the odds.

JB: Vine Deloria complained, in an interview in 1977 in *Sun Tracks*
that so many young American Indian writers turned to verse rather
than writing in what he thought was a more useful form to communicate with the Anglo world, fiction or prose. Yet you're saying that
really isn't so much of a choice, as a natural step.
Momaday: I think so. At least, that's how I think of it.

JB: I have noticed that certain themes appear to turn up again and
again in your work. What are those themes? Do you think about them
or are they there subconsciously?
Momaday: I would say that much of my writing has been concerned
with the question of man's relationship to the earth, for one thing.
Another theme that has interested me is man's relationship to himself,
to his past, his heritage. When I was growing up on the reservations
of the Southwest, I saw people who were deeply involved in their
traditional life, in the memories of their blood. They had, as far as I
could see, a certain strength and beauty that I find missing in the
modern world at large. I like to celebrate that involvement in my
writing.

JB: You don't think of yourself, though, as a person who is sort of
conserving something that's disappearing, do you? I've heard that
description of their work given by many non-Indian writers who have
written about Indian ways. And I'm not just talking about anthropologists, but also some of the novelists of the early part of the century
who thought of themselves as both celebrating and preserving—
almost like an artifact—something which was vanishing. Yet I don't
think that is characteristic of your approach.
Momaday: No, I wouldn't say so. There is an aspect of this matter
that has to do with preservation, of course—with a realization that
things are passing. I feel this very keenly. But I'm not concerned to

preserve relics and artifacts. Only superficially have things changed in the world I knew as a child. I can enumerate them. When I was growing up at Jemez Pueblo—I lived there for several years from the time I was twelve—I saw things that are not to be seen now. I wrote about some of them in *The Names*. I remember one day looking out upon a dirt road and seeing a caravan of covered wagons that reached as far as the eye could see. These were the Navajos coming in from Torreon to the annual Jemez feast on November 12, 1946. It was simply an unforgettable sight. But the next year it had changed considerably; there were fewer wagons, and there were some pickups, and the year after that there were still fewer wagons and more pickups, and the year after that there were no wagons. And I had later the sense that I had been in the right place at the right time, that I had seen something that will not be seen again, and I thank God for that. But the loss is less important to me than the spirit which informs the remembrance, the spirit that informs that pageantry across all ages and which persists in the imagination of every man everywhere.

JB: Yes, that's a great example. Are words magical?
Momaday: Oh, yes.

JB: How so?
Momaday: Well, words are powerful beyond our knowledge, certainly. And they are beautiful. Words are intrinsically powerful, I believe. And there is magic in that. Words come from nothing into being. They are created in the imagination and given life on the human voice. You know, we used to believe—and I'm talking now about all of us, regardless of our ethnic backgrounds—in the magic of words. The Anglo-Saxon who uttered spells over his fields so that the seeds would come out of the ground on the sheer strength of his voice knew a good deal about language, and he believed absolutely in the efficacy of language. That man's faith—and may I say, wisdom—has been lost upon modern man, by and large. It survives in the poets of the world, I suppose, the singers. We do not now know what we can do with words. But as long as there are those among us who try to find out, literature will be secure; literature will remain a thing worthy of our highest level of human being.

JB: You mention poets and singers. Are they related or are they different?

Momaday: I think they are the same thing. You might make this sort of superficial distinction. The poet is concerned to construct his expression according to traditional and prescribed forms. The singer, too, composes his expression according to strict rules, but he is a more religious being, on the whole, less concerned with form than with the most fundamental and creative possibilities of language. The American Indian would be in the second of these categories. This distinction, of course, requires elucidation, but, for the time being, I shall spare you that.

JB: And do you think there are some Indian poets who are still singers or vice versa?
Momaday: Yes.

JB: Could I ask you to read this one? I think it goes well with what we were just talking about.
Momaday: Yes.

The Delight Song of Tsoai-Talee

I am a feather on the bright sky
I am the blue horse that runs in the plain
I am the fish that rolls, shining, in the water
I am the shadow that follows a child
I am the evening light, the lustre of meadows
I am an eagle playing with the wind
I am a cluster of bright beads
I am the farthest star
I am the cold of the dawn
I am the roaring of the rain
I am the glitter on the crust of the snow
I am the long track of the moon in a lake
I am a flame of four colors
I am a deer standing away in the dusk
I am a field of sumac and the pomme blanche
I am an angle of geese in the winter sky
I am the hunger of a young wolf
I am the whole dream of these things

You see, I am alive, I am alive
I stand in good relation to the earth

I stand in good relation to the gods
I stand in good relation to all that is beautiful
I stand in good relation to the daughter of Tsen-tainte
You see, I am alive, I am alive

JB: I've always liked this poem of yours very much. As you may know I chose it for translation into some European languages. This is your own song, isn't it?

Momaday: Yes.

JB: This is the name which you were given by an older relative?

Momaday: The name was given to me by an old man, a paternal relative, actually. His name was Pohd-lohk, and he gave me the name when I was very young, less than a year old. Tsoai-talee means "rock-tree boy." It commemorates my having been taken, at the age of six months or so, to Devils Tower, Wyoming, which is a sacred place in Kiowa tradition. And the Kiowas call it "rock-tree." Therefore, Pohd-lohk gave me the name. All of this is set down in detail in *The Names*.

JB: This poem or song makes me think of some very traditional poems or songs. I feel as though I can see, for example, that south-western influence, the traditional songs of the Navajos and Pueblo people. Especially the Navajo people. I also feel I see something which comes out of Plains Indians' structures, a statement of who you are. Not so much a boasting song as a definition of being alive. Do you see all those things coming together in this? Is this part of what you did consciously or did the form of the poem come in and of itself?

Momaday: I see those things in it, but I'm not sure that I set out to reflect them consciously in the poem. As I recall, the writing of it came quickly, without effort . . . it's not a poem that I crafted over a long period of time. It is more spontaneous than most of my poems.

JB: Yes, you mention the word "dream" in here. Again it seems to me like the poem that comes out of a dream . . . the poem that traditionally would come as an inspiration from another voice.

Momaday: Dreams, I suppose, are also a constant theme in my work. I'm very much aware of the visionary aspect of the Plains culture, especially the vision quest, so-called. I have more to say about that, I think, in another context. I'm writing a piece now, based upon a vision quest. It will be a novel, I think.

JB: The idea of dreams, then . . . what are dreams?

Momaday: Yeah, what are dreams? Has there ever been an answer to that? There is so much we have yet to know about dreams and dreaming. Dreams are prophetic, meaningful, revealing of inmost life. But no one knows how they work, as far as I know. I have powerful dreams, and I believe they determine who I am and what I do. But how, I'm not sure. Maybe that is how it ought to be. Mystery is, perhaps, the necessary condition of dreams.

JB: The term, "the great mystery," is often used by some of the Plains people to describe the Creator or that life force which is beyond and above all human, in other life. That's not a mystery that, I sense, native people wish to pierce. It's a mystery which they live in the knowledge of, without wanting to know "what" it is. It seems rather counter to the Western approach to things. The Anglo approach is to *always* know.

Momaday: Yes, yes. I don't know.

JB: I was talking about the contrast between the Western, Anglo, view and the American Indian view. I'd like to take that back directly to literature and ask what you think the difference is between, let's say, an Indian view of what literature is, and I don't mean just a traditional Indian person, but, let's say someone who has been raised in the twentieth century and who is writing still as an Indian, as that of a writer who is non-Indian.

Momaday: I think there is only one real difference between the two, and that is that the Indian has the advantage of a very rich spiritual experience. As much can be said, certainly, of some non-Indian writers. But the non-Indian writers of today are culturally deprived, I think, in the sense that they don't have the same sense of heritage that the Indian has. I'm told this time and time again by my students, who say, "Oh, I wish I knew more about my grandparents; I wish I knew more about my ancestors and where they came from and what they did." I've come to believe them. It seems to me that the Indian writer ought to make use of that advantage. One of his subjects ought certainly to be his cultural investment in the world. It is a unique and complete experience, and it is a great subject in itself.

JB: One thing which I'm concerned with is a sense of the continuance and the survival of various things which seem to be central to a number of American Indian writers. Do you see your work as continuing some tradition?

Momaday: Yes. I think that my work proceeds from the American Indian oral tradition, and I think it sustains that tradition and carries it along. And vice versa. And my writing is also of a piece. I've written several books, but to me they are all parts of the same story. And I like to repeat myself, if you will, from book to book, in the way that Faulkner did—in an even more obvious way, perhaps. My purpose is to carry on what was begun a long time ago; there's no end to it that I can see.

JB: That's a question that I was going to ask. I'm glad you led into it. In *House Made of Dawn* there is a sermon which is given by a Kiowa character. He's not terribly likable in some ways. Yet those words turn up again in *The Way to Rainy Mountain* out of, I assume, your own lips. The things that happen in *The Gourd Dancer* also seem to be a continuance of that same voice and, of course, in *The Names* you have that repetition. I've heard some people say, "Momaday's repeating himself. Doesn't he have any new material?" But I've suspected this repetition was a conscious thing.

Momaday: Oh, yes. In a sense I'm not concerned to change my subject from book to book. Rather, I'm concerned to keep the story going. I mean to keep the same subject, to carry it farther with each telling.

JB: Some traditional songs and stories begin each new movement by repeating. They repeat and then go a bit further. That's the structure in your work?

Momaday: Yes, indeed, and I believe that it is a good way in which to proceed. It establishes a continuity that is important to me.

JB: What are the links in your everyday life to American Indian traditions?

Momaday: Well, I have the conviction that I am an Indian. I have an idea of myself as an Indian, and that idea is quite secure. My father was Huan-toa; my grandfather was Mammedaty; my great-grandfather was Guipagho. How can I not be an Indian? I'm a member of the

Gourd Dance society in the Kiowa tribe, and when I can, I go to the annual meeting of that society, and it is a great thing for me, full of excitement and restoration, the deepest meaning. Since I've returned to the Southwest I feel new and stronger links with the Indian world than I felt in California, where I was for twenty years in exile. Then, too, I have children. And my children are, much to my delight, greatly interested in their stake in the Indian world. So that's another link for me as well as for them. Of course I have Indian relatives. I lost my father, who was my closest tie with the Kiowa world; he died last year. But there are others who sustain me. I keep in touch.

JB: You could say then, perhaps, of "The Gourd Dancer," of your poem, although it's dedicated to your grandfather, that Gourd Dancer is also you.

Momaday: Oh, yes, yes. Again the continuity. That part of the poem which refers to the giving away of a horse: I wasn't there, of course. But it really did happen; my father was only eight years old, but it remained in his memory as long as he lived. And I absorbed it when I was the same age, so that it became my memory as well. This is a profound continuity, something at the very center of the Indian perception of the world. We are talking about immortality, or something very close to it, though the American Indian would not have that name for it. He would say, perhaps, if he were Kiowa, *Akeahde,* "they were camping." In that word is the seed of the same idea.

JB: The American writer some people might link you most closely to who is non-Indian is Walt Whitman. Whitman's life was a single work, *Leaves of Grass,* which went through different stages of development. Vine Deloria and Geary Hobson have both pointed out (Geary in an article in *New America Magazine* and Vine in that *Sun Tracks* interview), that there have been cycles of interest in American Indians and in the publication of American Indian literary work. As you know, D'Arcy McNickle more or less stopped being published after a certain point in the late thirties and only was published just before his death in the current resurgence in the later seventies. In the thirties, it was Luther Standing Bear, twenty years before that Charles Eastman. Do you think that this kind of cycle will happen again with American Indian literature or is there something different about the current surge of writing by American Indians and interest in their writing?

Momaday: I really don't know the answer to that. Oh, I suppose there will be cycles; the popularity of books by and about American Indians will pass, and then there will be regenerations of interest, *ad infinitum*. That's the nature of the publishing world, isn't it? I'm not worried about it. The American Indian is indispensable to the soil and the dream and the destiny of America. That's the important thing. He always was and always will be a central figure in the American imagination, a central figure in American literature. We can't very well do without him.

JB: I also wonder if it might not be different this time because we now have more Indian people who are literate, who do read. We now have also our own audience as opposed to an audience of people who are non-Indian.

Momaday: I'm sure that's true.

JB: What is it that contemporary American Indian poetry has to offer to the world of literature or to the world as a whole?

Momaday: Well, I think it's a legitimate and artistic expression in itself, first of all. Here is my voice, and my voice proceeds out of an intelligence that touches upon the inexorable motions of the world. There is design and symmetry in the pattern of my speech, my words. That in itself is a noteworthy thing. Another such thing is the perception that we were talking about a moment ago. I believe that the Indian has an understanding of the physical world and of the earth as a spiritual entity that is his, very much his own. The non-Indian can benefit a good deal by having that perception revealed to him.

JB: I've been interested in the place that women seem to be taking in American Indian literature. There seems to be a good deal of strong writing coming from American Indian women, perhaps more so than any other ethnic minority, if you want to call it that, in America. Why is that so? Do you have any ideas on that subject?

Momaday: No. It's not something that I have thought much about. But it doesn't surprise me, what you say. Women in the Indian world have always had strong, sometimes supernatural, voices. In Plains culture those voices were often understated for obvious reasons—it was a warrior society, after all—but even in that culture women have always had a prominent position. And it is appropriate that we see Indian women writing now. You're right, there are many, and more to come. And some are doing remarkably fine work. I spoke at the Institute of American Indian Arts in Santa Fe a few months ago. I was speaking particularly to the creative writing students there, and I met several young women, in particular, whose work was very impressive. I met very good young men who were writing well, too, but the women won the day.

JB: In a recent interview, as a part of a National Public Radio program that focused on American Indian women poets called *The Key Is in Remembering,* Paula Gunn Allen said that reading *House Made of Dawn* was one of the major turning points in her life. It made things possible for her that were never possible before. And it is certainly true that you've been a very important inspiration for many American Indian writers. Just the fact that the two best anthologies of American Indian writing, *Carriers of the Dream Wheel* and *The Remembered Earth,* both draw their titles from your work, is a very clear indication of how important people think you are to them. What do you feel about your place as a sort of, to use an academic term, dean of American Indian writers?

Momaday: It's something that I don't often think about. I don't know what that's worth, really. I do very much appreciate people who say the sorts of things that Paula Gunn Allen said on that occasion. But I'm not conscious of my place in that whole scheme of things as yet. And I'm rather reluctant to think in those terms, really, because I want to get on with my work. I'm afraid that if I started thinking of myself as the dean of American Indian writers I might not work so well. I might be tempted to slow down and accept the deanship when I really want to be out there among the subordinates doing my thing.

JB: Deans tend to be administrators, right?
Momaday: Exactly.

Shouting at the Machine: An Interview with N. Scott Momaday

Persona / 1982

From *Persona: The University of Arizona Undergraduate Magazine of Literature and Art* (Spring 1982), 24–44. Reprinted by permission of Lawrence J. Evers.

The interview took place one afternoon at Dr. Momaday's home in the Northwest foothills of Tucson. A warm, comfortable house of red brick and glass, it is set off by an unlikely and beautiful flower garden in the backyard. From inside the living room, looking through a large window, one is made acutely conscious of the contrast between the brightness of the flowers and greenery in the foreground, and the bleakness of the desert sand and plants visible everywhere beyond. One senses that this place is both an oasis and a fortress of sorts, verdant and yet protective.

It is a most appropriate setting for Scott Momaday. He is a large, impressive man who speaks in a deep, rich voice that immediately makes you feel comfortable and aware that words are valuable things, that he does not spend them indiscriminately. Author of many works, including the Pulitzer Prize winning *House Made of Dawn, The Way to Rainy Mountain, The Journey of Tai-me,* and *The Gourd Dancer,* he has recently turned towards the painting of watercolors as the major channel for his talents. He is currently a professor at the University of Arizona, and had just arrived home from a morning spent on the campus the afternoon he spoke with us.

Persona: I was struck by the mention in your memoir that when you were young and attending grammar school, the Kiowa tales were the things that most pre-occupied you, rather than mathematics or history. What do you think your subsequent education has done to that pre-occupation?

Momaday: I don't think it changed the pre-occupation, really. These things are still very important to me. I guess the education really represented a complication of some sort; it gave me other things to be interested in, but not at the expense of that, my dedication to the oral tradition of the Kiowas. That still remains a very important thing to

111

my mind. Though I'm interested in Melville and Emily Dickinson and such, it is not that I've become less interested in Kiowa tales.

P: To ask a double-pronged question: What are the advantages of being a Kiowa author? And what are the disadvantages?

M: To be a Kiowa is to have a subject—but then everybody can say that about his experience, whatever it happens to have been. It is a very rich experience, it is a very rich part of my heritage, and it's a fascinating one. It's a romantic thing in itself, you know, if you think about the nineteenth-century culture of the plains. It's highly colorful and romantic and it's a great subject. So that's the advantage. I have that and very few people have that rich a subject, I think. The disadvantage . . . I don't know about that. I don't see that there's a disadvantage particularly. Of course, there are people who want to categorize you, and I suppose that's a disadvantage, but it seems a very minor one. Every writer is categorized, every author, you know. That's just something you deal with. You can't let that bother you. I've known people who were defensive about being called a Jewish author, but it doesn't bother me at all to be called an Indian author. That's what I am.

P: It does seem, though, that you manage in all your work to escape what one would expect to be constraining about an Indian heritage by making that specific experience much more general, so that being Indian becomes incidental to being a man. How do you think you manage to so transcend the particular and reach the more general, the more accessible?

M: The particular is universal. That's the only answer to that. Someone once said something that I appreciate very much—and I paraphrase it probably badly—"Only by being supremely regional can one be truly universal." I believe that is true, I believe that is true. Faulkner writes about Yoknapatawpha county, but that county becomes the whole world to the reader. The regional aspect of his writing does not exclude you; it includes you. And that's the way writing should be. I simply don't care about categories, they don't mean much to me. A writer is a writer and the great common denominator that interests one is the English language. I write in English, and I'm willing to compete with anybody who writes in English, regardless of his region, or his heritage, or his ethnic background. These things are to be transcended. The idea is for the writer to write. He must express his spirit, whatever his spirit is, and he does it in the only way he can, and that is to write in words, and that is what matters.

P: Do you ever feel trapped by that, trapped by the language?
M: Sure, absolutely. Language is a trap.

P: In what ways do you feel trapped by language?
M: Oh, I don't really feel trapped, that's not the way to put it, but I recognize that there are limitations to language. There are ineffable experiences. There are things that happen to you that cannot be expressed in words. That's entrapment, in a way.

P: What was the first thing you ever had published?
M: It was a poem called "Earth and I Gave You Turquoise," which is in *The Gourd Dancer*. That was published the year after I graduated from college, 1958 I guess it was.

P: Was that a great feeling of re-affirmation, or was it anti-climactic in that you already knew you had something before it was accepted?
M: No, it wasn't quite the same, and it was a great good feeling to publish, the first publication. I thought that I'd done it, and that now I was a professional. And it was a very good feeling.

P: Before that, perhaps in your earliest years of college, did you doubt yourself very much, or did you feel some kind of difference, a certainty?
M: No. I think people who aspire to be writers and especially when they're young, in college say, haven't much doubt. You're not plagued by doubt at that age, you're very positive in your thinking. I pal-ed around with other aspiring writers and we all knew that we were going to burn up the world eventually. No, I don't think there was any doubt. There should have been; perhaps if we'd been more rational about it we would have been more doubtful, but no, we were all great authors!

P: Who did you pal around with?
M: Well, my best friend is . . . his name is Bobby Nelson.

P: The novelist?
M: He is a novelist. He was at New Mexico when I was there. We

met, in fact, in the registration line as entering freshmen. We became very close and pal-ed around all the time, and kept up with each other. He has written a couple of novels. The first one is called *The Last Station* and is set in Australia; he wrote one called *Brothers*, which is about two boys growing up in Texas; and he's published short stories and other things.

P: And who else?

M: Nobody, I think, who's gone on to become a household word or anything . . . but anyway, there were a number of people who thought of themselves as writers—which you do, you know, you think of yourself as a writer long before you are entitled to.

P: Did that ever, do you think, in any way inhibit the learning process by making you say to yourself, "Oh, but I already know that, I'll just go on to the next thing"?

M: I don't know about that. That's an interesting question because it might, it might very well have been an inhibition one way or the other. I don't know, though. There was competition even in those days. We were always trying to outdo each other. Though we were not published, there were contests, you know, creative writing contests at the university. We entered those and placed a great deal of store in any recognition we were given.

P: You seem to emphasize the "first word" a lot in your writing, getting to the first word as a writer. I wondered whether you think that creative writing programs can help you to get to the "first word"? Do you believe they can? Do you think they try to?

M: I have never placed much faith in creative writing courses, though I have taught my share of them and been in them as a student, too. And some of them, I must say, were valuable, although not in the way that one might expect. When I went to Stanford as a graduate, I went as a Creative Writing fellow, and so I was expected to take Yvor Winters's course in the writing of poetry, and I did, I took it five times. I found it extremely valuable, not because it taught me how to write—though it might have done that in ways of which I am not aware—but because I think it was most valuable as a course in criticism. I learned more about reading poetry and evaluating it, than I did about writing it. When I was at Stanford in my first year, I

received a telegram from Paul Engel, who was then directing the
creative writing workshop in Iowa. He offered me a wonderful kind of
fellowship to come there, and his big selling point to me was "Well,
listen, you will be in a community of writers, and you can benefit
enormously from each other." Which turned me completely off. I felt
that the last thing I wanted was to become a member of a community
of writers at that point. I've always felt that way about it. It seems to
me that writing is essentially an isolated and lonely business. I don't
particularly like to talk about writing when I'm writing. I am not
interested in hearing what other people's anguish is as they're writing;
I know enough about that without talking about it, and I don't find
any consolation in talking about it.

I don't believe that one can be taught to write creatively. One can
be taught how to write technically, and one can be taught how to
appreciate good writing, but finally it becomes a matter, to my mind,
of having the aptitude, or the genius, or the gift of God, whatever it
is. If you have that you'll find a way by yourself to express yourself
in writing. No matter how many classes you attend, no matter how
many people you listen to on the subject of creative writing, I don't
think any of that is going to change the course of things. I know I
might represent a minority view there, but it is my view.

P: Did you, though, in your workshops at Stanford, perhaps become
exposed to things you had not been exposed to beforehand? Did you,
for example, write a lot of free verse? Did you read a lot of free verse?

M: Well, that's correct, that's just right, I can answer that easily by
telling you that what I learned in English 201, the writing of poetry
under Yvor Winters, were the traditional forms in English. I knew
almost nothing about them when I went there. I was writing what
amounts to free verse, I didn't know an iamb from a dactyl, and the
course was enormously beneficial to me in that sense. When I came
out of there I did know what an iamb was, and I knew something
about traditional forms. I had been told that I would be much more
flexible in my writing if I knew the forms and could measure my
departure from them, and I think that's true. I gained an awful lot of
technical knowledge; I found out a lot about prosody in that course,
and the more you know about it, the greater your possibilities of
expression are.

P: So part of what you are saying is that form and discipline frees you rather than constricts you?

M: Absolutely, I believe that. That's, that's—why didn't I say that? (Laughter)

P: Is there a certain kind of education that you would recommend, or that you believe is a good education for somebody who feels that they are a writer, no matter how silly that notion is at a younger age? Do you feel that there is a way of going about it—

M: No. I don't think there is any one way to do it, and I think so much depends upon the temperament of the individual. I mentioned my friend Bobby Nelson. When we started out as freshmen at the University of New Mexico, we were both determined to be writers. I went pretty much through the orthodox business of attending classes and going straight through college. Bobby had the idea that a writer ought to have strong doses of the world, and dropped out of the university after one semester in order to fight bulls in Mexico. He sent me his press clippings. He fought nine bulls. Then he came back and went to school for another semester. Then he decided that in order to write he had to know what it was like to work in the oil fields, so he dropped out and went to West Texas and worked in the oil fields. Then he came back to school another semester and decided he had to know what it was like to fly jet-planes. That's how he got into the naval air-cadet program at Pensacola. He's lived his whole life that way, and for him I have no doubt that that's the sort of education he ought to have, and that enables him to be a writer—but it wouldn't work for me. It depends on the individual and his temperament.

P: Did you ever experience any confusion about whether you should write poetry or fiction? I mean that question to apply to both levels, both as what your "role" might be, and at the level of expressing a particular experience or idea.

M: No, I guess. There probably were times when I hesitated a bit about writing fiction because I had so committed myself to poetry when I was at graduate school. But even there I wrote a short story, for example, and Winters said to me, "Nobody's done *that* before." I wasn't completely comfortable changing gears there, but it seemed completely natural to me later, especially after I'd left Stanford. I had worked so hard learning these forms and imitating them, writing exercises, for example, in iambic pentameter and tetrameter, that I felt myself very much constricted by the end of that four year stint at Stanford, and so when I got out of there I just needed elbow room, and fiction was the way to go from there. So I wrote fiction without ever giving up poetry. I've always kept my hand in the writing of poetry, but I would not have wanted to write poetry exclusively.

P: It is interesting to me that your reaction was to do a different book each time you've done a book. *Rainy Mountain* is a completely different genre than *House Made of Dawn*. *The Names* is different again.

M: I think that there is some sort of impulse in me to try things that I haven't tried before. I want to write a play. I'm not going to be happy until I write a play. Simply because I've never written a play, and I'm curious to know what it's like. I became a painter for the same reason—I want to know what that is like. I like trying out new things. I would not like to write one novel right after another, and never write a poem or a play, or an autobiography.

P: Are you working on anything right now?

M: Yes, well, I have several things going. I'm painting a lot now, so . . . I think I'm giving a lot more energy to that than to writing at the moment. But I have begun what I hope might become a novel, although it's impossible at this point to say where it's going. At least I've got a start on it, and I'm, you know, turning that business around in my head to see what I'm going to work at.

P: Is that the way that most of your work begins, with just such a vague notion?

M: Yes, the best works, anyway, the ones that I'm most interested in. I have to deal with essays and various kinds of "assigned writing" that I just polish off as it comes, but for my creative works, novels and poems, things like that, I have to deal with them for a long time in my mind before I really get down to the sustained writing.

P: So you just mull them around until some sort of structure emerges?

M: You just live with them as seeds in the mind and then eventually they take shape and that's when you can begin to work them out on the page. But for a thing to germinate it takes a long time, thinking about it, sleeping on it.

P: Do you find that you will seize on a particular form by making a more cold-blooded decision, or does that develop itself along with the rest?

M: For me it seems to work the latter way you described. I never know what the form is going to be. No matter how carefully I outline the thing. I always find that I really develop the form as I go along. I can have fifteen chapters outlined, but I never keep to the outline. I find that once I get into the narrative rhythms of the thing it inevitably becomes something I had not foreseen.

P: This happened with *House Made of Dawn?*
M: Oh yeah, sure.

P: That's interesting, because it seems to make very conscious decisions in shifting point of view and focus.

M: I am sort of glad to hear that it gives you that impression, but I can assure you that the finished thing looks nothing like the outline I had for the novel.

P: Why do you think that *House Made of Dawn* came out as it did, why was there the necessity to move within it from one point of view to another?

M: Well, I don't know the answer to that, I suppose it finally came out in the way that seemed most appropriate as I was writing it. I guess I had begun with an omniscient narrator and had the idea of continuing in that narrative style throughout. However, as I came to certain points it seemed preferable to tell the story in the voice of one of the characters. That's the way it happened—and it seemed the way to do it as I got into it.

P: It did not present you with any great obstacle?
M: No, it never did seem to me to be an obstacle. I'm told by some readers that there are obstacles in the book. . . . (Laughter) But in the writing of it, it seemed the way to do it.

P: How do you develop the names you use in your writing?
M: There is no particular process. One of the first things that you think about is the name of your main character. Abel happens to be

the name of a neighbor who blew his brains out at the reservation. Quite a common name, you know, in the Pueblo society, most of the names are Christian. A lot of people have wanted to make some symbolic sense out of the name Abel, but suppose I'd used the equally common name, Jesús? What would they have made of that?

P: Did you ever feel very constricted in using the forms that might have been perfectly tailored to expressing, say, my experience, but which were entirely foreign to the environment in which you were raised, the environment you experienced? Did you feel that in some ways you have to break through the forms of other people?

M: I suspect that the answer is yes. I did feel, without being so much aware of it, at least consciously, that I had to arrive at a way in which to express my experience, and it was nobody else's experience, and consequently the expression could be no one else's. But I don't know that that is not true of every writer. My experience was unusual. As I was growing up I was placed in very different worlds, worlds that I think my readers know very little about. So in a way that was to my advantage, and in another way there was a problem as to how to present this unique experience to people to whom it was so foreign.

P: This problem of communicating with others who use a totally different system and structure seems to be precisely the one Abel is faced with when he is put on trial in *House Made of Dawn*. How do you think you managed to communicate this clash between completely contrasting cultures without getting the language tied up?

M: I don't know, but it happened. I mean I didn't have any great method in mind, but I did want to convey that idea, the very one that you are talking about. One of Abel's great wounds has to do with his voice; he becomes inarticulate, he cannot express himself in language, which in his culture is a terrible, terrible thing. I wasn't sure when I was writing it, I was very much aware that this might be difficult to do, and I wasn't sure I had done it even after I had finished the novel. But I *had* done it, because people do understand that, they do understand that this is part of his identity. He's a man without a voice.

P: And Abel loses his voice not as just an Indian, but as a man? He becomes almost *L'Étranger,* the Stranger?

M: That's right. He becomes steadily more estranged from the human race.

P: So in this episode of the trial of Abel, we are deliberately left slightly in the dark? The defense bases its case on the idea that Abel did not really kill what to him was a man, but rather an evil spirit, yet we are never sure if this really is what Abel felt, although we feel sympathetic to him. It is left entirely open to interpretation.

M: That's what I had in mind when I was writing it. It becomes a problem of how to indicate it in the best way, knowing that you can't be explicit about it, knowing that there is an ineffable aspect to it, and so you simply point to it.

P: When the whole concept of *House Made of Dawn* was germinating within you, what were your very initial ideas? Did you know you were going to write a novel, for instance? You must have had a starting point, the "first word" . . .

M: Well, as I say, I had thought about it a long time. I guess I first got the idea of writing a novel, oh, I can't give you a date (laughter), but I got the idea sometime after I graduated from the University of New Mexico and before I started my graduate work. There was a year in-between, and I think it was in that year that I really started thinking about writing the novel. All the time I was in graduate school, this was in the back of my mind, and the thing was turning over, you know, in my mind. I started it almost directly thereafter, I think, and wrote it during the next two years, something like that—but not steadily. I was writing sporadically, and if you put all the writing time together as a piece, it would probably turn out to be something like six or eight months. But it took much longer than that.

P: What did it feel like to finish writing *House Made of Dawn?* Was there a feeling of completion, or was it just the final working out of something that had long been inside you?

M: When I finished the manuscript itself I guess the main feeling was one of relief—Thank God *that*'s over! The elation had come before that when it was accepted by the publisher, which was long before it was finished. I submitted two or three chapters and the publisher gave me a contract, and it was great. There was a lot of elation; I mean I was really sky-high at that point. And in a way it's too bad that the elation came that early, because it was more drudgery than it might otherwise have been. I knew it was to be published and that it was a matter of turning it out. It would have been nice to have the elation at the end, in a way—though, I must say, I felt very good about finishing.

P: Do you think that the ending of *House Made of Dawn* is Rosseau-like in any way, a suggestion of a return to nature?

M: That seems a fair statement. The life at the Pueblo is predicated on a solar calendar, and it is much closer to nature than most twentieth-century communities. His going back into that traditional world represents a return to nature, so yes, I think that's a fair statement.

P: Is that a philosophy you are suggesting for other people, or is it just for Abel in the book?

M: Oh, only in the book. No, I wouldn't make a philosophy of it. I wouldn't advocate that everybody ought to return to nature. Though I . . . Well, I have feelings about that, too. I've lived for the last twenty years in one of the great cities of the country, San Francisco, and I enjoyed it immensely, but I also felt that it was a much more superficial world than the one in which I had grown up. That being the Southwest, and I always knew that I would return to the Southwest, to the real world, if you will. So I have this kind of prejudice about nature and the wilderness. To me it's more real than city life.

P: Even Tucson?

M: Tucson, well, Tucson is . . . you've got both things here, but it's unmistakably the desert, and that means something to me.

P: Did you ever, after you received the Pulitzer Prize, get the feeling that "now they've got me"? Did it ever seem to you that winning such an award might cause more problems in your writing?

M: That's a good question, and I'm not sure that I have thought about it sufficiently to give you a good answer—but it is certainly a mixed blessing. I've been aware of certain negative aspects to it. When I was awarded the prize, it came as a complete surprise. I had no idea that I was being considered for it at all. It came out of the blue, and that was a very great feeling, I mean "Wow." I was completely elated. But after a while, when the elation wore off, I found that I was inhibited to a certain extent. What do you do after you win the Pulitzer? Go for the Nobel the next year? The negative aspects are really, really trivial, but to this day I get far more junk mail, I'm sure, than I would have, far more invitations to speak here and there—which again is a mixed blessing. Sometimes it's good—it's lucrative—but it also represents a kind of invasion of your time, and you have to live with that. More demands are made on my time by virtue of having won a Pulitzer Prize than I like. I sometimes wish that I had more privacy than I have because I think I could convert it into something good. But it isn't there—not so much as I'd like.

P: How do you write? Do you write directly onto the typewriter, or do you write by hand and then transcribe?

M: I sit at the typewriter, but I always have a pad of paper next to that, and I go back and forth. I guess I spend most of the time at the typewriter, but when I get stuck I work it out on the pad and then return to the typewriter. I find myself going to the pad a lot. I like that! (Laughter) Going to the canvas a lot, going to the mattresses.

When I write I put myself into a kind of routine; writing is a ritualistic business for me. When I am really working well, I have a pattern and I keep to it. When I was writing *House Made of Dawn* and doing most of that writing, I was getting up at a certain time, about five o'clock in the morning, and I went out to have coffee and read the newspaper. I got back to my study about six-thirty or seven, and worked until twelve-thirty, every day. I got so that the routine was so comfortable for me that I could turn out a great deal in that period of time. I found that even though I had time after that in which to write, it didn't do me much good, because I had exhausted myself after five hours or so.

P: Do you do much final revision, or does the pad take care of all that?

M: The pad takes care of that. I do the revising on the spot. I am not the sort of writer who does a draft, then returns and revises it. I have to revise it paragraph by paragraph, and sometimes sentence by sentence, so that at the end of the day I have—and I'm going to generalize here—at the end of a good day I have maybe a page of typescript, but it has been thoroughly revised, and it is what I want it to be. I don't go beyond a piece until I have it where I want it. So the revision takes place on the spot, daily, and once I have put together a manuscript, it's finished.

P: Are you disappointed with the critical reception of your poems?

M: No. It seems to me that my poems have been well received.

P: How do you react when somebody, for example, criticizes your writing as being "precious"?

M: Well, I know what that critic means.

P: What does he mean?

M: That I sometimes write very tightly. I'm not sure "precious" was the word he used, I don't remember now. But he was making the point that it was stilted in a way—and my writing can be that. It's not as informal or conversational as a lot of writing is—but then I don't want it to be.

P: Does it seem, then, to be more poetic to you? *House Made of Dawn,* for example, seems to be a very poetic book.

M: Well, I'm concerned to be lyrical. I like to be lyrical. I think of my writing as being lyrical, poetic in that sense. That's what I strive for. Who wants to write a prosaic book?

P: Do you ever find that your work in criticism ever interferes with your authorship in any way? Are they completely separate elements of you, or do they operate concurrently?

M: I keep them separate, and I do not think of myself as a critic at all. I've written very little critical matter. Reviews are about as close as I come to criticism. I don't particularly like it. When somebody asks me to write a review, I do it if I'm interested in the book at all, but I don't like to do it; it's not a kind of writing that I find satisfying; it is just work and you are just not inspired. Inspiration is very important. You can become inspired very easily, I think. At least I can if you're talking about a poem or a novel, but not the introduction to a catalogue, or a review, or a lecture that someone wants you to hand over as a manuscript for publication at the time you deliver the lecture—all of that goes against my grain, and I have a terrible time writing those things. But they have to be done. So I'm enormously pleased with myself when they are done because it is like pulling teeth.

P: What do you think about the most recent schools of criticism. Derrida-ism, etcetera? Do you think these are at all threatening in some way to new writers?

M: I think if it were taken seriously it might be a threat, but I do not see it as something that will be taken very seriously by very many people very long. It's like painting. There are fads, and the fads can become schools, even chapters in art history, but their energy is limited and they expire after a while, and I suspect that is true of most contemporary literary schools. And I'm a little bit out of my depth here because I don't keep up with criticism; I'm not sure what's happening in the "realms" of criticism. Nor am I particularly interested.

P: What writers have exerted a major influence on you?

M: I don't know. I've been asked that question a good many times, and I'm always a little perplexed by it because I can't say who had been an influence. I can say that I would *like* to have been influenced by this writer or that, and perhaps they are influential in ways that I don't understand. I went through a period of time in my youth when I admired very much such writers as D. H. Lawrence and William Faulkner. I admire them less now than I did then, but I was so much caught up in them at one point that they may very well have influenced me. When my critical sense was more highly developed I became more interested in such writers as Isak Dinesen and Wallace Stevens, and I would like to think that they have been of some influence in my work, but I can't say. I really don't know.

P: I felt all through *House Made of Dawn* that you had been influenced by Camus's *The Stranger*. Is that at all a possibility?

M: It is a possibility because I know that book rather well, and have taught it on occasion. I was trying to remember when I first became aware of it. I guess as an undergraduate. So it could be. I also very much like the writing of Gide, who was like Camus in some ways, and there again is a possibility.

P: There seems to be a very Gide-like comment made in *House Made of Dawn* and much of what else you have written, a questioning of the novel form itself. Is that, too, part of the whole process, or more of a conscious decision?

M: It is part of the whole process, I think. Most writing, I find as I think about it, is subjective. You are not really aware where you are getting things; you just have them and set them down without really questioning them. If it's there, you're so damn grateful for it that you just set it down while you have it, and you never, at least I never, stop to analyze it, and ask myself where it came from.

P: Why did you become an English professor?

M: It was all a complete fluke. What happened was that when I graduated from college, I took a job teaching at a school on the Jicarilla reservation. It was a combined grammar school and high school, started with grade one, pre-school, and went on through twelfth grade. All the students, or virtually all of the students, were Apache kids. I was recruited right out of the University of New Mexico to go and teach. They had just started a program, the State Department of Education started a program, on the teaching of oral English. I had a minor in Speech and a major in English, and I was Indian, so I was just what they were looking for. They came and hired me. I was delighted because I didn't have anything better to do and having a steady job sounded great to me. So I went up there to teach, and I did for one year. And in that year I applied for the Stanford Creative Writing fellowship and won it, got it.

All of this is a very amusing story if it's told the right way. I didn't even know about the fellowships, but my friend Bobby Nelson who was then a naval air-cadet at Pensacola wrote to me one day and told me about this fellowship, and I said, hey, this sounds like a good idea; I'm going to apply for it. In his letter he had included the flyer for this, so I took a look at it and said, well, I'm going to apply for it too. So I did, and damned if I didn't get it, and I was so happy at Dulce on the Jicarilla that I was reluctant to leave. But here I had this opportunity, and so I applied for a year's leave of absence and got it. But I fully intended to go back at the end of that year and take up my job at Dulce. But I fell into the clutches of Yvor Winters, who turned out to be one of the great men in my life. He took me by the hand and told me I had been admitted to one of the prestigious schools in the country and I'd be a damn fool if I didn't work towards an advanced degree. So I did. I allowed myself to be talked into that. I took the Masters, completed it in three quarters, then just went right through, took my Ph.D., and was offered jobs at the end of that time; so that's how I got into the business of teaching at the university level. I went to the University of Santa Barbara, and have been with one institution

or another ever since. But I didn't start out to do that at all. It still
surprises me a bit.

P: You do come, though, from a family of teachers.

M: My parents were both teachers, that's right. But it is not a future
I thought of for myself. When I was little, I never dreamed of being
a teacher.

P: What did you dream of being?

M: Oh, a cowboy. At one point, even as late as my undergraduate
years, I was hell-bent on becoming a lawyer. I was going to law
school. So my whole destiny was changed in that business of the
fellowship. And I still, as I say, look back upon that with a sense of
surprise because it was not what I had expected at all—but that's how
it happened. I'm glad it did; I have no regrets about that.

P: One of the things you say in your memoir is that you "invented
history," and I wonder how this ties into your writing?

M: I think it is my writing. That can be a definition of writing.
Writing is an invention of history as I see it. I'm teaching a course
right now called "The Autobiographical Narrative" and we talk about
this very point a good deal. People like Nabokov in *Speak, Memory,*
one of the texts we are using, says at one point, "I must confess I do
not believe in time." And when you hear someone say something like
that you are arrested, you know—"How can someone make such a
blatant repudiation as that?" And yet, when you start thinking about
it you understand that, well, of course, he doesn't believe in time, it's
his business not to believe in it, that's what enables him to write.
When I think about my growing up, that history is largely of my
invention as a writer. I see it with a writer's eyes, I deal with it as a
writer, it is mine to interpret. There is experience there, but it means
nothing until I have explained it, and explaining it is an invention
of history.

P: How does this tie into being a Kiowa?

M: Well, I don't want to become too metaphysical here, we're right
on the verge of it—but I think that the Kiowa, a Kiowa, if I can be
definitive for a moment, is someone who thinks of himself as a Kiowa.
And what does that mean? It means that he has an experience in a
way that enables him to think of himself in a way that other people

cannot think of themselves; his experience is unique. It involves a history, a history of their migration from the Yellowstone to the Washita. Each time a Kiowa ponders his Kiowaness, he invents that whole history—and it is his invention, it is whatever he makes of it in his own mind. It is not written down, and he can't go to a book and find out what happened to the Kiowas in the Black Hills. All he can do is imagine. But it is his invention, finally. I think what I'm saying is an over-simplification, but it is also true that we all invent history; history is an invention. It is not there except that we think of it and make something of it in our minds.

P: In music there have been recent trends towards the "commercial" elements of composition and performance. Many great jazz players, like George Benson, have come out with "fusion" records with strings and vocals etcetera. The same thing has happened in rock music as well, resulting in "corporate rock," which is the music we hear on the pop radio stations. Do you think that something similar is happening in writing?

M: I think there are things like that happening. I don't know what the relationships are exactly, but every once in a while there is a phenomenal kind of happening in the world of books, publishing. One case in point is the paperback boom and the publication of a book in paperback exclusively, without going through a hard-back edition at all, contracts being given to authors by paper-back companies. That is a fairly new development, but economically I think it is even more viable right now than publishing first in a hard-back edition, then the publisher selling the rights to a paper-back publisher. God, I don't know, there's so many things. I'm sure that we're about to come out with computer books. We are coming close to that with word processors; we're verging in that direction. I wouldn't be surprised if very soon now somebody punched eight hundred keys on a keyboard somewhere and out of a gigantic machine will come a novel, and the writer will be at several removes somehow. That's sad to contemplate, but I think it will happen, and I think it will be a flash in the pan. I think all the critical schools we are talking about are flashes in the pan, and I hope that corporate jazz business you're talking about is a flash in the pan.

P: Whenever I pick up a book written past 1960, with a few exceptions, I have this immediate sense that the author probably sat down beforehand with his agent and worked out what the publisher would be most likely to buy and what sort of price they could get—and then proceeded to write this. Do you think that feeling is valid?

M: It is entirely valid. That is happening all the time, and we're being forced, writers are being forced to think in those terms now. The publishing world is in such a state that you cannot succeed on merit now. I hope that, too is a flash in the pan. But it is perfectly true that very good things are being written and turned down simply because the publisher can no longer risk the business of publishing a book that doesn't sell out. He has to make money on it, that's his business. And it's a terrible, terrible thing; it's very unhealthy, because it means that only the most established writers are being published. Since their track record is good, they will make money, whether they write well or not. So the publisher goes with them. The younger, unproven writers, half of whom are doing much better work, are not given the chance, they're not published. That is a terrible mistake, and it will eventually represent a great deterioration in our literature. Unless the thing is reversed in some way. It may be. I hope so.

P: Do you ever feel threatened by the fear that you might lapse into a state like, say, that of the latter Wordsworth where you might start to only follow the role of "writer" rather than actually writing?

M: I am aware of it, but I'm sure it hasn't become an obsession yet (Laughter). I have long since come to the conclusion that it is my business to write what is in me, and if it comes to the point where I know I am not going to earn money by writing, that has to be somehow beside the point. I still have to write what I feel I can write. But so many of us are compromised and placed in a position where we are greatly encouraged, if not made, to write what is economically acceptable.

P: Did you consider these elements when writing *House Made of Dawn?*

M: No, it wasn't the problem then that it is now. I can tell you this, that when Harper and Row accepted the book for publication, they had no expectation of making money. That is a foregone conclusion with any first novel; it will turn up in the red, that goes without saying, and all trade departments operate in the red. At the time that book was published, there were editors in the big houses who were willing to publish on that basis; if something was worthwhile in their estimation, they would run it, knowing it was going to take a loss. It happens that *House Made of Dawn* happily surprised us all and ended up very much in the black, but it was the exception, and was not published on any expectation of making money for the House. That's the way it ought to be, but it no longer is.

P: When we were first discussing this interview among ourselves, we thought that the scene from all your writing that most epitomized what we felt about your work is that in which Abel is seen shouting and gesturing at the tank, and we had thought about calling the interview "Shouting at the Machine." (Laughter) We feel that that is in some way what you do in your writing.

M: I had lots of fun writing that particular scene. I just delighted in picturing the whole thing in my mind, and I wanted to indicate all the frustration of this poor guy who is there against his will, caught up in all the tumult and chaos of action at the front. My God, what sort of an equation is that, this poor bewildered man against the machine? He dealt with it in the only way he could, as I saw it. He simply made a caricature of himself, released his frustration.

P: Is this what you have done in your writing?

M: It is what every writer does with his writing, I'm sure. The machine in my garden is that damn typewriter; it becomes your enemy, and you exorcise all your evil spirits by pounding away at it. The harder you hit the keys, the better. The more pain you can inflict on it, the better.

N. Scott Momaday: Interview

Kay Bonetti / 1983

The following interview with Native American poet and novelist N. Scott Momaday was conducted by Kay Bonetti for the American Audio Prose Library in March of 1983 at Mr. Momaday's home in Tuscon, Arizona. Momaday began the interview by reading from a work-in-progress.

K.B.: I'd like to begin by asking you to set the piece that you read, "Tsoai and the Shield Maker," which is from a work-in-progress, in context. Can you give us a picture of what you're working on right now?

M.: Like most writers I don't want to talk too much about the work-in-progress because I'm superstitious, but the piece I read called "Tsoai and the Shield Maker" is the prologue to what I think is going to become a novel. This prologue is an extension of the story about the boy who turns into a bear, and I think the novel itself is going to be a further extension of it. I'm curious about the boy. We know what happened to the girls; they become stars, but nothing is told of the boy, and he interested me. So I'm working with that idea, imagining certain things about who he was, who he may still be, what happened to him, how it may be that he roams about the world reincarnated, struggling with his bear power.

K.B.: Is there any suggestion of the bear in that story being an archetypal artist figure?

M.: Well, that's a thought. I think so, in the sense that it seems to me the whole question of transformation is creative. And of course American Indian oral tradition is full of allusions to men who were turned into animals, birds, things other than men. So I think there is something creative and very old about that idea.

K.B.: Well, I was thinking of what you say at the beginning of *The Names* when you refer to it as an autobiographical account and an act of the imagination; the artist has that sensibility or that way of looking at the world which necessitates transformation.

M.: You're right. The storyteller, whether he be a writer or a singer, is chiefly involved with creativity. He creates himself. He creates his listener in the process of story telling, and that's how I want to think of writing. It's very much at the center of my mind as I'm writing this present piece because it does stem from that story, and there is so much creativity in the story itself.

K.B.: And then there's this shield maker who transforms himself on another level, too, which is very suggestive.

M.: That's an adjunct, of course, to the story of the boy who becomes a bear, but I myself am fascinated by shields and used the shield as a motif in much of my artwork. I just finished an etching in Sun Valley, Idaho, which has a shield at the center; and my first exhibit of paintings in 1979 had as its motif shields. I believe that shields are intrinsically powerful, as of course did the Indians of the Plains in the nineteenth century and before. So that's an important subject to me, and I want to go on with that.

K.B.: I'm very interested in what you did in "Tsoai and the Shield Maker" that you read today. You used the story which is from "Colors of the Night."

M.: I incorporated one of those into this prologue with slight changes. I do that a lot; for example, the introduction to *The Way to Rainy Mountain* appears as one of the sermons in *House Made of Dawn*. I like to take things that I have written and published and incorporate them into other things to be written and published. To me, that's a kind of continuity that I want to keep. Somebody was asking me the other day about that. That's really quite an interesting thing in itself. It's as if you were writing one story over your lifetime, and I said, "yes, that's precisely what it is." I think of what I do as telling one story; it's long, and I can't get it all into one book. So what I do is I write a chapter at a time, as it were, and I publish it as a book. But it's all one story.

K.B.: While speaking of recurring things, let's go back and pursue the shield. Would you please explain for our listeners and for me the significance of the shield?

M.: It's a personal talisman, it's a flag, it's like a coat of arms except that it belongs to one person. And it stands for him. It's like a name, if you will. My shield stands for me. I must live up to it. It protects me. Not because it repels missiles, which it might do, incidentally, but much more importantly because it contains power. Usually a shield is determined by a dream. I dream of something that is my power, and then I incorporate the images of that dream in a shield, and forever that is my medicine. So the shield is an important symbol in the Plains tradition and in other traditions as well.

K.B.: Did a warrior make his own shield, or who is the shield maker?

M.: It happened both ways. A man might make his own shield and then some men in the tribe became renowned as shield makers. They did a good job of it, and so they were commissioned by warriors to make shields according to the warriors' dreams. I tell you, the shield maker, what I dreamed and ask for a shield to be made on that basis. That's how it happened much of the time.

K.B.: You're the son of a painter and a writer; you paint but are primarily known as a writer. Can you say at what point you chose the written word?

M.: No, probably not. It happened very early in my life. I thought of myself as a writer, I suppose, when I was a child because my mother was a writer. There were always books around the house, and she was a great influence in that way. She interested me in literature very early. And so I had, as you suggest, on both sides a strong creative influence, and I elected writing. I didn't think of myself as a painter until I was well into my adult years. But I thought of myself as a writer when I was very small, and it's a dream that I held on to, and eventually I did become a writer.

K.B.: I'm extremely interested in your mother, and I wondered if you would mind telling us more about her.

M.: Well, I spell all that out in *The Names*. But briefly, my mother was born in Kentucky, and her great-grandfather was a man about whom I've been able to find very little. His name was Galyen, and he married a Cherokee woman. That is how the Indian came into my mother's side of the family. So my mother has less than half Indian blood in her; much less than half, as a matter of fact. But that little bit became very important to her when she reached a certain age. She began to think of herself as an Indian, and she, in some way that I don't begin to understand, was the reincarnation of that old Cherokee woman who was her grandmother across the generations. That became a very important identity for my mother, and she from that point on thought of herself as an Indian. She chose that identity among several that she might have chosen.

K.B.: Has she ever told you what her youth was like? She grew up in a white world. What were the details that took her to the Indian school in Kansas?

M.: Haskell Institute.

K.B.: Haskell Institute! Did her father, a widower who had reared his children by himself, approve of this move on her part? Did she have to earn her own way or did he help? Do you know any of those details?

M.: I think he helped but basically she earned her own way. It was simply a very decisive act of the imagination. She decided that she wanted to go to school with Indians. Haskell was the logical place to go. She told her father; my grandfather and my mother were very close. I suppose because my mother had lost her mother when she was just a child, my grandfather had to be both parents to my mother and succeeded brilliantly. He was greatly devoted to her and she to him. So when she had made that decision, he backed her and assisted her in every way that he could. I think there must have been a lot of disapproval or a lot of looking askance at my mother by her relatives when she was growing up, but that didn't seem to manifest itself in my childhood at all.

K.B.: So you grew up in this part of the country (Oklahoma) and your mother's family was back in Kentucky.

M.: That's right! I was much closer geographically to my father's relatives. I grew up on Indian reservations which I think fortified my association with my Kiowa relatives who were extensively Indian and spoke Indian.

K.B.: In *The Names* there's this very brief statement you make that really took hold of my imagination when I read it in reaction to so many things that I have read about you and other American Indian writers. "There was at Jemez a climate of the mind in which we, my parents and I, realized ourselves, understood who we were, not perfectly, it may be, but well enough. It was not our native world, but we appropriated it, as it were, to ourselves; we invested much of our lives in it, and in the end it was the remembered place of our hopes, our dreams, and our deep love." I realize this is a very large question, but this comes up over and over again with Momaday the writer. The business of that which is Indian about your identity; that you went away and became an Emily Dickinson scholar; that you teach as a professor, and yet you feel your identity to be Indian. The whole dynamic of the artist's self, the question of form and substance, is what I'm trying to get at: of finding integration with the Indian self while having to live within a white framework.

M.: Well, I think I know what you're saying. A lot of people have come to me about that and asked, "How is it possible for you to remain an Indian and live in a world which includes a lot of non-Indian areas and entities?" And I say, well, because that's simply my experience; all I can be is what I became on the basis of having lived in my time and place. I spent my boyhood growing up on Indian reservations. So I have a very keen sense and an understanding of that world, of certain perceptions of it, a loyalty to it, a love of it. But on the other hand, it was possible for me to enter into the non-Indian world at a certain point in my life and to succeed as I could in that dimension, and it just happens that I became a professor. It just happens that I had whatever it takes to become a writer, a certain kind of incentive, I guess, a certain gift, namely the influences of other people; and I'm thinking of course primarily of my parents. So it all happened. I don't think of it as being strange or hard to account for this experience. It was simply mine, and that after all is what a writer must deal with; his experience, whatever it is. I happen to have a very rich experience for which I'm very grateful, and I think as a writer that has been a very great advantage for me.

K.B.: Well, I guess the basis of the question was that so much of the white world is alien to, even antagonistic to the American Indian or Native American culture.

M.: I think that's true, and certainly one of my great advantages has been a kind of dual vision. I can see from both sides not only in my writing but in my understanding of the world and in my understanding of myself. I can perhaps cross over that boundary, whatever it is, between the Indian world and the non-Indian world more easily than other people by virtue, again, of my experience. So I'm not antagonistic in either direction. I can accept both worlds and take, I hope, what is valuable from both of them and contribute equally to both of them.

K.B.: When you published *House Made of Dawn,* I read a review in which a critic said that "Momaday created difficulty for a reviewer right away. American Indians do not write novels and poetry as a rule or teach English at top ranking universities either, but we can not be patronizing. N. Scott Momaday's book is superb in its own right." I guess that was one thing that I was trying to get at in terms of antagonism, and it also works both ways with respect to your publishing history. Did you encounter that sort of a response?

M.: I'm sure that a lot of people who have read *House Made of Dawn,* for example, and *The Way to Rainy Mountain,* have not known quite how to judge those books because the experience in them is, after all, rather special. Most people who review books do not grow up on reservations, so they do not have the same frame of reference, and I can imagine that I've caused people trouble in that way. But that's good, you know, that's as it ought to be. Critics should be challenged at every point.

K.B.: Was there a very startled response when you got the Pulitzer Prize, as this piece of writing that I was reading from suggests?

M.: Well, certainly I was startled! I don't know beyond that. I was completely unknown, and I am sure that a lot people reacted in this way, "Well, who's he? What's this? What have we got here? What's happened?"

K.B.: But you don't think it was a reaction of bigotry at all? Perhaps I'm misreading this reviewer in taking his words out of context here. It struck me that he was doing the very thing that he spoke against. He was being extremely patronizing in his remark.

M.: I can't say that I found a lot of patronizing reactions to any of my books. What do I want to say about that? I think that there is bigotry, of course, on the part of a lot of people. American Indians have no tradition of writing books; this is a little presumptuous, isn't it. But the same people who have such bigoted ideas about other minorities may be minorities in general.

K.B.: Well, I think there's one question one might ask about your coming to be a writer as an American Indian. You said you are a product of your experience and your experience was unique; you are the child of a writer and a painter. You grew up in a school house. After the end of WW II, you spent the rest of your childhood essentially in a school house. You lived at Jemez, where your parents taught at the pueblo school. But when one reads a lot of Native American literature, there is the sense that somehow the written tradition appears to be antagonistic to Native American tradition and story telling and art.

M.: Only in a technical way, I think. Writing is made of words; the Indian is very much at home in the element of words. So we're talking about some sort of technical distinction, it seems to me.

K.B.: Aren't there taboos though regarding the power of the word. I noticed that in *House Made of Dawn* you side step the Kiva ceremonies. Aren't there things like that that are very difficult to write about without violating . . .

M: Yes, but those are not taboos of language, I think. I didn't write about Kiva ceremonies because, in the first place, I never attended Kiva ceremonies and, in the second place, they are secret and their secrecy ought to be protected. So even if I did know what went on in the Kivas, I would probably not write about it. But that's apart from the language. I mean it's not because I'm afraid of the words, it's because I respect the traditions.

K.B.: In *House Made of Dawn,* there's a whole section in "The Priest of the Sun" where the Right Reverend John Big Bluff Tosamah talks about the word as seen from the Christian perspective of St. John. "In the beginning was the word and the word was with God and the word was God." Is that how it goes?

M.: I think so.

K.B.: And are we to take his sermon seriously?

M.: Well, I take it seriously. I think it represents one of my fundamental attitudes towards language.

K.B.: Well, he goes on to say that St. John went too far.

M.: That's right! What he's saying in that sermon is that the white man has abused language, that he says too much. He's talking about word inflation from which, God knows, we suffer greatly in our time. We're bombarded with junk mail and words in print. Words in general are cheap. But that attitude toward language is alien to the Indian attitude toward language which is much more economical. The Indian tends to take language more seriously, to believe more deeply in the efficiency of language. So that's what I think we have in that sermon, and it does represent my attitude towards language.

K.B.: So then that's not to say that there is an antagonism at all toward the form of a novel, toward writing as a form which is thought to be a Western form, a secular form?

M.: Depends on how you do it. If you write with respect for language and you write without wasting words, that's very much within the tradition. Writing itself; of course, is new, isn't it? The Indian oral tradition is immeasurably old. Writing is new to the Indian, but then it's also new to the white man, if you stop to think about it. Writing is only about six thousand years old. That's not a very long time in the tenure of man on the planet.

K.B.: With regard to the form of the novel there's been a lot written about Momaday, about the sacred text and the secular form. What I'm trying to get at is the function of the storyteller within the Indian tradition. It is a sacred function, is it not?

M.: Yes.

K.B.: Is your view of art such that you see the novel too as a sacred, or a potentially sacred form?

M.: Well, that's what it ought to be, and that's what I want it to be for myself. But I understand that probably most novelists do not think of it in that way. But because my regard for language does stem from the Indian attitude towards language as manifested in the oral tradition, I think I regard story telling, whether it be writing a poem or writing a novel or telling a story to my child as sacred matters. I think that ought to be what happens when a person takes it upon himself to speak or to write, to deal in language. He ought to do it not only with responsibility, but with great reverence, as words are sacred. There was a time I think when all people, and I'm thinking about biblical times, had that kind of respect and reverence for language. People in the Anglo-Saxon period, for example, uttered charms over their fields so that the seeds would grow into harvest. They believed that they could bring that about by exercising the power of the voice; they could affect physical change in the world. Now, that is believing in language! And that's the way I want to believe in it. That's the way the American Indian has traditionally believed in it, and it's the way I would have everyone believe in it.

K.B.: Well, to turn to the workings of *House Made of Dawn* as a novel. In *The Names,* you say, "The first word gives origin to second, the first and second to the third, the first, second, and third to the fourth, and so on. You cannot begin with the second word and tell the story, for the telling of the story is a cumulative process, a chain of becoming, at last of being." And you have mentioned the continuity within your work of using the same stories over and over again. It seems to me that that's also very much a part of the sacredness in your work. But I would like to turn this to a more technical question and ask you, in *House Made of Dawn,* what was, figuratively speaking, the first word of *House Made of Dawn?* What was the germ of the novel?

M.: The image of Abel running, I suppose, is the first, most cohesive, the most integrating element, if you can put it that way, in the novel. I'm not a good person to ask about *House Made of Dawn.* The author is the least trustworthy person to ask about his work. But as I think about the structure of it after these many years, it does have a kind of circular structure I set out to achieve. So it begins and ends with the same image. And time in the usual chronological sense is left out of that novel. There is a lot of going back and forth in time in *House Made of Dawn.* I wanted to do certain things with my principal character's perceptions, so there are a lot of things that we have inside of Abel's mind. And then there is another confusion of narration in the book. There are several characters who tell the story, parts of the story, and they must all come together to form a cohesive unit. So I would describe the structure of that book as unorthodox, but it is nonetheless a whole piece. And I like doing things that way. *The Way to Rainy Mountain* is again a book that is composed on different levels of narration. There are three voices in the book, and they alternate. And one of the things I like about that book, which is my favorite of my books, is the design, the physical design of the book, which I had nothing to do with. But Bruce Gentry who designed it did a wonderful job, so that you can open it at any place and you have three voices on facing pages, each in its own type face, and I think you not only hear them as different voices, but you see them as different things on the page. It's a wonderful book in that sense.

K.B.: Well, the thing that fascinated me in *House Made of Dawn* was the fact that Abel says in the beginning that he is inarticulate. And I couldn't help but think of that line of Emily Dickinson's, "tell the truth, but tell it slant."

M.: (Laughs). Yes.

K.B.: That is the way the book is structured. His story is told slant. "The Longhair" in the beginning deals with both Abel as longhair in the sense that the Right Rev. John speaks of longhairs, but it also deals a lot with Francisco, his grandfather. He doesn't really at any point tell his own story, does he? Then we have "The Priest of the Sun," then "The Night Chanter" who is Ben Benally, and then finally "The Dawn Runner" in which really the consciousness of the grand-father takes over. And it's through indirection that we come to hear the story.

M.: Yes, I would agree; I think that's true. I think that is a very effective way of telling a story. I like to approach things indirectly. I like to have people, various people, give their own ideas of the same thing, so that you have several points of view. I think that's by and large the method of storytellers, too. If you tell something perfectly, if you narrate it straightly and there are no indirections, I think you run the risk that it's boring, a little too predictable perhaps. But if you have several points of view and you keep going round and round the thing until you can see it from all sides, that becomes interesting in itself, it seems to me. There are lots of devices, of course, the novelist has available to him. And one is the incorporation of stories within stories. There are other such stories in *House Made of Dawn*. The old woman whose hamster dies is another such insert. And in a sense, these things are digressions, but in a greater sense they're not. They're integrating principles.

K.B.: Exactly. And over and over again, that kind of story is used, that recurring motif of the death of someone young and precious— Vidal, Abel's brother, and Francisco's stillborn baby.

M.: Precisely. I think that's a good point. The effect must be cumulative, and there is finally one effect to all of them: they accumulate until finally they become an important force in the novel.

K.B.: Yes, that's what I wanted to get at, to explain what that force is. Even though they are not Abel's stories, they are things that come to Abel or surround Abel and reflect his own preoccupation with a death of something in himself, which he must work his way through to some kind of a healing or rebirth. And the one that triggers it is his memory of Vidal, his young brother, and that of his mother. Take the early deaths that he remembers in the beginning and the cumulative effect is that elegiac tone which seems to move through *House Made of Dawn*. Were you conscious of *House Made of Dawn* as having an elegiac tone?

M.: Oh yes! Indeed, Benally really does put his finger on that at the end, when he reminisces and talks about going out at dawn. "And for the last time, for the last time . . ."; he keeps repeating that; which I wanted very much to be a kind of a threnody, an elegiac symbolism that is pronounced at the end of the novel.

K.B.: Do you see the end of the novel as problematic for the reader at all?

M.: Yes, I do. Because a good many people have expressed to me that it's problematic. They say, what happened to Abel? And I say, your idea is as good as mine. I wrote the last page and that's it. And I don't have any idea beyond that. Other people have asked whether it does end upon a note of hope or of despair. And I say, I don't see that it must do either. Abel is making an effort at the end of the novel, I think, to get back into his traditional world, and I am not concerned whether or not he can succeed in that. As a novelist, I'm not concerned. I didn't want to indicate one thing or the other in the novel. So it is open-ended, and I can see that people think it's problematic in that sense.

K.B.: Well, it seems like at the end all those roles are so mixed up that storytelling as a sacred act seems to be fused with the idea of

healing. Abel's progress through the novel is the same progress that
we've seen with the Eaglewatchers who take him hunting after he has
seen the eagles and the snake. The logical implication would be that
the next step for Abel is that he will become a storyteller.

M.: It's an interesting question you're raising of whether Abel can
become a storyteller. It's one of the things that interests me about
Abel's condition in the novel. One of his great risks is that of the
voice itself; he loses his voice, he becomes inarticulate. Finally, he
cannot speak. And that idea, it seems to me, is crucial in the novel.
One of the prayers in the night chant which begins *House Made of
Dawn* is "restore my voice for me." And that's Abel's prayer, I think.
That's the thing he needs most, to have his voice restored. If he could
just speak as he once could, that would be a great sign of recovery.
But that's in question. At the very end he runs out of breath, and he
can no longer sing the song. He has not the voice, but the song is in
his throat or his heart. That's the question: can he recover his voice?
There is no answer to that.

K.B.: Well, the thing that struck me and overwhelmed me was of
course the image of the eagle and the snake in the air, fused together
as an ancient symbol. Is it not the power of spirit and matter, brought
together? It's Quetzalcoatl, isn't it, in the Aztec tradition?

M.: It is an ancient symbol, though I wasn't thinking of that
particularly when I was writing it.

K.B.: Really? Because that's what struck me; when the snake fell,
to me it was a symbol of some kind of terrible disintegration that was
going on, both in Abel and in his tradition, and then he goes to war.
In American Indian writing, does it seem to you that WW II is in the
American Indian experience comparable, say, to WW I in Western
intellectual history?

M.: I think it was in the sense that never before had the Indian been
involved in that chaos. Very few Indians I suspect took part in the
First World War, but a great many took part in the Second. And it
turned out to be a very unsettling experience, of course. That's why I
wrote about that generation. At Jemez, I knew a lot of young men
who had been in the Navy or the Army, and they had come back from
WW II. And they were a sad lot of people in that they had been
disoriented in a way that Abel is. Terrible things happened to them;

they murdered each other. And they drank themselves to death. And they were involved in terrible car crashes. And they died violent deaths. So that was a very dramatic generation to write about, and I happened to have known it quite well, and so it was the logical thing for one to do.

K.B.: Well, you do say in *The Names,* "I try now to think of the war, of what it was to me as a child. It was almost nothing, and nothing of my innocence was lost in it. It was only later that I realized what had happened, what ancient histories had been made and re-marked and set aside in a fraction of my lifetime, in an instant. And *there* is the loss of innocence, in retrospection, in the safe distance of time. There are the clocks of shame; we tell the lie of time, and our hearts are broken." I had two questions based on that remark. In terms of what ancient histories have been made and remarked and set aside in a fraction of my lifetime, we could say that of the Japanese, we could say that of any number of cultures. But I assume you were talking about your own, the American Indian culture, in that remark?

M.: If I remember rightly, I was talking about the great impact of war upon human history. When I was a child during the years of the war, I wasn't aware of what was going on. It was all a newsreel to me. But later I came to realize that very important things had happened in World history, not only on the level that I wrote about in *House Made of Dawn,* not only as far as the Indians are concerned, but also as far as everyone else is concerned. I think the Second World War was one of the great moments, if that's the word for it, in human history. And to have lived through it, even as a child, is a significant thing.

K.B.: Could you explain that remark, "There are the clocks of shame, we tell the lie of time and our hearts are broken"?

M.: Well, (laughs), how am I going to answer that? It's a metaphysi-cal statement, isn't it? But what I'm saying there is that the Second World War, about which I'm writing, is the context to that passage. The war is, was, a shameful thing. The clocks of shame, those are the clocks that kept the time of the Second World War. In moments of shame, we tell the lie of time and our hearts are broken; we believe that we overcome such madness and eradicate it, but that's a lie. Of course, we don't. The shame is still there. The Holocaust, the bombing of Japan, Hiroshima, those things constitute a shame with which we must live. That's where our innocence is truly lost.

K.B.: What do you think of the work of white men who've made Native American tradition their life in literature? Men like John Neihardt and Frank Waters. How do you assess their work?

M.: I don't assess it, I don't know enough about it. I've read *The Man Who Killed the Deer,* and I've read *Black Elk Speaks.* So I know a little bit about these men. I like both works that I've just mentioned. Then, of course, I've read other things by non-Indian writers that center upon the Indian World, such as *Laughing Boy,* which I think is a very fine novel in its way. Dee Brown has written with great responsibility, it seems to me, and sensitivity of the Indian world. There are any number of others. And as I say, I don't assess them; I don't judge. Some of those works I respect, and some more than others, but probably on the basis of literature rather than anything else have I made any distinctions.

K.B.: What does happen at the base of your spine when you hear words like Native American literature?

M.: Well, nothing happens really at the base of my spine; it's not a very accurate or precise term, is it? Native American literature might mean any number of different things and probably does to various people. Native American literature means a body of literature that somehow represents the Native American experience, and when one can put together a certain number of books that shed light upon that subject from one direction or another, one can make a course out of it.

K.B.: But how do you feel about doing this to literature, to any kind of literature? Do you feel that this is a healthy thing, or is it a ghetto situation?

M.: Oh, I think it's a healthy thing, or can be. One has to categorize literatures in order to deal with them. You can't have a course on world literature, for example. There are such courses, I'm aware, but they're pretty hard for me to put together. If somebody asked me to teach a course on world literature, it would be a pretty arbitrary and random sampling of World literature by definition. So you have to categorize literatures, and you have to say we'll teach a course on Southern literature and we'll include Faulkner and this writer and that. And to that extent Native American literature is a useful idea as a category. Native American literature, we can handle that in a semester. (Laughs).

K.B.: But, how do you place it? How do you place something like Native American literature within American literature?

M: It's the most viable American literature. If you think of literature as writing, it is not as highly developed as Jewish literature or transcendentalist literature, but there are reasons why it isn't, and it will become more highly developed in time.

K.B.: It is hard for me, being raised in the literary tradition I was raised in, to speak to someone like yourself. It's hard for me to say I can read *House Made of Dawn* and see things in there that look like fine writing out of Western traditions. I guess there's something about your writing that is distinctly Indian. Do you feel there is in fact something that can be distilled out and that's separate from the larger white tradition?

M: Of course, that's the way it ought to be.

K.B.: And some writers get angry if you speak in terms of universals. There are writers who feel that the minute you start talking about universals, you start talking about Western white literature.

M.: Oh no, I don't think so. That's certainly not my point of view, and I don't remember having encountered anybody who argued that. Universals are universals. They don't belong to any particular literature, nor to any particular ethnic experience. I think there are a lot of universals in my work, which is to say that the Indian has as valid a human experience as anyone else. And what is human experience but the accumulation of universal experience. Abel is every man at every time and every situation, just as Ishmael.

K.B.: What would you say is most distinctly Indian about what you do?

M.: Attitude toward language, I would probably cite first; attitude toward nature; attitude toward personal relationships; ideas of kinship; attitudes towards old people. Those are very broad statements, but I think of each of them as having a particular meaning in the Indian World. The Indian feels differently on those levels about life, as far as I can see. He has a more highly developed idea of language,

I think, than have other peoples in general, because in Western civilization our attitudes towards language have deteriorated over the centuries. The Indian's has not. He has an understanding of nature that sets him apart because attitudes towards nature in Western civilization have deteriorated over a long period of time. Western man in general tends to look at the earth as dead matter. His idea is to use it, to exploit it, to take out of it what can accommodate his lifestyle at the moment. The Indian doesn't. He thinks of it as living, vital, possessed of spirit. One can construct a catalogue of these things and say that this is where the Indian differs from other people. But it would be hard to answer the question completely because it's a big question and requires a big answer.

K.B.: Do you write out of sense of mission, of wanting to transmit these values into the world at large?

M.: No, I don't write out of a sense of mission beyond my own mission and compulsion to write for my own satisfaction. I'm not a political writer, and I don't construct political or social messages in my writing. Who knows what you write out of, what intelligence you write out of, finally. I'm sure that a lot of my writing and a lot of most people's writing is subconscious. It stems from observations and information that you don't know you have at any given moment, but they're there.

K.B.: Another thing that I was trying to get at earlier when I was talking about a basic antagonism between the form of writing, whether it be poetry or the novel, and the Indian tradition out of which you are writing is the fact that you tell the same story over and over again. You use things, you take them from one context and put them in another. It seems that the very vitality of the oral tradition, whether it be Indian or any other oral tradition, is in fact that it has to live from generation to generation. It seems necessary to change the stories. They have to be retold, they have to be somehow re-created with each generation in order for them to continue to live and to really be myth or legend. Otherwise, they're nothing but dead form. And you feel no contradiction in the act of writing, of putting it down on paper? Because once it's there on paper and in print, it's there.

M.: Yes, I agree with that. You're asking me if I know how I feel about having it there forever and ever in print?

K.B.: Yes.

M.: I don't have any trouble with that so long as you understand that when you do transcribe from the oral tradition, translate what is in the tradition into writing, it's not by any means the end of the oral tradition. One can keep telling the same story, for that matter, again and again, and it will always be a unique performance. It will never be the same thing twice. So to write it down is simply to place it in another tradition. And that's neither good nor bad, as I see it. It's just a fact.

K.B.: And it doesn't take away from the sacredness of the language.

M.: No, on the face of it I don't think that it detracts from the sacred nature of language. Writing doesn't. Writing can be sacred in a great many instances. The Bible, of course, is a sacred text. And the Koran. Many examples of writing are sacred and were created as sacred matter. So writing, by no means, negates the sacred. On the one hand, it is fixed, and once you have written something down, it remains fixed on a page as visible text. It is not necessarily available in the same way to different people. That's a very complicated way of saying that people read things differently. So that even if you have a fixed text on a page before you, it is not going to be the same thing to two people. It is going to vary according to the reader's intelligence and perception and experience. So the written text is not as frozen as we sometimes think it is.

K.B.: I want to ask you about your attraction to Emily Dickinson.

M.: Emily Dickinson did simply appeal to my imagination in the way that some writers do, and you don't know particularly why. The first time I read her I thought this is really excellent stuff. And though I didn't understand it very well, I admired it greatly. And then as a graduate student I got closer and began looking more deeply into Emily Dickinson, and finally ended up spending a Guggenheim year reading her in manuscript. So, I feel that she has been an important writer in my life, and I have read most of her work, if not all of it. And I enjoy teaching her. I still find her poems fresh, even though I've been at them for many years now. They still come at me with a burst of clarity that very few things in my experience have had.

K.B.: Would you say that she's been an influence on your own writing?

M.: I wouldn't know about that. I don't know who has been an influence on my writing. If those people whose work I admire most have been the influences, she would certainly be one of them. I wouldn't presume to say that I write anything like her. I don't know of anyone who can write like Emily Dickinson. Her style of writing, her precision and economy, are so completely her own that I think you'd be making a mistake trying to emulate her. But if by admiring her work and seeing ways in which she deals with images and points of view that she brings to this subject or that, if those things can be learned from her work, then perhaps she has been an influence upon me.

K.B.: What about Yvor Winters? You were a student of his, were you not?

M.: He was a very close friend. And he taught me a great deal about poetry, particularly the traditional forms of poetry. When I went to Stanford, I thought I was a poet, but I didn't know much about poetry, as a matter of fact. After studying with Winters for the four years that I was there, I came away knowing something. I did learn things about poetry, but that's about as much as I can say.

K.B.: Did he approve of your work?

M: Oh yes, he said wonderful things about it, and we carried on a wonderful correspondence after I left Stanford, between the time I left and the time he did. I came to think of him as one of the great minds in my experience. He had a formidable intellect and a fine critical sense when it came to poetry.

K.B.: If I understood you correctly, you said that it would be hard for you to say what your influences were, what your models were in terms of writing. Do you feel that you had to find your own way?

M.: Yes, I think I'm like every other writer in that way. I did have models; I admired people's writing and read them carefully. Emily Dickinson would be a case in point. I admire the poetry of Wallace Stevens. I admire the prose of Isak Dinesen very much. I think maybe she's almost the equal of Emily Dickinson, in her imagination and in her ability to express herself in words. But this is not to say that these are influences. I just don't know.

K.B.: As an American Indian, choosing to write about an American-Indian experience, did you feel when you started maturing as a writer

that somehow there really were no written models for what you
wanted to do in your writing?

M.: Yes, I had that sense, I wanted to do something original and
that's something that I bring to everything I write. I don't want it to
be derivative, I don't want it to be like anything. I want it to be unique.

K.B.: Well, thanks for talking to us this afternoon.
M.: You're more than welcome. Thank you for coming all this way.

A *MELUS* Interview: N. Scott Momaday—Literature and the Native Writer

Tom King / 1983

From *MELUS*, 10, no. 4 (Winter 1983), 66–72. © 1983 The Society for the Study of Multi-Ethnic Literature of the United States. Reprinted by permission.

One of the early images of Indians in film and literature was that of a mute, a silent, stoic primitive who never spoke, who seemed to be without voice. It was an image, like many images of the Indian, that had little relationship to reality.

Indian people were never mute, but until the middle of the 20th century the Native voice was a voice that was seldom heard. In the 1960s, when it was heard, it was raised in complaint, in protest against the injustices that Indian people had been forced to endure.

And along with this voice of protest, a literary voice began to be heard. It rose, not out of the protests so much as out of the imaginations of a creative people and the oral traditions of many nations. It was a voice that, for centuries, Indian people had reserved for themselves, a voice that would now be shared.

The emergence of Native writers, the emergence of a Native voice, should probably be dated from the publication of N. Scott Momaday's novel *House Made of Dawn*. This is not to say that Indians were not writing fiction prior to 1968. Novels by Native writers began appearing at least as early as 1899 with the publication of Chief Simon Pokagon's *Queen of the Woods*. Others would appear during the first half of the twentieth century—John M. Oskison's *Wild Harvest* (1925), John Joseph Mathews's *Wah'Kon-Tah* (1932), and D'Arcy McNickle's *The Surrounded* (1936). Many of these early books and others dealt with the way Indians had been and suggested that Indian culture was either a thing of the past or that it was slowly dying.

House Made of Dawn was a novel about the present and about living. It did not treat the Indian and Indian culture as though it were a cultural dinosaur up to its knees in sticky tar and slowly sinking into a pit. It saw the Indian world as alive and in reasonably good health, resistant and tenacious. "The invaders," Momaday wrote concerning the Pueblo response to the Spanish,

> were a long time in conquering them; and now after four
> centuries of Christianity, they still pray in Tanoan to the

old deities of the earth and sky and make their living from the things that are and have always been within their reach . . . They have assumed the names and gestures of their enemies, but have held on to their own secret souls; and in this there is a resistance and an overcoming, a long outwaiting.

For critics who had insisted that the Indian and Indian culture were dead or at least so changed over the years that they scarcely resembled the original, Momaday's description of this resistance, this "outwaiting," provides a key to understanding the Indian world. It is a notion that is well understood by Indian people. Simon Ortiz, in a presentation at the MLA convention in 1981, talked about language, culture, and the question of authenticity. "This is the crucial item that has to be understood," insisted Ortiz,

that it is entirely possible for a people to retain and maintain their lives through the use of any language. There is not a question of authenticity here; rather it is the way that Indian people have creatively responded to forced colonization. And this response has been one of resistance; there is no clearer word for it than resistance.

House Made of Dawn was one of the first Native responses that used a "foreign" language, a non-oral system of communication, the complication of an enforced religion, and the limitations and advantages of a technological culture to create a world in fiction that mirrored the world in which many Indians live. It was a response of resistance for it argued that Indian culture was not slouching towards oblivion. It was a creative response in that it did not try to describe the world of the Indian (in this case the Pueblo); rather, it sought to define the essential qualities that give that world life, strength, and continuance.

N. Scott Momaday, like his novel, is a creative response to the impositions of a second civilization. He is both a Kiowa and a university professor. He is a writer and a storyteller. In the following interview, he discusses some of the problems that face Native writers as they attempt to create an image of the Indian and his universe in literature.

Interviewer: Most of the major novels that have been written by Indian writers have dealt with the present or the immediate past. For the Indian writer, is there a problem with using the historical past? Are the historical stereotypes that have been created by non-Indian writers so formidable that Indian writers avoid the period?

Momaday: The stereotypes are indeed formidable and they are inhibiting. I have, as you know, dealt with Kiowa history to some degree, especially in *The Way to Rainy Mountain*. But that is not a novel. It does not occur to me to write an historical novel about Indian life. Books like *Hanta Yo* do not appeal to me very much. The mythological distance, rather than the historical distance, appeals to me greatly. Why should this be so, and can one generalize some sort of meaning from it? I suspect that the Indian, even the contemporary Indian novelist or poet, has a different concept of history than has the non-Indian, and the so-called "historical novel" is not congenial to that understanding. I think of the Indian calendars, the "winter counts." They are predicated upon a very special notion of the past, aren't they? They are not the stuff of which historical novels are made. You look at them and say, "Ah, so this is the essence, rather than the whole story, of what a people brought away from the winter of 1837." In a way, history for the Indian is an account in shorthand; it is an image, a pictograph. Generally speaking, Indian writing ought to reflect that concept of history, I suppose. I mean, that's probably what you ought to expect. But finally, of course, writing, literature, ought to defeat all expectations.

Interviewer: Non-Indian writers have used the Indian as a character in fiction for a good many years. Do you notice any differences in the way Indian writers use the Indian as a character in fiction? Do they give the character new dimensions or do they simply re-work an old image?

Momaday: Well, I would hope that the Indian writer brings more that is authentic to his creation of an Indian character. But in the long run, of course, an Indian character, as such, is worth less than a character who is recognizably human, whose characteristics are universal.

Interviewer: When you began to conceive the character of Abel in *House Made of Dawn* and were confronted with the need to create a character that was recognizably human and at the same time recognizably Indian, what were some of the attributes, characteristics, and/or thoughts that you felt were necessary to incorporate in the character in order to successfully portray an Indian man?

Momaday: You know, I didn't think about that specifically. That is, I was not concerned, at least consciously concerned, to compile a list of attributes and characteristics that identify Abel as an Indian. I thought of him, then, and I think of him now, as a man, a human being. Of course he is an Indian man, which is to say that he thinks of himself as an Indian man, according to his experience. It's all he can do, isn't it? Abel's Indianness is certainly important, for it determines the way in which he sees the world, but I think it probably ought not get in the way of the reading of the novel, if you see what I mean. Abel reflects his ethnic experience in virtually everything he does. I find it impossible to break him down into "Indian" attributes and characteristics. He is recognizably Indian. And, for my purposes, at least, this means nothing so much as that he is recognizably human.

Interviewer: James Fenimore Cooper, in *The Leatherstocking Tales,* developed the notion of "gifts." They were a means of separating the two races and establishing certain boundaries within which each race should operate. Scalping, according to Cooper, was acceptable behavior for an Indian because it was one of his "gifts," but it was not acceptable for a non-Indian. In the writings of Indians and non-Indians, do you see any vestiges of this notion of "gifts"?

Momaday: There is one, which interests me a great deal. It is a stereotype, of course, and yet it isn't; it is based upon a fundamental difference in the way various peoples perceive the world. I have in mind the notion of language, the belief which one places in the power of the word. You have heard the expression, "white man speaks with forked tongue," a formula that probably came about in Hollywood with the "Grade B Western." Yet it seems to me to reach farther into basic perceptions than most of us would understand at first. It is, unwittingly or not, a sensitive commentary upon the way in which the Indian and the non-Indian look at language. Interestingly, this is one of the few aphorisms in our idiom that reflects more favorably upon the Indian than upon the white man.

Interviewer: James Welch, Leslie Silko, and yourself create protagonists that have suffered a loss of identity. This loss is, of course, a form of alienation and is a major theme in many modern novels. Is the alienation that affects Abel, Tayo, and Welch's unnamed character different from the alienation that other characters in American literature suffer? Or, is the alienation they suffer basically of the same sort that affects characters such as Ahab, Joe Christmas, and Nick Adams?

Momaday: No, I don't think so, if we are talking in very basic terms. We are all alienated in one way or another, I suppose. The historical alienation of the Indian is rather obvious. More subtle is the alienation of children, say, in a world in which nuclear holocaust is a real possibility. What I'm saying is that the "alienation" of the Indian, real as it is, isn't worth a great deal to the writer as I can see. It's only what he makes of it, in any given case.

Interviewer: There seems to be the notion that the oral material gathered in the 18th and 19th centuries by anthropologists, folklorists, and ethnographers is more "authentic" than the efforts of contemporary novelists. One of the arguments is that the oral materials that were gathered in this period were gathered from people who were very much a part of the culture while the contemporary literature is produced by individuals who stand at some distance from their culture. How valuable is this body of early work and how valid is this complaint of "cultural distance"?

Momaday: The materials gathered by early anthropologists and ethnographers and artists are extremely important, obviously. I'm thinking of such field researchers as Washington Matthews, and James Mooney. And I'm thinking, too, of such artists as George Catlin and Edward Curtis. One could mention others. Their work is indispensable. If they had not lived and worked and recorded their observations, we would know far less than we do about American Indian culture before the twentieth century. But there are also very important people of more recent times. Oliver LaFarge, Ruth Underhill, Alice Marriott, to name but three. I see no reason why contemporary writers, whether they be scientists or novelists, should be farther from their subject.

Interviewer: The Bureau of American Ethnology, the Bureau of Indian Affairs, and the records of Indian field agents represent potential materials for fiction. To date, Indian writers have made little use of these. Have you any thoughts on how these sources might be used?

Momaday: No, not really. The sources are there. If they appeal strongly to some writer looking for a subject, he will make use of them.

Interviewer: The obligation of any writer is to write well, to use his gifts to the best of his ability. Do you feel that there are any additional burdens that are placed on the Native writer by either the non-Indian reading public, by tribes, or by Indian people in general?

Momaday: No. To write well is all that one can ask.

Interviewer: While both *The Names* and *The Way to Rainy Mountain* contain autobiographical material, they do not seem to be autobiographies. Yet they are not fiction. What exactly are these books? Do they represent a form that is suggested by the oral materials or by the Kiowa culture itself?

Momaday: I think of both books as memoirs, though admittedly they are not much alike, and I suppose they depart more or less obviously from what we call "autobiography." *The Names* is a book about growing up in America. Dee Brown, God bless him, once said that it was perhaps the most American book ever written. That is, of course, extremely generous, but it is true that I wrote that book out of the conviction of having lived, in my ancestors, for many thousands of years in North America. And *The Way To Rainy Mountain* proceeds also from that conviction, but it is more mythological in its character. There are three voices in that book, and only one is directly personal. The others are historical and, what shall I say, original. Some critics have used the word "epic" to describe it. I very much like the sound of that, but I'm not sure I know what it means.

Interviewer: Two of the main concerns of Indian people today are the preservation of the culture and self-determination. Does contemporary Native literature help to attain either of these goals?

Momaday: Yes, all literature functions in this way, I believe.

Interviewer: Is there a relationship between the "oral tradition" and contemporary Native poetry? Are there certain themes that proceed from that tradition?

Momaday: The works of Indian poets proceed from the oral tradition, I believe. That tradition is there in the background, and it can scarcely be ignored. We are talking about a sensitivity to language, a faith in the efficacy of the word. That is an important legacy for the Indian writer. Beyond that, there are certain themes, certain attitudes and perceptions that demand expression. Among these are the relationships between Man and the other creatures of the earth, between Man and the landscape, between Man and supernatural beings.

Interviewer: There has been little drama produced by Native playwrights. Hanay Geiogamah's plays stand out as some of the few examples. Does drama present a difficulty to Native writers or is it simply a form of expression, in written form of course, that Native writers have not gotten around to yet?

Momaday: I really do not know the answer to this question. As far as I can see, the Indian has a very highly developed sense of the dramatic. It is present in virtually every expression of his life. Perhaps it is so prevalent that he doesn't feel the need to translate it to the stage. An interesting question; I wish that I could do it justice.

Interviewer: Can we, or should we, try to put together a definition of Native literature that is more than simply literature by Native writers?

Momaday: I have never been able to think of literature in such precise and exclusive terms. I don't know what "Native literature" is and "literature by Indians" is, I suppose, like literature by Germans or Jews or, if you will, cowboys. Literature, in the best sense, is to my way of thinking writing that deserves to be preserved for its own sake. All other distinctions are by the way.

Interviewer: Within some of the fiction written particularly by Indian authors, there is the idea that Indians have access to another world that is exclusively Indian. Do you think that such a world exists or does it appear to be a romantic idea that is simply a part of the creation of "Indianness" in fiction?

Momaday: There is most certainly a world that is exclusively Indian. I have been privileged to live in that world, and I have written about it from within. That world is very important to me, but I do not think that it is necessarily important to others, others than Indians, I mean. The reflection of the Indian world in *House Made of Dawn* is of course a matter of literary considerations, and it is important on that level. But there is a distinction to be made between the Indian world and the Indian world reflected in literature. As a writer, it is the reflection, the appearance that matters to me (literature is made up of surfaces, appearances); as an Indian it is the reality that matters. The one thing is negotiable by definition; the other is indeed exclusive.

N. Scott Momaday

Laura Coltelli / 1985

From *Winged Words: American Indian Writers Speak,* ed.
Laura Coltelli, Lincoln: University of Nebraska Press, 1990,
89–100. Reprinted by permission of the University of Nebraska
Press. Copyright © 1990 by the University of Nebraska Press.

N. Scott Momaday was born in 1934 at Lawton, Oklahoma. His
father, Al Momaday, a Kiowa, was an accomplished artist, and
for many years he was principal of the day school at the
Pueblo of Jemez, New Mexico. His mother, Natachee Scott, of
Cherokee descent, is a well-known writer, painter, and teacher,
educated at Haskell Institute in Lawrence, Kansas, and then at
the University of New Mexico.

When Momaday was two, the family left Oklahoma and lived
in various places in the Southwest, especially in the Navajo
country. In 1946 they moved to the Pueblo of Jemez, a Towa-
speaking village, where Momaday's parents were each offered
teaching positions. He attended high school in Santa Fe and
Albuquerque and, in his final year, at Augustus Military Academy, Fort Defiance, Virginia. In 1958 he received his bachelor's
degree in political science from the University of New Mexico.

Urged by a friend to apply for the Wallace Stegner Creative
Scholarship at Stanford University, he won the award and began
to study under Yvor Winters. Momaday received his doctoral
degree in 1963; his dissertation, on Frederick Goddard Tuckerman's poetry, was published two years later. After his doctoral
degree, he taught English and comparative literature at the
University of California at Santa Barbara and Berkeley, Stanford University, and the University of Arizona, Tucson, where
he currently teaches and lives. He is the father of four
daughters.

The Journey of Tai-Me, privately printed in Santa Barbara in
1967, was his first publication devoted to the mythical lore of
the Kiowa. It was followed in 1968 by *House Made of Dawn,*
which won the 1969 Pulitzer Prize. This success marked the
beginning of a new Native American literature and paved the
way for young Indian writers. *The Way to Rainy Mountain*
(1969) continues Momaday's journey into his tribal past, a
journey which is defined by the writer himself in that book as
"The history of an idea, man's idea of himself."

The Names (1976) is an autobiographical account shaping his
own Indian identity and giving voice to his personal past. His
poetry has appeared in two collections, *Angle of Geese and*

Other Poems (1974) and *The Gourd Dancer* (1976). His many essays, short prose, and articles witness his commitment to issues concerning Indian culture. Some of them, widely anthologized, are exceptional assessments of Native American thought, as indicated by a selection of titles: "The Man Made of Words," "An American Land Ethic," "A First American Views His Land," "The Morality of Indian Hating," "Native American Attitudes toward the Environment."

In the past few years Momaday has also gained an increasingly high reputation as a painter: in 1979 he had his first show at the University of North Dakota, and since then he has exhibited in Minneapolis; Norman, Oklahoma; Santa Fe, New Mexico; Phoenix, Tucson, and Scottsdale, Arizona; Basel; and Heidelberg.

The interview took place on September 25, 1985, at Momaday's house, on the outskirts of Tucson. Some of the desert plants surrounding the area were still in full bloom, brilliant and colorful against the gray lightness of the sand. Once inside, his imposing yet warm voice quietly took hold of the room.

LC: The understanding of the landscape is one of the most important aspects of Indian oral tradition. As you said, "I should affirm myself in the spirit of the land," or just to use one of your favorite expressions in defining this relationship, "There are places where you have *invested* your life," but you suggest that there is also a process of appropriation. Would you elaborate on that?

Momaday: Well, yes, I think that the sense of place is very important in American Indian oral tradition. And the question is how does one acquire such a sense? I think it is a long process of appropriation. The American Indian has a very long experience of the North American continent, say, going back thousands of years, maybe thirty thousand. So I think of that as being a very great investment, a kind of spiritual investment in the landscape, and because he has that experience he is able to think of himself in a particular way, think of himself in relation to the land, and he is able to define for himself a sense of place, belonging, and to me that is very important and characterizes much of the American Indian oral tradition. Probably writing too, more recently, because the writing, I think, springs in a natural way from the oral tradition, and the sense of place is crucial to both.

LC: And does it work this way in literature?
Momaday: Literature at large?

LC: Yes.

Momaday: I think so. I think that in most literature that I know of, the sense of place is important. It differs, of course; when I talk about the American Indian and his many thousands of years in America, I think of that as a unique experience, but certainly there are other unique experiences in other parts of the world and involving other peoples. But the sense of place, I think, across the board, is important in literature.

LC: But could you say that the spirit of the place is better interpreted and understood in literature by western and southern writers? I am speaking of American literature.

Momaday: Talking about American Indian literature, certainly the center of that literature is in the West, I think, because the oldest surviving societies are in the West. We have communities of people in Arizona, New Mexico, Nevada, Montana, and so on, whose way of life has continued in a way that is not so in other parts of the country. I don't know, I can't really speak to the Northeast as a geographical area; I just don't know enough about it, but I do know that the oral tradition, the Indian oral tradition, is very strong in the West, and in American literature exclusive of Native American literature the tradition seems to be very strong in the South.

LC: Can you see any difference between these two approaches, between the western and the southern?

Momaday: Yes, sure. I think of southern literature as focusing largely upon the War Between the States and the development before that war, of an agrarian society in the South, which was aristocratic in large measure, and then the collapse of that society.

LC: Decadent, white society.

Momaday: Yes. Faulkner, of course, is the person who comes to mind as the spokesman of that ideal; and he says something to the effect in one of his books that for every boy who grows up in the South and so on, there is still that moment at Gettysburg. But the West, on the other hand, the western literature deals with another question, and that is the opening of the frontier, which in a sense, I think, is still going on. So that in one way the literature of the West is newer, I think, than the literature of the South; it deals with a more

recent and ongoing experience in the American imagination. I am
fond of dealing with the history of the West and the imaging of the
West in the American mind. I think it's a rich kind of field to explore.
The American Indian experience is part of that as well.

LC: As you yourself said, *House Made of Dawn* is very symmetrical. Is it a design coming out of the cultural world in which the events
take place?

Momaday: Yes, I think so. I think that the novel reflects a kind of
shape that is real in the American Indian world.

LC: *The Names* is the title of your memoir. In one of your poems
the carriers of the dream wheel "spin the names of the earth and
sky." Thus is language, in shaping "the aboriginal names," the first
creative act?

Momaday: Is it the first creative act? Probably, probably. I think
there is inherent in the Native American world view the idea that
naming is coincidental with creation; that, when you bestow a name
upon someone or something you at the same time invest it with being.
It's not an idea, by the way, that's peculiar to Native American
experience; it's a worldwide kind of idea, but it is certainly important
in American Indian society. And I think, yes, this is where things
begin—naming.

LC: "A man's name is his own." Even the dead take their names
with them.

Momaday: Yes, that's true in certain American Indian societies; the
Kiowa is what I had in mind. That was true of that society; when
someone died in the tribe he was thought to take his name with him,
out of the world, unless he had given it away before he died, and that
frequently happened. It was a great honor to be given a name,
someone's name.

LC: So the investment of the self in the spirit of the land, and the
investment of the self in language.

Momaday: Yes, yes, I think so.

LC: And how can the written language continue and develop the
oral tradition?

Momaday: It's not a question that one can answer quickly or simply, but it seems to me that the things that inform oral tradition, the very best oral tradition, are the things that ought to inform the best literature, the best of the written tradition. In other words, I think that the two traditions are probably more apparently different than they are really different, one from the other. At some point they converge, and they share, I think, the same qualities. And the story-teller in the oral tradition is doing—or maybe better to put it the other way round—the writer who is writing a novel, say, is engaged in pretty much the same activity, it seems to me, as the storyteller who is telling a story in the oral tradition. There are differences, of course, but in the main, I think, they are probably closer together than we realize.

LC: What's the real relationship, the essence of their relationship?

Momaday: Well, the writer, like the storyteller, I think, is concerned to create himself and his audience in language. That's probably the most important single common denominator. Both are acts of creation and so are in some sense indivisible.

LC: So we have storyteller-audience, writer-reader.

Momaday: Yes. And that relationship, between the storyteller and the listener, is pretty much the same relationship as that between the writer and the reader, with some obvious distinctions.

LC: There are recurrent patterns in contemporary American Indian literature. Do you think that we can speak then of some common denominators?

Momaday: Well, what occurs to me is that all of modern American Indian writing, it seems to me, proceeds from the same national experience, if I can put it that way. It proceeds from the same general history and prehistory; that is to say, I think that one of the things that characterizes or ought to characterize American Indian literature is a procession from the oral tradition. Oral tradition is at the root of modern American Indian literature, and everybody, every Indian who is writing out of his Indianness, I think, has that in mind, whether consciously or not; but he is working with precedents that go back into oral tradition.

LC: In *Ceremony* and *House Made of Dawn,* for instance, the main characters are both veterans coming back from their war experience and both of them become "inarticulate" in that they can't speak or communicate to other people. I am not speaking just in terms of a literature coming out of the oral tradition, but of themes, characters, events.

Momaday: Well, the figure—I can speak about *House Made of Dawn*—of Abel is commonplace in the sense that he is a kind of, a kind of—I can't think of the word I want—he represents a great many people of his generation, the Indian who returns from the war, the Second World War. He is an important figure in the whole history of the American experience in this country. It represents such a dislocation of the psyche in our time. Almost no Indian of my generation or of Abel's generation escaped that dislocation, that sense of having to deal immediately, not only with the traditional world, but with the other world which was placed over the traditional world so abruptly and with great violence. Abel's generation is a good one to write about, simply because it's a tragic generation. It is not the same, the generation after Abel did not have the same experience, nor the one before. So it is, in some sense, the logical one to deal with in literature.

LC: Yes. There are always three generations, and the main characters come out from the third generation.
Momaday: Yes, Yes.

LC: It understood that individual tribal thought and traditions are indispensable in analyzing structure and content of these works because they come from very different cultural worlds.
Momaday: Exactly. That's right. That's very important, very important.

LC: Do you feel that in your prose poems there is a stronger link with the oral tradition?
Momaday: I think that the prose poems are very close to oral tradition, to Indian oral tradition, and probably closer than most of the poems that are composed in verse. The oral tradition of the Indian has a closer model, represents a closer model, for the prose poem than for the poem. It's storytelling traditions, and it's in one sense easier to tell a story in a prose poem than in a poem.

LC: In 1970 you wrote in "Learning from the Indian" that "more than ever before, the Indian is in possession of his future as well as of his past" and that "he stands to make a major contribution to the modern world" in terms of "Indian land ethic, his integrity as a man and a race, capacity for wonder, delight and belief." Contemporary American Indian literature is playing a remarkable role in American literature at large, it's a very innovating contribution to it. Is American Indian literature a major vehicle for that?

Momaday: Yes, I think so, because the Indian has always had such a keen regard for language. So literature as such is a large part of his experience and one of his great contributions, I think. And you are right, American Indian literature is becoming a very important, recognizably important, part of American literature as a whole. And we are just now rethinking the boundaries of American literature, and we are obliged, I think, to include oral tradition, elements of oral tradition, that we did not even think of including twenty-five years ago.

LC: And just in terms of contributions, what's the major contribution to American literature at large?

Momaday: That whole oral tradition which goes back probably to beyond the invention of the alphabet; the storyteller was the man who was standing with a piece of charcoal in his hand making, placing, the wonderful images in his mind's eye on the wall of the cave; that's probably one of the origins of American literature. He has begun to tell a story, and he develops in the course of time that storytelling capacity in himself to such a wonderful degree that we have to recognize it as being somewhere in the line, in the evolution of what we think of American literature. I have an idea that American literature really begins with the first human expression of man in the American landscape, and who knows how far back that goes; but it certainly antedates writing, and it probably goes back a thousand years or more. So we have to admit it now, and always think in terms of it. We cannot think of Melville without thinking of American Indian antecedents in the oral tradition, because the two things are not to be separated logically at all.

LC: What about language and imagery?

Momaday: I think there is a close correlation: before a man could write, he could draw; but writing is drawing, and so the image and the word cannot be divided.

LC: Let us now speak about structure. As you said before, the structure of your novel *House Made of Dawn* comes out from your cultural world.

Momaday: That's right. That's right.

LC: So there is also a major contribution in terms of technique.

Momaday: Yes, I am sure of that.

LC: Writing on white-Indian relations in 1964, you stated that "the morality of intolerance has become in the twentieth century a morality of pity" and that the contemporary white American, on the whole, is ambiguous and even contradictory with respect to Indians. In your opinion, is there any significant change more than twenty years later?

Momaday: Yes, I think so. I think that the morality of pity has given way to something else.

LC: So there is another stage?

Momaday: There is another stage. Maybe a present and ongoing stage. The Indian has made remarkable strides in the direction of assimilation. He gets along in the larger world beyond the boundaries of the reservation much better now than he did twenty years ago. He has made tremendous strides in that respect and he has made them without having to sacrifice, I think, his most intrinsic and important values. He remains an Indian, which is the whole point of it. He brings his Indianness, as he always has, really, with him into new experiences, into new territories. There was at one time a real danger of the Indian simply being frozen as an image in the America mind. But I think we have largely dislodged that image, and he also becomes something more vital and infinitely more adaptable than the figure on the screen who is being chased by John Wayne.

LC: You are a writer and a painter as well, like your father. Quite a number of American Indian writers are also painters. Do you think that there is a special reason for it? Is it because there is a remarkable aesthetic perception in the Indian universe?

Momaday: I think that's part of it, and I think also that the real answer to it probably lies in the very thing we were talking about a moment ago, the proximity of the image and the word to things. In one sense the painter is doing what the writer is doing, that is, he's constructing images that represent reality in one way or another, and when you start to think about it that's what the writer does too. He constructs images that represent reality. Words are artificial in the way that paint on canvas is artificial; it's not the real world; it's a reflection, one remove from the real world, and in some ways the reflection is truer than the things it represents as it passes through the intelligence of the painter or of the writer. But the activities, the two activities, seem to me very much alike.

LC: Speaking of modern Indian painters such as R. C. Gorman, C. F. Lovato, Harry Fonseca, Fritz Scholder, T. C. Cannon, Neil Parsons, can you see in their subjects, color techniques, any connections with contemporary American Indian writers?

Momaday: Sure. Yes. Lots of them. If you take for one example Jim Welch's *Winter in the Blood,* you can find that story or that narrative illustrated in the work of Fritz Scholder. I can think of, I can bring to mind paintings and prints that Fritz has made which might very well illustrate a passage in Welch. And I think that's probably true of a great many painters and writers. They are dealing with the same subjects in obvious ways.

LC: What about your paintings?

Momaday: I am late to come to painting. I've only been at it for about twelve years, seriously painting. And I'm still feeling my way. I have come from more or less abstract images and drawing to something else; I have recently taken up watercolor for the first time, and I find it terribly exacting to work in watercolor. It's very different from acrylics with which I have been working for some years, and before that, ink-and-brush work on paper, drawing in a real sense. So it's hard for me to talk about my painting because it seems to me in flux at the moment. I don't know where it is, where it's going.

LC: Just in progress.

Momaday: But it is in progress. And I feel very good about that, and I feel that I am coming closer to realizing whatever talent I have for painting as I go. And that's always a good sense, you know, a sense of accomplishment.

LC: What do you think of the non-Indian critics of your work and of American Indian literature in general?

Momaday: Well, I don't know. I think that critics are critics whether they are looking at American Indian writing or painting or whatever. It's like everything else, some critics are wonderfully astute and intelligent and others are wonderfully stupid. So the writer and the painter, I think, had best ignore the critics as far as they can. Too much praise is bad for the writer or the painter, and certainly negative reception of his work is an impairment too. I don't pay much attention to people who write glowing things about my work because I think that can be deceptive, it can get in my way, and I pay even less attention to people who take me to task, for one reason or another, because that too gets in my way. It's rather nice to work with blinds on, if you know what I mean, and profitable, I think.

LC: What about the critical reception of your work in Europe?

Momaday: Well, it's been very gratifying, I think. I am always a little amazed when I read things that have been written about my work, and I think I can say that most of what has been written about my work has been altogether favorable, and of course that's the way I would have it. But on the other hand, you know, I think, to repeat myself, I think that for me anyway, it's best to keep working and to pay not so much attention to what people have said about what I have done in the past.

LC: How has your work evolved in the past few years?

Momaday: Oh, I think I just spoke to that point with respect to painting. I don't know, it's hard for me to see, hard for me to look at my own work and draw any conclusions about it. The novel that I am writing is not like anything I have written before, so that it represents some sort of new direction in my work, I think. It's contemporary in the main, but it does draw a lot upon historical facts and prehistoric, mythological elements. So that it covers a wide range of things. It is basically the story about a man, and the setting is for the most part in the present, but there are a lot of references to, as I said, things in the past. It has got an Indian character to it, but has also got a kind of non-Indian dimension to it. The principal character is an Indian who does not know he is an Indian, and part of the story has to do with his finding out he is an Indian, what it means to him. But in any case, I can't talk much about it because probably I am not even half through it yet, and so I have no idea what it's going to become. I'm happy with what it is now; it's fun working on it, gratifying to work on it, but it's too early to describe it in any real way.

LC: Would you describe your writing process?

Momaday: Well, I think of myself as being a very undisciplined kind of writer. I have moments of inspiration: I never know when they are going to come upon me, and when they do I try to take advantage of them. I write now in the early part of the day, when I am really rolling along. I like to get up early and get to work early, and I can work, I find, for maybe six hours at the most, writing, and then I have to back away and do something else; but if I can write, say, four hours a day consistently, that's as much as I ask of myself.

LC: Do you have any book of poetry in progress?

Momaday: Well, I have some poems which have not been published, several poems, maybe half a dozen; and these are, I hope, to be part of a forthcoming book, but I write poetry so slowly that I don't even envision a book of poems by a certain date. It will happen when it happens, that's all I can say. But I like some of the recent poems I have written, and so I keep that going too, you know, in addition to the painting and the novel.

LC: Is there an evolution as a poet as well?

Momaday: Yes. I started off writing poetry without knowing what poetry was, and so it was very ragged. Then I went to study under a man who knew a great deal about poetic forms, and he taught me a lot, and I changed; my writing changed under his teaching, so that it became much more clearly defined in traditional ways.

LC: You are speaking of Winters?

Momaday: Yes, Yvor Winters. And when I left Stanford and after Winters had retired and then died, my writing of poems changed again, I think, and it became freer. I had backed myself into a corner, and I was so conscious of the traditional English forms of poetry that I left myself very little place to maneuver. So I opened up a bit and my verse became freer, not free verse, not entirely free, but more flexible, I think. I keep writing in that more flexible way, though now that I think about it, it's rather interesting to me that of the maybe last six poems I have written, at least two of them are sonnets, the very tightly controlled forms. But I have achieved, I think, in those traditional forms, a kind of freedom that I did not have before. So that's probably to the good.

N. Scott Momaday: Storyteller

Dagmar Weiler / 1986

From *Journal of Ethnic Studies,* 16, no. 1 (Spring 1988), 118–26.
Reprinted by permission.

Q: You told the "Bear Story" today, and I noticed that your stories are never finished. I always want to go back and ask questions such as "What happened when the bear meets the man?" or "Does the pregnant woman in the old Kiowa myth of the people who came through the log give birth to a new tribe?"

Momaday: I do think about these things. I wonder: What happened? Where were they? What was on the other side of the wall? Where did they come from? The story doesn't tell us what happened to that pregnant woman. She's in a terrible predicament. She's stuck in the log. What happened? We're not told. But the more I understand about storytelling, the more I realize that there is always a part of the story which leaves us wondering about this or that. Many things are not given us, and for the Western man this jars a little bit because we want to know. We expect to be told. We don't expect loose ends in a story. But in Indian tradition, it's not that way at all. There are always loose ends, and that is what you'd expect in a story.

Q: Since you stressed the Indian side, I'd like to talk very briefly about your position as an Indian writer. Last semester, I took an undergraduate class in which we read Leslie's Silko's *Ceremony* and *Storyteller,* and I remember that some of the students had problems with those works. We also read *House Made of Dawn,* which I think was the last novel, and they found difficulty there, too. They asked the question: "Where is the message [in *House Made of Dawn*] comparable to that of an angry woman like Leslie Silko, or that found in some of the poems by Joy Harjo, and what enables them to take a stand?" The students seemed to be missing this. I remember two years ago in an interview you said that you didn't make social comments. In connection with this "Indian" issue, how do you see yourself?

Momaday: I don't see myself as an Indian writer. I don't know what that means. I am an Indian, and I am a writer, but I don't just

want to say "Indian writer" or talk about Indian literature. I don't
know what that means, exactly, and I don't identify with it at all.

Q: You did a review of several books in 1971. You talked then about
Vine Deloria and other Indian writers. I had the impression you
criticized them somewhat for stressing their Indian stand. Let me
quote this. You said: "As far as I can see, the Indians who are giving
the best account of themselves at present are doing so without any
particular regard to movement as such or to the ways in which they
are accounted for by the others." So you would say that first of all
you are a storyteller, a writer who happens to be an Indian?

Momaday: Or I'm an Indian who happens to be a storyteller. I don't
order those things in any particular way. I am an Indian and a writer,
but I'm a lot of other things as well. They are all very important to me.

Q: It just struck me that you have had many discussions with these
young people. They were looking, especially in the early 70s, to Red
Power, and these young students were expecting something out of,
for example, *House Made of Dawn*. You know, what the Indian
should do, and they didn't find it there. Maybe they missed something.
They immediately realized or thought that the Albino was the symbol
for the White man. It was easier with an angry woman like Silko. It
was much more out in the open: the social, political, and economic
problems. You stress the fact that you are a poet, but I would like to
talk about the prose. "The Way to Rainy Mountain": it appeared as
an essay; it has been anthologized.

Momaday: Yes, the introduction.

Q: The introduction appeared as an essay: you published it as a
book together with short Kiowa tales, and later the priest Tosamah
uses it in *House Made of Dawn*. Is there a difference between the
three forms? Would you say the impact is different?

Momaday: Well, yes. I say that it functions as the introduction to
The Way to Rainy Mountain. In *House Made of Dawn,* it functions in
a different way because it tells us something about one of the characters in the novel. It is the delineation of Tosamah's character, among
other things, so it's completely different.

Q: That is one thing that I had problems with—that Tosamah was
telling the story. *House Made of Dawn* fascinates me. It is disturbing—

Momaday: Good!

Q: —mainly because there are many beautiful voices. Let's talk about Father Olguin and Angela, or maybe not so much about Father Olguin but Frey Nicolas. How did Nicolas appear in *House Made of Dawn?* Did you rely on old manuscripts? Is he right out of old missionary ledgers?

Momaday: I didn't research the book at all. It just came right out of my imagination. I don't know how I happened to get the idea of the character of Nicolas. He's very much in place because he's a mission-ary, and the missionaries, especially the Catholic missionaries in pueblos, are very important. I think they have, in over four hundred years, made a great difference. Well, I'm not sure I want to say that. I don't know if they have made a difference or not, but they have become a kind of institution in the pueblos over that period of time, and they are interesting, you know, the priests and the pueblos. I got to thinking about their lives and what they must feel, being the representatives of the Catholic church to what in the past certainly had been a pagan society. They must have felt very isolated, and I wanted a character that would represent that sort of dichotomy in pueblo life. Frey Nicolas was the answer for me. He could occupy that position of an intermediary in the pueblo and articulate some of the conflicts that informed the pueblo world. In a sense, Father Olguin comes as a later representative of that same conflict; Angela comes as a later representative of that conflict. So it seemed that such a character would be interesting and, indeed, I enjoyed working with both Frey Nicolas and Father Olguin.

Q: I think many of us find it fascinating that all the voices are distinctive. Nicolas, for example, in the first entry: the voice is that of missionary who is still in concert with his belief. It's "They will, Lord" and "Have mercy" and "I pray." And later he falls apart. There is also this beautiful scene—"Dear Lord," I think he is talking about Francisco. He remembers watching this boy, and what fasci-nated me is that, by the time you tell this story, this man is dead. But still, through your style, you make him come alive. We can hear him.
Momaday: Yes.

Q: And that is why it seems as if you opened a ledger and copied it.
Momaday: Well, that's wonderful. I'm glad that you have that sense of it because that was my intention.

Q: You mentioned Angela. I have a problem there. Angela seems to me to be the only one whose voice is not convincing. What is Angela's role?

Momaday: Angela's role is to be a kind of foil to Abel. She represents the antithesis of the pueblo world. Yet, she and Abel are able to relate to one another on one level although they are so diametrically opposed in most of their cultural attitudes. So she enables us, I think, to see the pueblo world and Abel in a particular way, a way in which you would not otherwise be able to see him in his traditional context.

Q: I think my criticism may derive from a comparison of Angela and Milly. Later in the book we hear Milly talk. It is a wonderful, almost Faulknerian passage as she remembers her life on the farm. It is printed in italics, but we hear her talk. Her voice is "listening"; she has her own style. Angela's is somewhat weird, a blurring sound, a compulsive cycle of sexual exploits; Angela is there, and then she vanishes. What about Milly? Would you say that while Angela is disturbing Abel, Milly has a human touch? I noticed that Milly is almost the only one Abel is communicating with. He hardly speaks throughout the whole book, except to Milly.

Momaday: Yes, I would say that. I think that Milly is much more selfless than Angela. Angela is motivated by things that are deep within her that we don't know much about and she is strange, a stranger, as you suggest. Milly is not that. She is concerned about Abel and she, I think it is fair to say, wants to help him. He's certainly aware of that. He's able to perceive that she means him well, so he responds to her in a very sympathetic way. And, you know, Angela's something else. It's a sexual relationship, and I think that Angela does not mean him well, and he understands that, so he is wary of her. In a way, he plays the game with Angela. He understands that she requires a certain response on his part, and he makes it. He's willing to make it; he's willing to go that far. But with Milly, I think, the feelings are much more genuine and deeper.

Q: The priest of the sun is one character who deals explicitly with the problem of language. He uses the introduction to "Rainy Mountain." I think he accuses other people of taking the word and convoluting it, overusing it.

Momaday: He says, in effect, that this is what the White man does. This is the Western tradition as far as language is concerned. They overdo it. They go too far. He talks about this in the sermon "According to John." He lets us know it's important.

Q: To exaggerate a bit, it is Tosamah whose speech seems to be a little convoluted.
Momaday: Of course. He's a trickster figure.

Q: This is a wonderful irony.
Momaday: Thank you. I agree.

Q: There is this hipster language, such as you hear in caricatures of almost all Black preachers.
Momaday: Yes. He's a trickster, and he takes advantage of language in the situation, and he's bright. Much of what he says, I think, is provocative and true. I think of his sermon as being a wonderful kind of commentary on language, even in his own ironic terms. What he says is thoughtful and makes sense.

Q: What is his position in the Indian world as created in the story we have been discussing?
Momaday: What is Tosamah's position? Well, I think of Tosamah as being uprooted and lost. He and Abel are poised somewhere apart from their traditional world. They are also apart from the other world, but they have fashioned an existence in that no man's land. And Tosamah has done it better than most people have because he's shrewd and a cynic and he takes advantage. He exists. He wears masks. He knows how to take a bad situation and make the best of it.

Q: Tosamah's voice seems to be the one that will be out there, the one person who will be heard by the White man as well as by uprooted Indians in the city.
Momaday: Well, perhaps that's true. Tosamah speaks the White man's language. He is able to turn the tables, as it were. He takes, after all, one of the great, classic doctrines of the Western world, *The Gospel According to St. John,* and he twists it around so that he condemns the whole White culture. It's a wonderful thing to do. It's a tour de force. In a way, it's fair to say that the White man, if he listens to any of these characters, will hear Tosamah. The Indian, if

he hears any of these characters, will probably be most receptive to Ben Benally. When Ben Benally talks of witchcraft in the traditional world and sees the sunrise on the red mesas, that's the reality of the Indian. Tosamah does both things. He speaks for both worlds, and he does it eloquently, you know. But you never know quite where he is in relation to the reality of any given moment. He wears masks.

Q: That's right. I found him one of the most disturbing figures, and that's one of the reasons why I asked about him. The first time I read it, I thought of the story in *Rainy Mountain* and Tosamah's voice. It's not right. After his ranting, there is that mythical voice, and I thought, why this man? Earlier you mentioned the traditional form of the novel.
Momaday: I did?

Q: Yes, today!
Momaday: Today? I don't remember. What did I say?

Q: I'm thinking of the plot, the straight story line, the main protagonist. Although Abel may be at the center of *House Made of Dawn,* I don't think it is really Abel's story. All the characters have their own stories, even if they appear only once briefly, like Milly. But they are evocative, even the dead man because he is so articulate and because he has his own voice. You can imagine his whole story. In the structure of the novel and the prologue we see Abel running— does the ritual of running have a healing effect on Abel?
Momaday: Well, yes!

Q: He runs again at the end.
Momaday: I think in the novel it says rather explicitly that his running provides him some of the rehabilitation. He is coming to terms again with his traditional world in the act of running. The question of whether or not he makes it is open. I mean a lot of people want to know what happens after the last page, and I don't know. I don't know what happens to Abel finally, and I don't want to know.

Q: I find that that is the wonderful thing about it. There's a structural circle. I have this image that Tosamah is building a house made of dawn that is not filled with furniture, but with these voices. Of course, in a year maybe I will remember Frey Nicolas and specifically, the priest. You have written several essays on the value of man and the land. In your essays, you say we must reestablish the connection to the landscape. Is that right?

Momaday: Yes, I believe that's important. I think that most people in the world today have broken a bond with the earth to their peril. I think we should reestablish a positive relationship to the earth.

Q: Do you believe that we can stop the changes, that we can go back?

Momaday: Yes, I think we can. There is no alternative but annihilation. I don't think we are by any means on an irreversible course. The earth is not as vulnerable as we sometimes think.

Q: The first time I read certain passages of yours describing the land, they reminded me of photographs of Ansel Adams. I'm not sure why yet. As far as I know, Adams would go back to Yosemite to re-photograph the land over a period of years to see what had happened.

Momaday: Maybe. I didn't know that.

Q: I have to admit that when I saw the Rand McNally full color atlas that you did the text for, I was a little disappointed because some of the photographs looked too good.

Momaday: Well, that's what I think of Ansel Adams. I don't like him. He's too postcardish. His view of nature is not mine. God knows that people like that sort of thing. It's removed from the real Yosemite. It's removed from the real world, and I agree that it's too true of the Colorado book, of all coffee table books that are always a little too glitzy. I don't care much for them. I would rather take my own photos of Colorado or Yosemite. They wouldn't be as slick as those of Ansel Adams or of David Muench. I prefer that. I suppose it's a matter of taste.

Q: Maybe the best camera is still the mind. I looked at the Billy the Kid story recently; what is the fascination with Billy the Kid?

Momaday: Well, Billy the Kid is a fascinating part of America. He was an outlaw. He became a legend in his own time. Isn't that fascinating. He was a man who lived to be 21 years old, and in that short time he became a legend on this earth. He became someone who inspired stories, songs, movies, and the great ballet, and how does that happen? It's all very fascinating, and, of course, I grew up in the very landscape in which Billy the Kid lived his 21 years. I fantasized as a boy that I rode with Billy the Kid, and what a wonderful thing that was!

Q: It struck me that "legend" is maybe the key word. It doesn't really matter whether his real name was Henry or George or whatever, because you take this as a starting point, this strange and true story, and recreate Billy the Kid.

Momaday: Well, yes, I'm interested in legend, and Americans are like other peoples of the world, manufacturers of legends. The legends that we manufacture are among the most valuable possessions that we have. I consider that to be what I do as a writer. The book I'm writing now is itself a legend, not only a kind of investigation of the legend-making process, but is itself the legend-making process.

Q: I was very interested in the format of "Billy the Kid." The pictures in it are your paintings. They remind me a little bit of the faces of people in your father's daguerrotypes.

Momaday: Well, most of these paintings are based on photographs. The one of Pat Garrett is curious because if you look at it closely, you will see that one of his eyes is a cat's eye and has a vertical kind of pupil, and he has only half of a mustache. In the photograph from which that painting was made, he has half a mustache and the pupil in one of his eyes is elongated and vertical. It's a strange photograph, but I was true to it.

Q: And this picture of his sister? Did you take that from a photo-graph too? She looked like a man a little bit, doesn't she.

Momaday: Yes. There is a photograph, and I did look at the photograph. The painting is based on the photograph, but the painting doesn't look a whole lot like the photograph.

Q: Your paintings are all in ink or water color. Are you trying to find new media.

Momaday: I have worked in various media. I have done pen and ink drawings and brush and ink acrylics on canvas and paper. Recently, for the last year or two, I've been working in watercolor a lot. Most of the show I've just mounted is composed of watercolor and acrylics, but not watercolor on paper.

Q: In "Billy the Kid," there are short stories, and wonderful poems. I love the way you go from Billy the Kid on a rocking horse to a lullaby. It's beautiful. Was this a new form for you?

Momaday: It was all my idea, but it didn't happen at once. I wrote the series first. In fact, did I write it as a series? I don't remember; to tell you the truth, I don't remember the evolution. I guess I had the idea of writing a piece on Billy the Kid, a series with 21 pieces, so I did that first. I got the idea of the Billy the Kid suite of paintings two or three years ago, and I painted Billy first of all, and then Sister Blandina, then Catherine McCarty and so on, and then I thought it would be nice to use these paintings to illustrate it, this piece that I had written, "The Strange and True Story of My Life with Billy the Kid." I had done some work for *American West,* and I know the publisher there; so I called him up and asked him to publish these paintings. That's how it happened.

Q: Some final questions about your 1974 trip to Russia. It must have been quite an experience. What did Moscow look like to you? What was your reaction?

Momaday: It was a fascinating place to me. I didn't know what to expect. The only knowledge I had of Russia I had gained by reading Russian literature. I'm always fascinated by the Russia of Dostoyevsky's writings, of Tolstoy's writings, so I was enthusiastic when the idea of going there was presented to me. It turned out to be a wonderful experience. I enjoyed every part of it. I taught one class at the University of Moscow; I met my class on Saturday afternoon for two hours. I taught 20th-century American literature. I had a large class, perhaps 100 students and faculty members. I had time to myself in which to wander around Moscow. I learned how to get around; they have a wonderful metro.

Q: You mentioned some problems with the telephone.

Momaday: Oh, I have a wonderful story about the telephone. I had a telephone in my suite of two rooms. They gave me very nice accommodations at the University. I had a telephone, a television set and a refrigerator. The story about the telephone is this: I was given a very generous stipend which was much more than I needed, so I thought that I could use this money that I was accumulating for telephone calls to the United States. So I set aside about half the money that was given to me. I made telephone calls to the United States, and I kept waiting for the phone bill. I had no idea what it was going to cost me, but I was reasonably sure I had it covered. After a month there was no bill, and I began to worry about it. I tried to find out what had happened. I wanted to know how much money I owed the phone people, but I couldn't find out. I couldn't get any satisfaction at all. I called the operator, told her I had called several times to the United States, requested the amount of money I owed, and asked for the bill. And the voice on the other end of the line said, "Oh, don't worry about that, it's all in order." I was led to believe that if I would just be patient, the bill would arrive. Well, to make a long story short, the bill never came, and when I left Russia, I was quite concerned. I thought, "They can't let me out of the country without the phone money." And, you know, I thought as I packed and departed for the airport that it's going to happen at the airport: that's where they'll get me. And then I went through customs and got on the plane and then I thought that out over the Baltic, MIGs are going to appear and force us down and say, "Mr. Momaday, what about the phone bill?" So it's a funny story. The bill just never came, and I left the money with a Russian friend, and I asked that if he could find out how much money I owed to please pay the bill, and that if he couldn't, to just spend it any way he wanted. So it was a great mystery to me. I never understood the Russian phone system at all.

Q: Maybe this would be inappropriate, but would it be right to say that finally, when all is said and done, that Scott Momaday is a story-teller?

Momaday: Yes, absolutely. You've got it. You have defined me.

N. Scott Momaday
Louis Owens / 1986

From *This Is About Vision: Interviews with Southwestern Writers,* eds. William Balassi, John F. Crawford, and Annie O. Eysturoy, Albuquerque: University of New Mexico Press, 1990. Reprinted by permission of the University of New Mexico Press.

N. Scott Momaday was born in Lawton, Oklahoma, in 1934, the son of artists Alfred Momaday and Natachee Scott Momaday. He defines himself first of all as "an American Indian (Kiowa) . . . vitally interested in American Indian art, history, and culture." Between 1935 and 1943, Momaday lived with his parents on the Navajo Reservation, an experience that would create a deep affinity for Navajo culture in the half-Kiowa child. In 1946 the family moved to the Jemez Pueblo in New Mexico, where Momaday would spend the formative years of his youth and where he would set *House Made of Dawn,* the Pulitzer Prize-winning novel published in 1968. Momaday received a bachelor's degree from the University of New Mexico in 1958 and immediately accepted his first teaching position at Dulce, on the Jicarilla Apache Reservation in northern New Mexico, where he began a long poem that would eventually evolve into *House Made of Dawn.* Lured by poet and professor Yvor Winters away from Dulce to Stanford University in 1959, Momaday completed his M.A. in creative writing at Stanford after one year and his Ph.D. in English from the same university in 1963. Since receiving his Ph.D., Momaday has taught on both the Santa Barbara and Berkeley campuses of the University of California as well as at Stanford University. He is currently Professor of English at the University of Arizona, where he teaches courses in the Native American oral tradition. Momaday's first published book was a revised version of his doctoral dissertation, *The Complete Poems of Frederick Goddard Tuckerman* (1965). In 1967 Momaday privately published *The Journey of Tai-Me,* a collection of Kiowa oral literature, which was republished in significantly revised form in 1969 as *The Way to Rainy Mountain.* When Momaday won the Pulitzer Prize for *House Made of Dawn,* the publishing world—seemingly ignorant of such important earlier novels by Indian authors as John Joseph Mathews's *Sundown* (1934) and D'Arcy McNickle's *The Surrounded* (1936)—was, in the words of Henry Ramont, "stunned at the selection."

Momaday has spoken often about his concern to avoid stereotypes of what "Indian" is assumed to mean in twentieth-century

America, and he has spoken just as often about the crucial place of landscape in Indian lives. A passage from his autobiographical work *The Names* (1976) recalls "the long wall of red rocks which extends eastward from Gallup" beneath which are "cattle and sheep, rabbits and roadrunners, all delightful to a child." In his most recent work, *The Ancient Child,* a novel published in 1989, Momaday's protagonist is, like the author, a painter who "sees the world in a particular way, in terms of lines, and shapes, and shadows, and forms." The "inner eye" that Momaday invokes in both of these passages extends throughout his work as a principal motif. In this interview, conducted by Louis Owens on April 3, 1986, Momaday speaks eloquently of his concern for ecology and reflects, once again, upon what it means to be an American Indian writer today.

Owens: I'll begin by asking what it means to you to be included in a volume focusing on "Southwestern Writers." Do you consider yourself a Southwest writer?

Momaday: Well, I think of myself as being a native of the Southwest. I've spent most of my life in the Southwest, so I identify with it very strongly.

Owens: Living in the West and Southwest, have you ever felt isolated from the publishing center in New York?

Momaday: Oh, no. I'm very much involved with the publishing houses in New York. I get to New York often enough, and besides, that's the sort of thing you can do by mail and telephone.

Owens: Well, let me shift to a different kind of question. How do you approach the act of writing, the mechanics of putting words on paper?

Momaday: I generally do my work in the morning. I like to write before noon, and when I'm really on a good schedule I start pretty early. I like to get going by eight o'clock or even earlier, if possible, and I find I can work for maybe six hours. I try to get up early and get to work early and then by noon I'm through.

Owens: During the past several years you've been spending a good deal of time with your painting, I understand. When do you paint?

Momaday: When I paint, it's generally afternoon.

Owens: You achieved early, impressive success as a writer, winning a Pulitzer Prize nearly two decades ago for *House Made of Dawn.* How successful has your painting been in recent years?

Momaday: Quite successful, actually. I have paintings currently in several galleries—in Santa Fe, in Scottsdale, and here in Tucson. And I have shows coming up in May and June of this year in Basel, Switzerland, and Heidelberg, West Germany. I've been very pleased.

Owens: I can think of no one who has written more eloquently about the landscapes of the Southwest, what you call in "The Man Made of Words" and *The Way to Rainy Mountain* "the remembered earth." Do you respond differently to landscape in painting than in writing?

Momaday: I don't paint landscapes. I prefer a closer focus in my painting. Lately I've become very interested in painting Indian shields, for example.

Owens: You've mentioned that you plan to spend time in Europe writing in between the shows in Basel and Heidelberg. How important is place to your art, particularly your writing? Do you find that you can write anywhere, or is a particular environment important to you?

Momaday: It's not the place so much. It seems that I *can* write almost anywhere. I don't know what the circumstances have to be for me to write, but I will say that I have been very productive in Europe. I've spent quite a bit of time in Europe in the last several years, and I seem to work there pretty well.

Owens: Since we're on the topic of Europe, do you have any thoughts as to why there is currently such a strong European interest in American Indian writing, perhaps a stronger interest than we find in this country?

Momaday: I don't know that it is only currently; I think there has consistently been a strong interest in Native American culture in Europe. This has been my experience from the first time I went there. There are a lot of factors. I think that in Europe, being older and having developed the land so long ago, there is a kind of deep appreciation for what we think of here as the frontier experience. They identify with that, and the American Indian represents to the European a kind of freedom, a relationship with the wilderness that is no longer practical in Europe so that it becomes a kind of vicarious experience.

Owens: You stated a long time ago, in "The Man Made of Words," that "Ecology is perhaps the most important subject of our time." Do you still feel this way?

Momaday: Yes. Today, of course, we think much more of nuclear war—that, too, is ecology.

Owens: Do you find a different ecological sensitivity in Europe, one that might be more sympathetic to an American Indian attitude toward the earth?

Momaday: I think so. For the reason I gave a moment ago, the fact that there is very little wilderness left in Europe, the European has a sense of loss where wilderness is concerned, and the fact that there is still wilderness somewhere is important to Europeans in a way that it may not be to Americans. I think this is becoming true all over the world.

Owens: It sounds as if you also may be talking about a need for a psychic wilderness.

Momaday: I think so.

Owens: The sixties, which saw what has been called a renaissance in Native American writing, also was a time of tremendous new interest or revitalized interest in ecology. How do you feel about our attitudes toward ecology today?

Momaday: I think a much-needed and real interest in ecology came about in the sixties, and I applaud that awareness. I think not nearly enough is being done to protect the earth from exploitation, but there is a greater awareness, certainly, and maybe one can be sanguine about that. Maybe we will take the steps to preserve the environment eventually. It's one of those things you just can't know. Sometimes I think the interest is waning and that we've passed the critical point. I hope that we all have become ecologists in a way, and there I think the American Indian stands to set an example.

Owens: When we spoke earlier this year, you mentioned the light pollution around Tucson.

Momaday: That's interesting to me. It's something I never thought about until I moved here, and something I understand at first hand now. Just seeing the stars is a very important thing, something I took for granted growing up in the rural Southwest. It's a moral issue now. I want my kids to see the stars, and their kids, and so on, and there's a possibility they won't.

Owens: Given your own sense of relationship that you bring out so well when you discuss the Kiowa myth of the sisters who ascended to the sky to become the stars of the dipper, there would seem to be a kind of dangerous "mythic" loss in being cut off from the stars.

Momaday: Oh, yes. I see it that way too. It's something that threatens me at my center. The stars are very important to me mythically. To think of losing the stars represents to me a very deep wound.

Owens: Do you see your own writing as political?

Momaday: Political? No, I don't think of it as political at all. That's not my disposition somehow. I'm not a political person. A lot of people I know will read my work as a political statement, and it can be read that way I suppose, but so can anything.

Owens: On a different subject, you have a Ph.D. in literature from Stanford, one of your first publications was an edition of the poems of Frederick Goddard Tuckerman, and you've taught at such universities as Berkeley, Stanford, U.C. Santa Barbara, and now Arizona. Still, you are known worldwide primarily as an American Indian writer. How has this education and training in very conventional Anglo-European scholarship affected your approach to American Indian materials? How have you been able to achieve a synthesis?

Momaday: I don't know that I can answer that. I think that the formal training that I had at Stanford under Yvor Winters was extremely important because there was an awful lot that I didn't know about traditional English poetry, and I learned a lot about that when I was a graduate student at Stanford. As to how I might have applied that learning to my work in American Indian tradition, I really don't know.

Owens: A large percentage of those writers identified from very early on as Indian—people like John Milton Oskison, John Joseph Mathews, D'Arcy McNickle and others—have been very highly educated, most having completed graduate as well as undergraduate study. Do you see this high level of formal education and corresponding affiliation with academia affecting what the general public perceives as "Indian" writing?

Momaday: I really haven't thought about that. I have a difficult time understanding what "American Indian" writing is. I know that I've read things on American Indian culture and American Indian experience by both Indians and non-Indians, and I'm not able to make for myself any important distinctions.

Owens: You were one of the few early positive reviewers of Hyemeyohsts Storm's *Seven Arrows,* as I recall, a novel that was controversial because of questions concerning Storm's identity as a Northern Cheyenne and his use of traditional Indian material. This whole question of identity becomes a rather troublesome one. Do you have difficulty with someone such as Gary Snyder assuming an Indianlike role, what has been called "white-shamanism," in his poetry?

Momaday: I don't see anything intrinsically problematic about that, though I think that someone who writes about an experience who does not himself have that experience runs a certain risk. That's just, I think, completely up to the writer. I've read non-Indians who have written about Indian matters and done it very well, and of course that works the other way around too. I've also read some things that were very bad because the writer was simply writing outside his experience.

Owens: During your recent reading at the University of New Mexico, you were asked by someone in the audience whether D'Arcy McNickle had been an influence on your writing, and you replied that he had not because you had not read very much of McNickle's work. Have any American Indian writers been influential in your own work?

Momaday: I can't think of any who were a particular influence. I don't know many Indian writers who wrote early enough to be an influence on me. I keep up now with Jim Welch and some writers of my own generation and younger writers, but I think that when my literary intelligence was being formed, I wasn't reading Indian writers. I just didn't know about them.

Owens: You weren't aware of such writers as John Joseph Mathews, Oskison, Mourning Dove, or McNickle?
Momaday: No.

Owens: Am I simply imagining the echoes of Hemingway and Faulkner in *House Made of Dawn,* or were you aware of such influences when you wrote the novel?
Momaday: I don't know of any such influences. I certainly read

Faulkner when I was an undergraduate and before I started writing
seriously. Hemingway is less likely, I think. I knew one or two things
by Hemingway well, especially *The Old Man and the Sea* and *A
Farewell to Arms,* but that's about it. I don't particularly care for
Hemingway. I admire Faulkner now and then. He exasperates me but
there are things about Faulkner that I admire very much.

Owens: Given your own fascination with totemic bears, how do you
feel about Faulkner's *The Bear?*

Momaday: I think that's very good. I read that very early on and I
admire it.

Owens: What about D. H. Lawrence?

Momaday: Lawrence was a man I liked as an undergraduate and
read widely, and I still admire Lawrence very much. He is more likely
to have been a kind of influence on me than either Faulkner or
Hemingway. And, of course, I admire the work of Isak Dinesen
very much.

Owens: When you were studying at the University of New Mexico
and later at Stanford, it was nearly impossible to specialize in American Indian literature as a legitimate area of study. Given the opportunity, do you think you might have preferred to have completed a
Ph.D. with, say, an emphasis upon the American Indian oral tradition?

Momaday: Oh, if such a thing had been possible I might have. But
it wasn't possible, so I didn't even think about that. I did draw upon
my experience of the Indian world when I was doing graduate writing
at Stanford, and I was encouraged to do that. But, you know, I took
the Ph.D. in American literature and got interested, of course, in the
oral tradition very soon after I left Stanford. I've been able to develop
that interest, but as a teacher rather than student. As you know, at
the University of Arizona I teach a course in the American Indian
oral tradition every year.

Owens: I seem to recall that you taught a course in Dickinson while
at Santa Barbara? Is that so?

Momaday: I don't remember, but it could be. In fact, it probably is
so. I had a Guggenheim Fellowship while I was teaching at Santa
Barbara, and I spent that year reading Emily Dickinson in manuscript.

Owens: Your essay "The Man Made of Words" contains your splendid definition of what an American Indian is. You say that "an Indian is an idea which a given man has of himself. And it is a moral idea. . . ." And you also say that "We are what we imagine. Our very existence consists in our imagination of ourselves." Would it be valid from your point of view to suggest that *The Way to Rainy Mountain* is your own act of imagination, a personal quest for identity?

Momaday: Yes. I would not argue with that. I think that's certainly true.

Owens: And I suppose *The Names* would be a continuation of this quest.

Momaday: That's right.

Owens: In *The Names* you write of yourself as a child curious about what it means to be Indian. How does this question of identity affect Indian writing as you see it, given the fact that so much of what we identify today as Indian writing is written by mixed-bloods, people of both Indian and European ancestry? Does that complicate the question?

Momaday: It seems logical to me that the mixed-bloods are most naturally curious about their cultural identity. My father being Kiowa and my mother being mostly European, I guess I had a sense of living in those two areas when I was a child, and it became important to me to understand as clearly as I could who I was and what my cultural resources were. And I daresay that's probably true of other people who are of mixed-blood. It seems to me that's where you would be most likely to find this business of identity being worked out in writing.

Owens: Would it be correct to say, then, that most contemporary Indian fiction represents a kind of identity quest? I'm thinking of writers like Janet Campbell Hale, Louise Erdrich, Leslie Silko, and so forth.

Momaday: I think so.

Owens: And then I think of someone like Jim Welch, who is a full blood and writes a novel such as *The Death of Jim Loney* about a young mixed-blood caught between Indian and white worlds.

Momaday: Well, Jim is also Gros Ventre, and maybe it can be a

tribal division as well as a cultural one. I've never talked to him
about that.

Owens: Given the fact that most of what is published as American
Indian literature is written by people of mixed Indian-European ancestry and culture, is this giving the reading public a slanted view of what
it means to be Indian today?

Momaday: I would reiterate that it's probably the people who have
some possibility of identifying themselves in more than one way who
are most interested in the question. And maybe they're in the best
position to write about Indian culture, those who have an investment
elsewhere as well and can bring a certain objectivity to bear.

Owens: Let me ask you a question about *House Made of Dawn,*
something that's intrigued me for some time. You once said that
Tosamah is your favorite character in that novel.

Momaday: Far and away. I think he's the most intricate. He's much
more interesting because he's more complicated and has many more
possibilities. He has a strange and lively mind, and I find him, and did
at the time I was writing the book, fascinating.

Owens: My students have almost always been fascinated with
Tosamah. In addition, however, he also strikes me as the most
displaced character in the novel.

Momaday: I think so. He's a kind of riddle, and he's extremely
skeptical, but has the kind of intelligence that makes the most of it.
But I think of him as being in some ways pathetic, too. He's very displaced.

Owens: He's a poignant figure.
Momaday: I think so.

Owens: I've read that one of your Kiowa names can be translated
as Red Bluff, is that true?
Momaday: Yes, that's true.

Owens: Does the name John Big Bluff Tosamah play on your own
identity, and is Tosamah a kind of self-portrait?
Momaday: Well, no, it's not a play upon the name. He is called Big
Bluff, but that's not the meaning of his name. I invented the name
Tosamah. There are names very much like it in Kiowa, and in Jemez

for that matter. There is a Tosa family in Jemez and a Tonomah family in Kiowa, so I think the name just came about.

Owens: But Tosamah does appropriate some of your own language.
Momaday: Oh yes, I used him. I took great advantage of him.

Owens: It seems as if he takes great advantage of you in some ways as well.
Momaday: (laughs) He acts as my mouthpiece here and there.

Owens: He's a wonderful trickster figure. I'd like to ask about your own peregrinations. Have your repeated movements from New Mexico to Stanford and Santa Barbara, Berkeley, Arizona, Europe, and so on affected what you have described as a "tenure in the land," a sense of intimacy with place?
Momaday: I don't know the answer to that. I still think of myself as having deep roots in the Southwest, and belonging in that landscape. But I have not been really rooted to that landscape in my adult life. I come and go. I get into it now and then but I've traveled widely. I sometimes wonder. In one sense I have driven a kind of wedge between myself and the ancestral land, but in another I've fulfilled the nomadic instincts of that culture, and I'm not sure what it all means.

Owens: Let me ask another question about identity. So much contemporary Indian fiction—that is, fiction written by people who identify as Indian—is very syncretic. Leslie Silko, for example, writes *Ceremony* using her knowledge of the Laguna Pueblo and of Pueblo and Navajo mythology, weaving a kind of tapestry. You yourself, who identifies as Kiowa, write a novel set in Jemez Pueblo, and again you weave different cultures together. Could all of this be achieving a kind of synthesis in the American imagination of what an Indian is, so that it obscures the diversity of American Indian cultures?
Momaday: Well, it may be. I think the effect of such writing is a working towards a synthesis of some kind. Maybe all writing is a working toward a similar synthesis. I'm not concerned to define or delineate American Indian experience, except to myself and for my own purposes. But I am very concerned to understand as much as I can about myth-making. The novel that I'm working on now is really a construction of different myths. I've taken a Kiowa myth to begin with and am bringing it up to modern times. I don't know how much

I've told you about this, but my main character, Set, is the reincarnation of a boy who figures in Kiowa mythology, a boy who turns into a bear. And I'm also working with Billy the Kid in the same novel. And there will be other elements like that, other mythic elements that will inform the story in one way or another. I regard what I'm doing as an inquiry into the nature of myth making.

Owens: The portions of the new novel that I've read or heard you read are very powerful. Is the Kiowa boy you mention the same boy who figures so prominently in the Kiowa story about Devil's Tower?

Momaday: That's the basic myth, the one that I start with. That myth is very important to me personally, and I have thought about that story a lot and now it seems that it's time for me to expand upon it, to follow through on some of the possibilities that I've seen in it.

Owens: This myth-making impulse, which seems to be at the center of *The Way to Rainy Mountain* as well, seems to be an impulse that leads us in the direction of an imagining of identity, a realization of who we are.

Momaday: I would say so.

Owens: What you've just been describing sounds like a synthesis of the quest for a personal identity that I see in *The Way to Rainy Mountain* and *The Names* and a larger concern for the myth-making impulse in general.

Momaday: That's something that I'm working on and it's important to me. I think you're right about that, and that's really what I'm concerned to do.

Owens: How do you explain the hiatus between the two novels? You won a Pulitzer Prize for *House Made of Dawn* in 1969, and you must have had tremendous pressure from your publishers, agents, whomever to come out with another novel quickly, yet here it is almost two decades later.

Momaday: (laughs) A lot of people have suggested to me that I should come out with another novel, but I don't think of myself as a novelist particularly. I happen to have written a novel, but I'm more concerned to write well in other forms as well as the novel. I've been fairly productive over the years—besides the one novel, I've also written a number of poems and prose pieces that are nonfiction.

Owens: You've certainly been productive, but what prompted you to move away from the novel and now back to it almost twenty years later?

Momaday: I think I wanted to see what writing in other forms was like, so I took my turn at autobiography and poetry and what have you, even travel literature, which I really like. I find myself very interested in writing about travel. I'm doing a piece on Bavaria now for the *New York Times*. But I think that the only way I can pursue this myth-making business is in the novel form now. It's possible to get at it in poems and to write about it in terms of scholarship perhaps, but the heart of it is a matter for fiction.

Owens: Could you say something about the novel form—what insights have you gained since your first novel?

Momaday: I don't know that I've ever really come to define the form of the novel to my own satisfaction. I think of a novel as a story first of all and therefore a narrative, and I believe that it should have a perceptible shape to it—a beginning and so on—but beyond that, I think there's a lot of room for experimentation in the novel form. Obviously a lot of other people do as well.

The novel I'm working on is experimental in certain ways because it deals with ancient matter, which has its own form; and it's an expansion of that form, a kind of reworking of it, and I hope to come up with perhaps new ideas of reflection or amplification or expansion. I think it's an unorthodox kind of novel.

Owens: Since you refer to it as experimental, are you very conscious of the experimental fiction of the last couple of decades by people like Robbe-Grillet?

Momaday: Really not at all. Every time I hear contemporary critics talking about fiction I'm completely confused. They're using terms that they weren't using in my day, and I just haven't kept up.

Owens: So your experimentation is not an impulse that rises in part from awareness of people like Donald Barthelme, Robert Coover, and that sort of new-fiction crowd?

Momaday: No, I'm well outside that camp. I was at the Salzburg Seminar in American Studies last summer, and I met such people. Deconstruction was very much in the air, and I must say that I wasn't understanding what was said. I'm not a critic.

Owens: There's a great sense of play in the portions of your new novel that I've seen. Will that element be consistent throughout the entire work?

Momaday: I think it's going to, though I won't know that until I get around to the final revisions. It certainly informs what I have down so far. It's going to have a kind of playfulness to it that I haven't really tried before.

Owens: It's something that seems characteristic of recent publications by Indian writers. There's a rich vein of black humor in Jim Welch's writing, and there's a great deal of playfulness in Louise Erdrich's *Love Medicine.* Of course, it was even more true of Gerald Vizenor's *Darkness in Saint Louis Bearheart* in 1978. Do you have any sense of writing by American Indians having matured since your seminal work in *House Made of Dawn,* with a new sense of confidence perhaps?

Momaday: I think so. I think that that's what ought to happen and what probably is happening. With every new step, with everything written by an American Indian now, I think there is a growing confidence. It will be a very important literature, probably is already, but it's certainly going to become more and more confident and secure.

Owens: Could you compare what has happened in American Indian writing during the last two decades with the Harlem Renaissance in black writing?

Momaday: I think of *Bury My Heart at Wounded Knee* as a kind of breakthrough. It seems to me that with the publication of that book there was a sudden disposition to understand the experience of the American Indian. The kind of burgeoning that we're talking about really happened in the publishing world rather than in any sort of social or political arena. It was really a willingness to look back at history and to say, "No, this isn't necessarily how it was." It seems to me that's what Dee Brown accomplished.

Owens: You've mentioned Jim Welch. Are there any other contemporary writers in particular whose work interests you?

Momaday: There are writers who interest me. But I don't find myself keeping up with any particular writer completely. I don't read contemporary fiction in great depth; I'm too busy with other things.

Owens: I recently came across a reference by Yvor Winters to you as a "post-symbolist," and elsewhere I've seen you described as a "lyrical imagist." You may not want to do this, but how would you describe your own poetry if you had to attach a phrase to it?

Momaday: I don't know that I'd want to do that. Post-symbolist is a term I heard a great deal as a graduate student, and I fail even now to understand it. I see my poetry as being also cross-cultural in a sense. When I was exercising my earliest knowledge of traditional English forms, I was doing a lot of very closely controlled writing, and I came to understand the value of such control. But at the same time I was concerned to develop my voice as a projection of the oral tradition. So I keep the two things going, and I think probably that it's good for me to work across those boundaries.

Owens: As a final question, do you have any overriding sense of what Native American fiction is today as opposed to 1969, when you won your Pulitzer for *House Made of Dawn?*

Momaday: Well, I think that it's very secure, that writing by Native Americans has certainly caught the attention of the world at large. There can be no doubt that now a good many people across the globe understand that there is an experience that is important in itself. I feel very good about so-called Native American literature.

The Ancient Child:
A Conversation with
N. Scott Momaday

Gaetano Prampolini / 1990

From *Native American Literatures, A Forum,* 2, no. 3 (1990/91), 77–99. Reprinted by permission of Gaetano Prampolini.

The conversation took place in Tucson, at the Momadays', on a clear and warm afternoon in November 1990. It started in the tile-paved yard, around an iron garden table painted white, to the accompaniment of a light, cooling breeze—a reminder of the open spaces reaching with no interposition all the way to Canada and an announcer of winter. It continued in the "Arizona room" of the house, while basketfuls of Guerrero ceremonial masks and bulwarks of recently arrived books on the tables, paintings on the walls by the Momadays, *père et fils,* and by other artist friends gradually sank into the gathering shadows of the night. It ended, or rather petered out, when the two interlocutors acknowledged, with a hearty guffaw, that they were both tired of the game, had enough of playing the roles of interviewed and interviewer.

A coda in three questions added itself to the original conversation on 4 June 1991, in the course of a collective interview session at the University of Pisa, during which Dr. Momaday was as elegant and insightful, patient and witty, as ever in answering the questions of a roomful of students and teachers.

All references to *The Ancient Child* in the following pages are to the first, hardcover edition of the novel: Doubleday, New York, 1989.

GP: I would like mostly to talk about your most recent novel, *The Ancient Child.* But before coming to, hopefully, more important questions, I have a few queries about some rather minor details of the novel which have raised my curiosity while reading. For instance, there is a Western song quoted twice in Chapter One: what is it?

NSM: "Cotton Eye Joe" is the name of it. I've never understood why it's called that, but it's an old American folk-song, and there are several versions of it. When I was in the seventh grade, it was very popular on the radio in Santa Fe—I lived in Santa Fe at the time, and I went to school at the Lee Harvey School there—and it was on the radio every morning, and I liked the tune. Then I came across this, which appears to be an older version, and so I believed that Billy the Kid might have known it.

GP: Several Navajo words appear in the novel. Like, presumably, many other readers, I don't understand them . . . There is one in particular, on p. 164, whose meaning I'd like to know.
NSM: "Nizhóni yei!"? It means "beautiful, very beautiful."

GP: And who were "the Regulators" (p. 170) that figure in Grey's fantasizing?
NSM: Men were hired to protect other men. For instance, John Chisholm, who was a great cattle owner, hired men to look out for his cattle, to protect his ranch and his possessions. These are called "Regulators." I'm not sure I understand why exactly, but that's the common term.

GP: And, of course, Annie Oakley is . . .
NSM: . . . the famous gunshot artist of the Wild West. She was a member of the "Wild West Show," she shot pennies out of people's fingers, and so on.

GP: From one of your conversations with Charles Woodard I understand that your current work is a book of poems, the title of which seems to be *Earth, Pray My Days,* and, also, let's say, a multi-media work, *A Round of Shields.* Is that so?
NSM: Yes, exactly. As to the book of poems, the problem with that is that I don't know when it's finished. It could be finished now but I keep adding to it, and so I don't know where to stop exactly. But this is to be a collection not only of new things but of selected poems from my earlier work, and right now I have a manuscript which contains maybe eighty poems, and I want to publish that, well, within a reasonable length of time, but I'm in no great hurry. *The Book of Shields* is composed of sixteen prose poems, each one the story of a Plains Indian shield, and I'm illustrating each of the shields. I have a drawing to accompany each of the stories. I'm finished with the text but I'm not finished with the drawings.

GP: Does it take more to write the text or to draw the shields?

NSM: Probably longer to do the text, you know; but that's something that I've just been putting together for the last two or three years. So I have . . .

GP: . . . something along the lines of those six shields that you interpolated to the "Tsoai and the Shield-Maker" piece in *Four Winds,* something like that, or would the prose poems be longer, more developed?

NSM: No, they would all be of the length of the things in *The Way to Rainy Mountain,* all one page or half a page.

GP: Can you tell me something about when and how you got the first flicker, so to speak, in your mind about the story that was to become *The Ancient Child*?

NSM: I don't know where I first got the idea. You know, it comes from that Kiowa story of the boy-bear which I've known all my life. So, somewhere along the way the seed of this book was planted, but I can't put my finger on it exactly. I suppose about four or five years ago I started thinking of taking that myth and expanding it in some way. So it just came together over a period of time.

GP: Did you feel at a certain point that this new work, this thing that was maturing in your mind, was going to supplement the previous work that you had written, that in some way it was going to enrich it, to complete it?

NSM: Yes. I seem to go from one thing to another and keep them related in some way. And, yes, at a certain point I knew that this was going to amplify *House Made of Dawn, The Way to Rainy Mountain* and some of my other things, *The Names* . . .

GP: Among the books that Grey reads and enjoys when she is very young is Oliver LaFarge's *Laughing Boy,* a book that I know you like a lot. As I read your novel, at some point the relationship between Grey and Set somehow reminded me of the relationship between the female and the male protagonists of *Laughing Boy* itself. To be more precise, in both novels the woman is the leading element of the couple.

NSM: I think I see what you mean but I can't tell you . . .

GP: I'm not suggesting that in your novel you have been influenced by LaFarge. I'm thinking rather of a similarity. How would you react to somebody pointing out such a similarity between the two novels?

NSM: Well, I would say that surely there is and must be because after all we are talking about a Navajo woman, a woman who is at least half Navajo, in my case, and it is a love story at a certain level, and, like Slim Girl in *Laughing Boy,* Grey is very intelligent, very perceptive, very beautiful, she knows how to bring about things as she wants them, and she is dedicated like Slim Girl to one man and she protects him and sees him to his destiny. So, there are natural similarities.

GP: Yes. And there are similar similarities, if I can say so, between *The Ancient Child* and some segments of Leslie Marmon Silko's *Ceremony* where the male protagonist, like Set, is in a mess and is guided for a while to his own safety by a woman who's endowed with power. I know that you have already talked about the substantial importance of women in Indian cultures. And so, maybe, these are instances of this very thing.

NSM: I think that a lot of people writing out of Native American tradition understand the power of women and it makes a good subject for a story: Leslie Marmon Silko, Linda Hogan in *Mean Spirit,* her new and first novel, Louise Erdrich . . . we all deal to some extent with medicine people and sometimes they are women, because women are powerful.

GP: In your conversation with Woodard the novel is always referred to as *Set,* the title seems to be *Set.* What made you change that title into the present one?

NSM: *Set* was the working title. I was thinking all the time I was writing that *Set* would be the title of the novel. But when I got toward the end of it, I thought it needed another title. I wasn't sure what "Set" would mean to someone just happening upon it for the first time, and so I fell upon this phrase "the ancient child" somewhere in the novel. I had used that, and I thought "Eh! that's a good title," and so I just changed it, there in midstream.

GP: "Set," however, means something in Kiowa.
NSM: Yes, Set is the Kiowa word for "bear."

GP: I'd like to talk a little about the shape of the book. One thing that strikes the reader is, once again, the presence of several typefaces, of different kinds of prints. There are four of them: one for the

Prologue and the epigraphs; one for what we may call "quotations,"
like "Cotton Eye Joe," or Grey's scrapbook on Billy the Kid; one for
the narrative proper and one for the telling of the myth of the boy
who turns into a bear. Is this last component of the text to be
understood as a kind of parallel tale that the storyteller interpolates
to his telling of Set's story?

NSM: Yes. Especially the part that deals with Koi-ehm-toya and the
story of the boy who turns into a bear in italics as it runs through the
text. It's a story within a story, and yet it comprehends the novel as
a whole. That was quite intentional. I wanted it to appear in its own
type and to run as a thread in the narrative. The others, though, I
wasn't aware that they were there. You see, you pointed out these
things to me for the first time. I didn't know there were, what did you
say, four different types?

GP: Yes.

NSM: I didn't know that. I'm sure that's true, now that you have
mentioned it.

GP: There's a larger one for the poems about Billy the Kid.

NSM: Well, I must say that I can't claim credit for that, that's the
publisher's doing, the other types, the distinct type-faces . . . I just
had the two in mind.

GP: Is that a part of your Faulknerian heritage?

NSM: Faulknerian heritage? What?

GP: The use of several type-faces for your narratives?

NSM: Well, not that I know of. You know, *The Way to Rainy
Mountain* is set in three voices, each with its own type-face.

GP: Yes, actually I had *House Made of Dawn* in mind, more than
The Way to Rainy Mountain . . .

NSM: No, I wasn't thinking of Faulkner when I made those distinctions.

GP: Another question on the shape of the book. The general
epigraph to the novel, the one quoted from Borges, reads, "For myth
is at the beginning of literature and also at its end." The first part of
it seems very clear, the second may be puzzling to some readers—as
it has been to me. Is the reader expected to discover the meaning of

the sentence (''myth is at the end of literature as well'') only at the
end of *The Ancient Child*?

NSM: The way I take that quotation from Borges is that one cannot
finally escape myth. It is encompassing, all encompassing. It is at the
beginning of literature; literature begins somewhere back in mythology and finally it is there at the end as well. You cannot get away from
it . . . that's how I interpret that quotation and that's what I meant
to convey.

GP: Thinking of the end of your novel, I took the Borges sentence
in a very definite sense. The action at the end of it is a reenactment of
the myth, if I read the last chapter correctly. And it seemed to me as
if you had embedded, so to speak, the meaning of the Borges quotation (that myth is at the end of literature and could not be otherwise)
in the very texture of the novel.

NSM: Yes. The novel begins with a myth, and in that sense fulfills
Borges's equation, and at the end it descends again into myth, it is
moving in the direction of myth. What I think is that this is true of all
literature: you can take the *Odyssey* and say the same thing, you
know, or the *Iliad*. Myth is at the beginning and ending of all story, of
all literature.

GP: The overall structure of the novel consists in a Prologue and an
Epilogue and in four books in between, and the second two books are
much shorter than the first two. Each book has a title: ''Planes,''
''Lines,'' ''Shapes,'' ''Shadows.'' All of these words but one appear
in Cole Blessing's instructions to Set about the art of painting, as the
latter remembers them (pp. 55 ff.). Is that correct?

NSM: Yes.

GP: Is it significant? How?

NSM: Yes, I think it is significant. The story in some way is a
reflection of Set's mind. Set is a painter and so he is more concerned
with these realities of shapes, shadows, lines than other people are in
general, and I wanted to indicate that in some way.

GP: And why is the word 'shape' the only one of the four missing
from that passage, the one in which Set recalls Cole Blessing's
briefing?

NSM: No particular reason, I wasn't omitting it to any purpose.

"Shape" seems such an obvious kind of dimension of painting, anyway.

GP: Can you say something about how it is that—I'm quoting from the same passage—describing a shadow can be "worthy of the substance" (p. 55)?

NSM: I'm trying to remember exactly the quote . . . Yes, "You can—maybe—describe a shadow that is worthy of the substance" . . . Yes. In painting as in writing, as a matter of fact, the substance is sometimes less important than the shadow or the reflection. You have reality, but reality finally is not very interesting or, to put it in another and better way, it is less interesting generally than appearance. Appearance and reality . . . you have a core of reality and then a circumference of appearance, and that's what the writer works with, as well as the painter. So, the shadows are very frequently more interesting, and more engaging, and more meaningful than is the substance.

GP: When I read that sentence, a prose poem of yours in *The Colors of Night* came to my mind; "Green," the one about the girl emerging from the tipi and seeing the tree and the tree is there and is not there. Is that relevant to what you are saying?

NSM: Yes, exactly. That's an example of what I'm trying to say. Substance and reality. You know, the appearance is finally what matters.

GP: Moving on, I would like to talk a little about the characters of the novel, starting with Grey. Early in the novel I read this sentence: "She had looked hard at these dolls [one is a Kiowa doll and the other is a Navajo doll], trying to see to their centers" (pp. 16–17). It's the point where the "center" motif, if I can call it so, begins. Would it be correct to say that there is a "center" motif through the novel?

NSM: Yes.

GP: In *House Made of Dawn* it was prominent, it seems to me, because the narrative kept taking stock of Abel's position in relation to a center—that is, his own center. You have something of the same kind here as relates to Set. It's again a story about trying to recover a kind of balance, a center.

NSM: Exactly. It's about restoration, and the restoration is, as you suggest, coming back to the center and to a balance.

GP: In *The Ancient Child,* one of the most cherished myths of your youth—that is, Billy the Kid—becomes the object of Grey's fantasies. She even writes a scrapbook in 21 pieces about her hero. But it seems to me that, as the novel progresses, Grey outgrows her passion for Billy the Kid.

NSM: Exactly, and it signifies her own maturity. She's growing up, she's committed to this obligation to be a medicine woman, and Billy the Kid stands in her way, actually. She has invested so much of her imagination in him and he has served a real purpose in the life of her mind; but there comes a time when he has fulfilled that purpose and he is no longer necessary in that sense. So, a real mark of her growth, I think, in the novel is in that final giving him away.

GP: It seems to me that it's very important when she contrasts two kinds of bravery, Billy the Kid's and Set-angya's. Is that too a part of her maturation, of her growing up?

NSM: Yes. Billy helps her in certain ways too. In this case, when she imagines that Set-angya and Billy the Kid meet, she talks to Billy about Set-angya's bravery, and she confuses them at that point, and she says, "Well, you know if you had been there at the time you would have been a member of the Kaitsenko society too," and he says, "No, that's not right, I'm not brave in that sense." And she says, ". . . remember the time you killed Sheriff Brady, and Brady dropped the rifle that he had taken from you in February and you ran out into the streets, in that hail of bullets, and you picked up the rifle and you were wounded: that was brave." And he says: "Brave? I wasn't brave, I was stupid!" So he does set her right on that, and she learns a little of what bravery is. That's a part of her growing up.

GP: By the way, who was it in history who helped Billy escape from Lincoln County jail?

NSM: We don't know.

GP: But we do know now!

NSM: (laughs) Yes! Of course, it was Grey all along! Well, it is believed and with good reason that someone planted the gun for him, but we don't know who it was.

GP: While composing her scrapbook about Billy the Kid, Grey laments the difficulty of using words in writing. But then the results of her efforts in literary composition are so beautiful, the artifacts of a masterful hand. How is it possible?

NSM: Well, I think it must be that she simply has the ability, she's in love with words and she has had the kind of experience, beginning with the accessibility of books when she was little. She is capable, and she finds that out but in the process she also finds how difficult it is to write, and she comments upon it. It's hard to do but she can do it and she does it well.

GP: As to Grey's readings, at a certain point I read: "She had assumed them [that is, literary texts and oral tradition], appropriated them to her being" (p. 185). The pleasure Grey finds with the written word and with writing is equal to Set's pleasure with planes and lines and shapes and shadows. Is this a reflection of the dual form in which you express and realize yourself—namely, literature and painting?

NSM: Yes. I could identify with her interest in words and with Set's vocation as a painter. Those to me were very personal things, and, of course, I was thinking of my own experience in both these endeavours when I wrote about Set and about Grey.

GP: I was struck by the continuity that *The Ancient Child* has with your previous work. It seems to me that, although no doubt it is a novel, it is also a further autobiographical act, after *The Way to Rainy Mountain* and *The Names*. You seem to invest yourself in the characters in a way similar to the way in which you invested yourself in Tosamah in *House Made of Dawn*. The only difference is that here you invest yourself in *two* characters instead of only one. Does this make sense to you?

NSM: Yes. I think I see what you mean. I identify strongly with Set . . . and you're thinking of Grey as the other?

GP: Yes.

NSM: Well, yes, to the extent that she writes and I write, that she is deeply invested in her Kiowa heritage as am I. But I don't identify with her in the same way. She's much better than I am.

GP: Grey has the inborn memory of the history of her own people, the Kiowas, but she is a Navajo, too. Did you deliberately plan to mix a nomadic culture and a relatively sedentary one in her ancestry?

NSM: Yes, and simply for the reason that I know a good deal about both those cultures, and they are very different one from another and yet there are great profundities in both of them, and I wanted her to reflect that. When I thought of Grey as a medicine woman, of course I wanted her to be this wild young woman who rides naked on a horse—that's one dimension of her being—but when I started thinking about the depths of her imagination and power as a medicine woman, the Navajo came quite naturally to mind because the Navajo is an extremely dignified people and, I think, a powerful people, and I wanted to show that side of Grey.

GP: Perfecto Atole, which is a crucial figure in Set's healing, is a bear's paw keeper and also has tortoiseshell shakers made from snakeskin boots. Are you trying here, in this combination, to suggest the two great cultural areas—the bear- and snake-power cultural areas?

NSM: I suppose I had something of that kind in mind but it wasn't terribly important. The tortoiseshells are used traditionally as shakers for dancing, and they are frequently made with the tops of cowboy boots. And so I simply wanted to taunt, to have Grey taunt Perfecto with the fact that she cut off the tops of these wonderful boots that he had given her once upon a time. Not much symbolism into that.

GP: Only toward the end of the novel we discover that Grey's Indian name is Koi-ehm-toya, and Koi-ehm-toya is, of course, the old lady who watches the children go away in the distance, to meet their destiny in the woods. Can you say something about this?

NSM: Of course I wanted to suggest a kind of relationship between Grey and this old woman who inhabits the myth. Koi-ehm-toya, by the way, means "Among the Kiowas": it's one of my daughters' name, by the way, and I love it . . . so I was playing with things there too, and, well, that's all I can say about it *(laughs)*. Actually, I could say much more but probably it wouldn't be true!

GP: Well, it could make a good story!
NSM: Yes, and that's what really matters! *(laughs)*

GP: The relationship between Grey and her dying grandmother is similar in more than one point to the relationship between Abel and his dying grandfather Francisco toward the end of *House Made of Dawn*. Would you agree with that?

NSM: Yes.

GP: Is that the moment of transmission of some values from one generation to another?

NSM: Yes, certainly.

GP: And, also, the intermediate generation is in both cases, in the case of Abel and in the case of Grey, almost completely missing: Grey's father is dead and Abel is an orphan, so that they've got to rely on an older generation. Is that something significant?

NSM: Yes, I think this is a reality of the Indian world, and maybe of all worlds. But certainly, as to Abel in *House Made of Dawn*, his only real link to the traditional past is through his grandfather; and in *The Ancient Child*, Grey is the student of the grandmother; and all of her learning about medicine and power comes from the old woman and, of course, it is significant that it comes even after the old woman dies, that Grey can still communicate with her grandmother.

GP: Let's move on to Set. At the beginning of the novel, he remembers a dream that he had when he was very young, of a "frail young woman, . . . her eyes holding on to something beyond his dream" (p. 42). It seems to me that the whole dream is a kind of premonition of things to come for him. Was it meant to be so? That frail young woman already has something of Grey.

NSM: Yes, this is a kind of prefiguration. That's right, in some sense. I'm not sure you are thinking about it in the same way that I am, but, yes, for me this is a kind of prophetic dream.

GP: In the same passage I was struck by the presence of the word "the altar"—an altar which is called the centerpiece of the story—and in the same passage such words as "rite of passage" are also present. By the time we are at the end of the novel, one important altar has figured in the story of Set. So, that's why I was talking of premonition.

NSM: I think that's a good observation; there is the premonition.

GP: Well, before leaving Grey and starting on his journey toward myth, toward his inevitable destiny, Set has a longing for something beyond memory. Is this something to be related to his (for the moment unrecognized) Indian ancestry? Rather early in the novel one reads: "in Loki there was a certain empty space and longing for something beyond memory" (p. 45). Probably. Here too there is predestination, probably.

NSM: Yes, I've been rather literal there, I think. I'm suggesting that the boy, Loki, hungers for something beyond his actual memory; there is something beyond that, and after all this is the whole point of his quest: to find out what is beyond his knowledge in his own being. And of course Grey helps him to find out, to discover that. But that's what I was getting at there, that he had more than a suspicion, a kind of realization, a recognition that there was more to him than he could remember of his own experience. He has to go back before his time, into the heritage, into the blood memory, into his ancestry. That's where the information he needs exists, and only by going back to that kind of primeval experience can he find his true identity.

GP: Set says that he wants to paint to astonish God, to save God from boredom. How much do your poetics coincide with Set's?

NSM: Considerably. I consider boredom the greatest sin of all. We must take every step possible to keep from being bored . . .

GP: . . . and boring?

NSM: (laughs) Yes, bored *and* boring!

GP: Set at forty-four, when the story starts, is a frustrated artist: he wanted to paint a tree but was obliged to paint a house, he wanted to paint small but was obliged to paint large etc. How much of it has been your experience as an artist?

NSM: Quite a bit of that. I have had that experience . . . It is quite true that people get into ruts, as we say.

GP: Do you mean the market rules, the market channels, the market constrictions?

NSM: You are determined by the market. One of the great risks that all creative people run is to be original because people like to talk a lot of originality. They say, well, you must do this or you must do that; to the extent that a writer or a painter listens to this advice, his creativity is damaged.

GP: As a matter of fact, in one of your conversations with Charles Woodard, at a certain point you say: "It's harder and harder to find a sentence that hasn't already been articulated.'' Now, it seems to me that in *The Ancient Child* the narrator avoids the difficulty which you pointed out to Woodard—the difficulty of finding a sentence that hasn't already been articulated—by assuming for long passages, a kind of, how shall I say?, ''nonchalant'' tone, a light pose, especially in transitional passages, passages that are not related to Set's healing or his transformation into a bear. For instance, there is this kind of light touch when you talk about Grey as a young woman, or when you talk of Set, not when he's engaged in his painful and terrible search, but when he's still an inhabitant of the city. I think there is really a light, a nonchalant tone there, which I didn't find in your previous works.

NSM: Well, I don't know what to say about that. It is true, though, that in *The Ancient Child* there are these light touches, when Grey is playing with her own appearance, or teaching Dog, the horse, how to run so that she can pick up the match. And there are light touches, of course, when Set's got that affair with that woman in Paris, Alais Sancerre . . . It is playful. . . .

GP: Woodard insists that the humor in your work has been under-valued. He finds, for instance, a lot of humor in the captions under the photographs in *The Names* and in some of the poems of the Billy the Kid sequence, and you seem to agree with that. And you also say that humor is an expanding dimension in your work. This seems true in *The Ancient Child,* but I don't think that it is present only in the delineation of characters. For instance, I found humor, or irony, when Lola Bourne does not recognize herself in the sketch that Set has made of her, and she says that the sketch is the perfect likeness of Vivienne, a medieval French girl who was said to understand the language of animals . . . This is an oblique reference to somebody else in the novel, I think . . .

NSM: Yes, I think Set says somewhere, referring to himself and Lola, that the two of them were engaged in a lot of wordplay. And this is an example of that . . . she's playing with him at words when she says this is Vivienne, etc. So there is that kind of humor. And I think that Milo Mottledmare is a very funny man too, and Worcester Meat. There is a lot of humor in the delineation of those characters, too. I have fun with them, and they have fun with each other and me, you know.

GP: What I had in mind was that Lola's attitude toward the sketch Set has drawn of her is quite different from Grey's toward her own. Grey's sketch means a lot to Grey. It's a very important object in her winning Set over to her.

NSM: Oh yes, the sketch of the grandmother, for example, is a very serious thing, you know, because it teaches him how to paint her face—all of that symbolic face.

GP: The first time I read the book, I was struck by something in particular: when Set has the medicine bundle in his hands, his reaction is to be afraid of it, and I asked myself: "Why is he not curious about it, or why could he not be indifferent?"

NSM: Because when he touches it, he feels the power of it, and he understands immediately that it is something beyond his knowledge and control, and so he is frightened by it. It's as if it were hot to the touch, you know, electric—some powerful force is there, and he can feel it.

GP: When Set is about to start the process of metamorphosis, he says: "Bent, be my father," with some urgency, and fear . . . Why? Bent is not his father, after all, he's just the adoptive father, and Set knows that.

NSM: Well, Bent is and is not his father. Bent is the man Set trusts beyond any other man, because he is a father for him and he has been all the things to Set that his real father might have been. There is deep love between the two, and so when he addresses the plea, "Bent, be my father," it is a desperate kind of plea. He speaks in great need because he *needs* a father, and his real father is not available to him except in a very esoteric way.

GP: But at a certain point we read that in the story the position of Catlin Setman is a strategic position.

NSM: What do you mean?

GP: What do *you* mean?

NSM: I don't know . . . ! (*laughs*) Strategic. It's an interesting word, but I'm not sure I know what you mean by that.

GP: "And she spoke, too, over Catlin Setman's grave; it was as a kind of intermediary that she thought of Catlin Setman . . ." (p.174).

Why does she think of Catlin Setman as an intermediary? Just because she has used his name in the telegram that has been sent to Set?

NSM: No . . . no . . . I have to recover more of the context than I have in my mind right now, but Catlin Setman is an intermediary in the way that the grandmother is . . . These two presences stand between Grey and Set, and they also stand as intermediaries between Set and his past, his ancestral past. "Intermediary" in that sense, if I remember how I used the word 'intermediary' there.

GP: When the story begins, Set is in trouble, we are told, on the verge of a nervous breakdown, in a non-harmonic situation, and his problem is one of "saving his soul" (p.38). Has he managed to save his soul at the end of the book?

NSM: Who knows? It's *not* there!

GP: That's the edge, the boundary of mystery that surrounds, that should surround any good story.

NSM: I think so. Many people, you know, have asked me about *House Made of Dawn,* the ending of that book: what happened to Abel, did he die? And I say: "I don't know." It's like asking what's on the next page, and there is no next page.

GP: It's like asking what happened to the boy after he disappeared from the Piegan camp.

NSM: Exactly. I think there are all kinds of possibilities at the end of *The Ancient Child.* The transformation has begun . . . what happens? Does Set emerge as himself from that experience or does he become the bear? What does it mean? I don't know . . . But that's the way I prefer it. I don't want to know.

GP: In the last chapter, in the last scene before the Epilogue which takes us back to the traditional story, Set finally sees, "rearing against Tsoai," "the image of a great bear" (p.312). Is it a reenactment of the old myth? In other words, Set seems to have reached a stage where he can see, understand, perceive the perennial reenactment of the myth. Is that one possible implication of the finale of the story?

NSM: Well, there's much more to it to be seen. Set is participating, he is inextricably bound up with it. He does start to become the bear . . . It is not as if he's observing something, he is *in* it. It is something that is happening to him.

GP: Are you saying that the bear is a kind of double, or that the bear is himself?

NSM: The bear is himself . . .

GP: It's taking over . . .

NSM: It appears that the bear is taking him over, and this has always been the risk. I mean, the bear was taking over also back in San Francisco when Set was slowly losing himself and getting sick. So the whole import of the novel is that Set comes always closer to becoming the bear but he is given, through Grey's intervention, some kind of medicine which enables him to confront the bear, if not on equal terms, on more nearly equal terms. You see? That is the crucial reality of the end of the book. On the last page when his sense of hearing, his sense of smell become acute, and his sense of sight diminishes . . . where is he? What stage is he in? When his sisters look at him and are terrified and when a couple of them take a step toward him and then turn away . . . And the idea is that "he suffers a loneliness like death." There is this isolation. He is retreating some- how from the human world into some other dimension of existence, and the question is: does he complete that crossing or is there some sort of intervention? Does Loki come back to us or not?

GP: According to the traditional story of the Kiowas, some hunters later meet a friendly bear and try to establish some kind of communi- cation with the animal. I remember the hunter, the one with a withered neck, comes back and says that he has met the bear. So, becoming a bear does not completely cut your ties with humanity.

NSM: No, that's right, the boy who turns into a bear is going forever to be related to the human strain.

GP: And there is always a possibility for the boy-bear of coming back.

NSM: Nothing is impossible. It's like the Kiowa twin in *The Way to Rainy Mountain* who becomes the water beast. He's gone but the other brother goes down and talks to him in the water. There is still the relationship somehow, and I think this is probably true of the boy- bear too. Though the myth doesn't say it, you know. This is just supposition; we speculate but we don't ever know it.

GP: You have seen similar situations in Greek myths of metamor- phosis. People change into things, into animals, into plants and still have something that keeps them in touch with their previous state.

NSM: Yes, this is an ancient story, isn't it? And there are many versions of it.

GP: It's interesting how Set's sickness is seen by the psychiatrist who says that his problem is that he is self-centered. But, actually, his problem seems to have rather to do with the fact that he's not enough in the center of himself.

NSM: Yes, who knows . . . Clearly the psychiatrist does not perceive the reality of Set's existence and so he plays upon Set's feelings, and he works completely out of his own bias, his training. He thinks he has the pat answer, and he spouts it out but of course he's not on line and Set understands that.

GP: The most violent scene in the novel is the one on the Navajo reservation when Perfecto Atole has to play his part in the healing of Set. I find it a very violent situation. Does it correspond to a particular rite which you read about, or did you invent the whole situation?

NSM: Both things. I know about the touching of the bear's paw— the striking. That's ritual and ceremonial, but also there is Perfecto's own heart as the centaur. I invented the two, I brought them together on my own. But I'm curious that you found it more violent than the rape scene.

GP: Probably I found it more violent because we've read so many rape scenes in contemporary literature.

NSM: But not many men are circumcised in the process, are they? You don't read that so often.

GP: No. But let me put it this way: Grey, after all, is rather merciful; sometimes men encounter a worse fate.

NSM: (*laughs*) That's true, though that was bad enough, I think. More than enough!

GP: All in all, the way the reader of *The Ancient Child* has to go about the discovery of the meaning of the novel is not dissimilar from the way required of the reader of *House Made of Dawn*. That is, in both novels there are some blocks of narrative, and the reader is expected to construe the meaning by placing the blocks, the different units, together.

NSM: That's absolutely so.

GP: So you expect that these blocks must be linked together, or rather, and more frequently, juxtaposed. In writing so, were you consciously using a modernist technique?

NSM: Yes. I didn't write either of these novels in the conventional way; they are not orthodox novels. I like the way you put it: blocks of time and narrative and the idea that the reader will play around them until he can fit them together in the pattern.

GP: That's what I meant.

NSM: That's good I think, I like it that way. One of the reviewers of *The Ancient Child* said: "Don't come to this with the idea of reading a conventional novel, but if you let it have its way, it will be worth the time." I like that, I take a certain satisfaction in being the novelist who does not write in the conventional way, who makes you work a bit to put it together . . . Why not?

GP: Why not? You are a great admirer of Faulkner's *As I Lay Dying*. And it is by the same method that the reader gets to the meaning of that novel.

NSM: Yes, that's right. I'm also a great admirer of Vladimir Nabokov who did the same sort of thing time and again. He plays tricks on readers, which is not a bad thing to do.

GP: He plays tricks *with* readers, which is more merciful.

NSM: Sometimes with, sometimes upon . . . *(laughs)*.

GP: At a crucial point in the novel Set thinks: "There is only one story . . . *[you] must be true to the story*" (p.216). This appears at the end of a chapter; and the next chapter begins: "She [that is, Grey] must be true to the story," and goes on saying: "there is one story and we tell it endlessly because we must, it is the definition of our being" (p.217). From that point on, has the idea that Set's story *must* be told got anything to do with the traditional Indian belief that whatever happens is just a repetition of something that has happened, not only once but many, many times—since everything that happens is already prefigured in myth, in the original myth?

NSM: I think so.

GP: Do you remember Silko's story "Storyteller"? The one that takes place up in Alaska? What happens in the story is the fulfillment of what the old storyteller has been telling all along. Things must happen in a certain way because it has been told that they should go that way.

NSM: Of course. This is an ancient idea which is not exclusive to Indian oral tradition. But yes, there is a story, we inhabit the story, we live our lives in the course of a story and we must play a part. We must live up to the story, and I believe that, as I believe that all literature is composed of the elements of one story.

GP: It's like believing in destiny.

NSM: Yes, fate . . .

GP: And as you said, this is not exclusive of the Indian tradition. It's a mark of the archaic mind, probably.

NSM: Yes, I think so.

GP: The pre-rationalistic mind. I mean, the pre-scientific mind.

NSM: Yes, though that is not to exclude science from the story, it's also part of it. When you say "pre-scientific," yes of course, but it incorporates science. Science is not alien to it, it comes along and has its space in the story.

GP: It's a component of the story.

NSM: Sure, absolutely.

GP: In her *Landmarks of Healing,* Susan Scarberry-García refers to Richard Ohman, who classified *House Made of Dawn* among "narratives of healing," as opposed to "unfulfilled narratives of illness." Do you feel that *The Ancient Child* falls into the same category with *House Made of Dawn* as affirmative literature, as wisdom literature?

NSM: I think so, and I'm dying to see what Scarberry-García says about *The Ancient Child.* I know that she admires it, she told me, and she has lectured on it but she has not written on it yet. I think she'll find the same healing motif in *The Ancient Child*: it's there. Many people do not see it, but she is very perceptive.

GP: I have the impression that in this later novel you depend on your knowledge of particular myths, rites, particular ceremonies less than you did in *House Made of Dawn.* And so this novel is more accessible to readers who don't know much about the Indian mind,

Indian cultures. This was not so in the case of *House Made of Dawn* where, for example, you have to understand what witchcraft is and what it means to Abel. Instead, there do not seem to be any points in *The Ancient Child* which need a similar kind of knowledge.

NSM: I don't know. I haven't thought about that. Just as you've posed the question, I'm thinking . . . Well, in *House Made of Dawn,* yes, there are certain ceremonial patterns, for example the peyote ritual . . . the reader is not expected to know much about that, but it doesn't really matter—you don't have to know about it except what you read there. What else? Witchcraft at Jemez Pueblo: you have to take my word for the importance of that but, you know, the writer has unlimited authority when he talks about witchcraft in the pueblo, the reader comes along and says, "Yes, that's the way it is . . . , I believe it, I take this literally, as far as I can." But it's the same thing in *The Ancient Child,* isn't it? When the presentation of the medicine bundle is made, at the level of ritual there, nobody clearly understands what's going on, but you don't need to. When Perfecto Atole strikes Set with the bear's paw, yes, it's ritual, there's something under the surface here, but you don't need to understand that in order to believe it. So I'm not sure what your question is, and I'm not sure that I'm getting to the answer . . .

GP: In other words, I think that this novel carries its meaning outside Indian cultures more easily than *House Made of Dawn* does.

NSM: This is not something that I have thought of particularly, you know . . . which one is the more accessible. I don't know. You can see this problem more clearly than I can.

GP: After reading Scarberry-García's book, I realized how much I had not understood, and I've read *House Made of Dawn* several times in my life. Still I would have missed those things even if I'd read it three hundred times.

NSM: But that's good, that's the way our story should work. You should not get all of it, certainly not in the first reading. There is more to come. It is more elaborate and more intricate and more complicated and so it reveals itself more and more as you read it again and again. My thinking is that it's good . . . and of course I'm right! (*laughs*).

GP: I think that a general problem for non-Indian readers, whether American or European, is to try to fathom, to see, how much they

ought to know of the cultural background of the book they are
reading. For instance, when I read your books, or James Welch's
books, I think I understand something, and probably I do. Then, I
read some piece of criticism, Scarberry García's on *House Made of
Dawn* or, say, William Thackeray writing of the "crying for pity" in
Winter in the Blood, and all of a sudden I feel as if I'd read another
book. It seems, alas!, that my encyclopaedia as a reader did not
include some very specific things belonging to the particular Indian
culture the book dealt with! So, how can an "ethnic" writer expect
to reach the widest audience if he builds on something that is so
strictly local? How do you reconcile the need for specificity, for
particularity, with the expectation of getting across your meaning to
every potential reader?

NSM: I do not envision an audience, a readership when I write. I
tell a story and I put down what is in me to put down. The book that
you refer to is a very specialized, in-depth, study of *House Made of
Dawn* in which the author talks about the healing aspect of the story
and of the mythologies that inform the story, especially the Navajo
mythology. Scarberry-García spent a long time researching these
things, and she knows more than you and I ever will about Navajo
ceremony, and she shows the way in which that very special knowledge informs *House Made of Dawn.* But I did not write the book for
her, obviously! I was not concerned that anyone bring that kind of
knowledge and research to the reading of my novel. But it is nonetheless impressive to me that she could see so deeply into it and write so
well about the mythological elements which inform the context of the
novel. It is gratifying to me that I can appeal to someone on that
basis, but I would not want to appeal any less to, say, a seventeen-
year-old student of electrical engineering who comes to the novel. I
would want him/her to read the novel with profit, with excitement and
with reward. So, I don't know whether this answers your question
. . . That book, Scarberry-García's book, is a very responsible piece
of scholarship, and that's basically what it is, it's a wonderful act of
the intelligence.

GP: Do you feel that the attitude of your readership towards your
own work, and towards the Indian writers' work in general, has
changed over the past twenty years?

NSM: Yes, I have that sense, particularly when someone comes up to me and tells me: "I have read what you wrote and I reacted to it." When I hear things like that I understand that I am making some sort of difference, I have elicited some sort of response. I think that when you're writing you don't think about that so much. This is a question, by the way, that is very important, and one that ought to be asked all the time. I have been asked, for example, "For whom do you write? Do you write for an audience, do you have a readership in mind, or do you write for yourself?" That question was asked to William Gass, and his answer to it—which is to me the ideal answer—was: "I don't write for an audience, that would be pandering; and I don't write for myself, that would be self-serving. I write for the thing that is trying to be born." Wonderful answer . . . I wish I had said that! I will always hold it against Gass that he said it before I did. So I do have a sense of that. Another thing, just as a footnote to this question, is that you write not always knowing what you write, or what effect it has—these things are discovered after the fact, very often. I write something and I see it from my own point of view, and I have one opinion of it. Then someone else comes along and reads it and formulates another opinion or another point of view, another idea of it. I've had this strange experience many times. Someone comes to me and says: "Let me ask you a question: I was reading *The Names,* and I came upon this passage and it caught my attention. I had to read it very closely, and then I began to see this and this in it, and I want to be sure that I'm right. Did you mean for me to think in this way about the passage?" I look at the passage as if for the first time, and I say, "Obviously I meant it . . . but I wasn't aware of it at the time. You show me things that I have done out of my subconscious intelligence." This is how a writer works, I think, most often. One does not always write consciously, but one writes out of the very deepest parts of the imagination and the intelligence. Sometimes it takes a while, and it takes other people to show you what you have done. It is also true of painting, of course. You paint a picture and you think you see what is there until someone comes along and shows you something there that you did not know was there. That's terribly exciting! That's very much the creative process, I think.

GP: Can you tell me in a few words what you think you have learned from your own work in over twenty years now of literary career—and of artistic career, too, if you want to include painting? What do you know now that you didn't know at the start?

NSM: The list would be very long . . . but I'll put it in a few words, as you said. I have learned in everything that I have written. I find that writing, and painting as well, are learning processes. I once had a very able teacher; he taught at Stanford, and I took his course called "The Writing of Poetry" every single year that I was there, and I repeated it again and again because it was never the same, and I always learned something new . . . But I remember that one day he said, "You know, if you write poetry long enough you will become a learned man." And I thought to myself I didn't understand what he meant then, but I understand *now*. It is true, when you write you bring your whole mind to bear upon the writing, and it is a learning process. I have any number of times begun a poem, say, thinking that I knew what I needed to know about the subject in order to write a poem, only to find that I needed to know more than I knew, I had to research it. One poem comes into mind especially . . . Very early in my graduate career I wrote a poem called "Buteo Regalis," which happens to be the scientific name of a hawk that is very common to the Western United States—it's called Western Ferruginous Rough-Legged Hawk. I had grown up looking at these birds but when the time came to write the poem, I discovered that I needed to know much more about the creature than I knew, and so it involved a great deal of research. I went to books and started to read about the Western Ferruginous Rough-Legged Hawk; I had to read about its hunting habits. There's a line in the poem which describes the motion of its wings in flight: "Angle and curve gathering momentum . . ." I had looked at photographs of the bird flying directly towards the camera; hawks beat, and when their wings are uplifted they form a "v," but when they beat downward the wings bend to form a parenthesis, curved rather than angled. So all of this came to my knowledge, into my understanding in the course of writing the poem, and that's how it has been with virtually everything I have written. In the course of my career to date I have found out a great deal about the things that I have written about, I found out that I *could* write . . . Well, when one starts out to be a writer he doesn't know whether he can do what he's setting out to do or not. When a book is published, the writer sits back and takes a deep breath and sighs and says, "Ah, it was possible after all!'' So you find out things of that kind. In painting it's the same thing: you start up with a blank picture plane, a canvas or a sheet of paper, and you wonder if it is possible for you to take this space, and place upon it something that is worth the effort. When I paint something and I stand back and say, ''Yes, that's what I meant to do!''—it's a great feeling. In *The Ancient Child,* the protagonist of which is a painter, there is a passage in which I write that ''Set painted in order to astonish God,'' and this is why I paint and write: I want to astonish God. And when I have the sense that I have done that, ah! it's my whole reason for being, I can't do better than that. . . . And then I eat a good pasta! (*laughs*).

GP: Who knows whether you have astonished God, after all. Certainly your work astonishes us!

Interview with N. Scott Momaday

Camille Adkins / 1993

Tucson, Arizona, 21 April 1993

CA: Do you mind being introduced always the same way: N. Scott Momaday, American Indian (Kiowa) and winner of the Pulitzer Prize?
NSM: That's pretty standard. It's all right with me.

CA: Do you mind talking about your personal background, particularly the Indian elements of it?
NSM: No.

CA: You've written about it in *The Names*.
NSM: To some extent in all my books, yes.

CA: Might you ever do a sequel to *The Names?*
NSM: You know, when I finished *The Names,* I didn't think so. But since then, I have thought I have enough of a life beyond that now to write about it, so it's a possibility. It's not something I have clearly carved out, but if I find myself in need of a project and with time to give to it, I might bring it forward.

CA: The photographs in *The Names* . . .
NSM: Aren't they wonderful?

CA: How did you locate them?
NSM: It was pretty much an accident. My father told his sister what I was doing, and she said, "Oh, I have a wonderful picture of our mother. I found it in the trunk." And it turns out to be the best photograph of my grandmother that I have ever seen.

CA: In *In the Presence of the Sun* you thank your parents first among the people you acknowledge. Would you say a few words about each of your parents?

NSM: My father was a full-blood Kiowa—really, there's no such thing. There was a French Canadian somewhere in his background and Mexicán. My great-great-grandmother was a Mexican captive. But on the rolls, he was a full-blood. He grew up in the Kiowa tradition, and he spoke Kiowa fluently. And he was a painter. Though he was a teacher most of his life, I think of him as a painter. He had a wonderful knack of teaching children to paint. In the Indian world, that is very important; Indian people seem to have a certain aesthetic principle. I have never known an Indian child who couldn't draw pretty well. At Jemez Pueblo, where he taught for twenty-five years, he would take these young children, and he would make artists of them. Very accomplished shows. His students had shows internationally.

CA: While they were still children?

NSM: Yes, one of his students won a national prize and went to Washington to meet the President. Things of that kind. A group of his students had a show in France. He was very well able to instruct young people in art; and he was himself a very accomplished painter.

CA: You've written about watching him paint.

NSM: I grew up watching him paint. He was always painting in his spare time, and I would watch. He did very detailed work, the kind of work that I can't do. I'm much more casual and spontaneous on the paper than he was. He was very meticulous. He liked to visit with other artists; it was so wonderful that people would come to our house and paint with him. I learned a lot, I think, watching him and his friends paint. Something that became realized in me much later, but that I learned very early.

CA: Can you describe his painting?

NSM: Wonderful sense of color, but in the Indian tradition, which is flat, two-dimensional; lots of color, lots of detail. I don't have that in me, but I think I learned a lot from him.

CA: Are his illustrations for *The Way to Rainy Mountain* pen and ink?

NSM: Pen and ink, yes.

CA: My favorite is the horse, the thunderstorm. Your mother still lives at Jemez?

NSM: She's in her eighties. She lives at Jemez Springs, New Mexico, and she has been a writer. She says she writes now, though I don't know what will become of it. She's become very detached from writing. She thinks of it still, and she goes to her desk to jot things down. She's full of memories at this point. But she's there, and she seems well enough. She is a remarkable woman. She was a teacher most of her life, and she says she loved every moment of her twenty-five years at Jemez working with children. She's been completely satisfied with her work and her life.

CA: Where did she grow up?

NSM: In Kentucky. Then came west when she was in college. She went to Haskell Indian School in Kansas. That's how she met my father. He wasn't there, but one of his cousins was, and the cousin brought my mother to Oklahoma, where she met my father.

CA: The MLA is now recognizing Native American literature as a category. Do you have any particular feelings about being categorized?

NSM: No . . . well, maybe I do. The label diminishes the writer somehow, slightly. But labels are inevitable.

CA: I've read that you prefer the term American Indian because you grew up with it and you're used to it, but today you've been saying Native American.

NSM: I use the terms interchangeably.

CA: Do you think that non-Indians can deal truly with Indian subjects?

NSM: I don't see why not. It depends on the writer. Take Oliver LaFarge's *Laughing Boy*. LaFarge was not Native American, but he was an expert on Navajo culture, and he wrote well about it. Look at Tony Hillerman's books. There are those who say that non-Native Americans can't or shouldn't deal with Native American material. But I don't subscribe to that.

CA: Who then, other than yourself, are the important Native American writers?

NSM: Jim [James] Welch. I think very highly of his first novel, *Winter in the Blood.* Louise Erdrich. Leslie Silko is an important writer. Simon Ortiz and Joy Harjo are very good poets.

CA: In the past you have denied that you are a spokesman for any group or any person other than yourself. Is this still so?

NSM: Yes. I tell what is mine to tell. Vine Deloria and others are able to speak out more politically, and to do it well. But that is not for me.

CA: Some would prefer that you apply your Indianness differently from the way you choose to?

NSM: Maybe so, but I do what I can.

CA: Would you respond to some names for ''American'' literature?

NSM: All right.

CA: Faulkner.

NSM: *The Sound and the Fury* is one of the great books of this century. I wish I had written it—and ''The Bear.''

CA: You heard Faulker read from *Go Down, Moses*?

NSM: No, it was *The Hamlet.* It was in Virginia. I sat on the front row. I had assumed that he would be tall, but he wasn't; he was well under six feet tall, five-eight at the most. Afterward I drew myself up and asked him, ''Mr. Faulkner, what do you read?'' He replied, contemptuously, I thought, ''Young man, I don't *read*.''

CA: Melville.

NSM: *Moby Dick,* all of it.

CA: Even the ''Cetology'' chapter?

NSM: Yes, even that has its place.

CA: Did you have ''The Whiteness of the Whale'' in mind when you wrote about Abel killing the white man?

NSM: Not consciously, no. There's a strong strain of albinism at Jemez. The white man was an albino; that's all. And I knew of a murder trial in which the defendant claimed that the man he killed had turned into a snake, so he had to kill him.

CA: A real trial, then?

NSM: Yes.

CA: But Melville . . .

NSM: He's probably the most important American writer, other than Emily Dickinson.

CA: You studied the Dickinson manuscripts at Amherst?

NSM: Yes, I had a Guggenheim to study there for a year, and I looked at the variants, the changes, in her own handwriting.

CA: The effects are different from seeing the poems in print?

NSM: Yes, far different. Her language was equal to her vision; that is very rare.

CA: Emerson. You don't treat the Transcendentalists too kindly in the Tuckerman preface.

NSM: Emerson wanted badly to be a mystic. He saw what he wanted to see, the Oversoul and so forth. Tuckerman and Dickinson were more scientific in their views of nature. They saw what was there.

CA: The landscape and mythology of the American West are very important to you?

NSM: The way people perceive the West, yes. People all over the world are fascinated by the West and hold it vividly, though not always accurately, in their imaginations.

CA: Would you talk now about each of your books? When you were writing *The Way to Rainy Mountain,* did you really have all those forms in mind—the three acts of classical tragedy, the twenty-four books of the epics—that are referred to in Martha Trimble's *N. Scott Momaday.*

NSM: No.

CA: But you do often divide things into four parts.

NSM: Yes, I think four is a sacred number.

CA: How did *The Way to Rainy Mountain* come about?

NSM: That's still my favorite of my books. We printed it on a hand press, and that was *The Journey of Tai-Me.* We printed a hundred copies of it on the most expensive paper we could find, and we had it bound in leather. It was a beautiful book. I sent Gus Blaisdell a copy; he was then an editor at New Mexico. He said, "We've got to do a trade edition of this." And I said, "Not likely. It's not big enough." But he kept after me, and I said, "Let me see if I can expand it someway." That's when I thought of the commentaries. When I got into it, somehow I thought of the historical commentaries and the autobiographical or personal commentaries. That's how it came about, and so I had the three voices going then, alternately. That was very exciting to me.

CA: *House Made of Dawn*—There must be a lot to say.

NSM: Yes. I guess from the time I lived at Jemez, taking that whole span, the novel grew out of that time. I had seen a lot of men, young men, come back from World War II. And I had seen what happened to them, terrible things. Some of them were very good friends of mine. All of them were older, but still we got along quite well. And when I began to think about writing a novel, the story of the returnee who could not fit himself back into the traditional way of life was ready-made. I had first-hand knowledge of that subject.

It's always a mystery to me how books are written. When I was at Stanford as a graduate student, I was working in poetry, exclusively. And that was such a rigorous time for me because I knew almost nothing about traditional forms of poetry, so I learned them there. I was exercising a lot, and I wrote some poems. But when I left, I felt that I had worked myself into a corner, that I had become so dedicated or committed to traditional English poetry that I felt suffocated. I wanted more elbow room. So I began writing fiction. And that's when I started *House Made of Dawn*.

I wrote the very first part of it at Jemez Springs. I kept it up when I went to my first teaching post at Santa Barbara, and wrote the balance of it there in fairly quick order. Then I finished it in Massachusetts, where I had the Guggenheim and was working on Emily Dickinson, or reading her. So that's really the genesis and the development of *House Made of Dawn;* most of it was written in retrospect, thinking back on that time at Jemez that was so important to me. As I say, I'm always amazed to have written a novel. It would seem so impossible at the outset. But it happens, and you look back on it with wonder.

CA: It is said that you are preoccupied with structure in that book, that the structure is perhaps overly complex.

NSM: It didn't seem a preoccupation to me at the time. It is an unorthodox book, a strangely structured book, but it works. And it is a reflection of the way time works in the Native American world. So it happens; the story happens this way.

CA: What about the names in the book—Abel and Angela?
NSM: Less than is imagined is there in the names.

CA: You still don't know what happens to Abel?
NSM: I will wonder about that until the day I die. But it's rather good, I think, that I don't know. If I knew, I might be disappointed.

CA: You leave him running on the day before your own birthday.
NSM: And certainly he's running towards re-entry; he's running back in the direction of his traditional world. And either he makes it or he doesn't. What do you think?

CA: I think he might eventually become a healer, as his grandfather did after his first drumming.
NSM: Could be. What the hell do you know? But I like that. I hope you're right.

CA: Do you think that the book might be somewhat inaccessible to those who aren't familiar with the festivals and ceremonies particular to that area of New Mexico. How well can the book be read without prior knowledge of those particulars?
NSM: I really don't think it matters, but I don't have a keen sense of that. Seems to me I've read novels in which there were feast days or important dates of which I was not aware, but it worked for me anyway. I could take it and place myself in it and appreciate it. So I don't think that is a matter of great importance. But maybe I am expecting too much of the reader. I don't know.

CA: The chicken pull at Jemez. Does that still go on?
NSM: I think the chicken pull is on two days. I've forgotten what they are, around the 29th of June maybe. The last chicken pull I saw was a kind of fiasco. It has lost much of its excitement, its glamour. It was being done by kids, little kids. They were having a great time, but they were not nearly as skillful as those men I first saw. They were terrific horsemen, and it was a great thing to see. So I think it's deteriorated. Whether it will come back, I don't know.

CA: *The Ancient Child*—twenty years between novels.

NSM: I guess I wanted to get the art into it. I wanted to write about an artist, a painter. And I wanted to work also with the business of transformation and the legend of the boy who turns into a bear, with which I, of course, identify very strongly. So Set is the reincarnation of that boy, just as I am. A lot of it is autobiographical in the sense that I was able to incorporate my knowledge of painting, incorporate my identity/identification with the boy in the legend. And Grey is a character that I greatly enjoyed working with. She's a little larger than life, I think. She's someone I would like to know. I think those two things in particular—the aspect of painting and of transformation—are the two things about the novel that interest me the most, and probably the two things that motivated me to the writing of it more than anything else.

CA: Grey. Maybe she *is* larger than life. Toward the end of the book, though, doesn't she subordinate herself to Set and to his medicine?

NSM: But that's her whole purpose from the beginning. She is to assist him in the realization of his bear power. Some while ago, someone asked me a question that I just was not expecting. The question was, ''When are you going to write the sequel to *The Ancient Child*? You can't just leave her pregnant and alone in the hogan.'' I had to think about that.

CA: Set's vision at the end of the book, in my view, keeps the ending from being too soft. I think the last word of the book is ''darkness.''

NSM: Yes. And as I don't know what happened to Abel, I don't know what happens to Set. What happens on the next page? He has turned into a bear, or he is in the process. That's exactly how it is also with the legend. The boy turns into a bear. We don't know anything else about him. What happens to him? I think that's how it ought to be. We ought not to know.

CA: Your newest book, *In the Presence of the Sun,* contains your own illustrations this time.

NSM: Yes, my own.

CA: I'm first drawn to the shield section.

NSM: I think that was the idea from the beginning, that this should be the centerpiece. I had published the shields separately as a fine press book. So this was in a way like *The Journey of Tai-Me*. The question was how to best expand it for a trade edition, and then I added all this other stuff to it. But the shields are the centerpiece.

CA: Did you miss your father when you were doing the illustrations?
NSM: Oh, yes. I have missed my father in many ways since he died. I keep dreaming of him.

CA: The poem about the father in this book is I think among the strongest ones.
NSM: Do you?

CA: What are the colors in this painting? [referring to page 132 of *In the Presence of the Sun,* accompanying the poem "December 29, 1890, Wounded Knee Creek" on page 133.]
NSM: There are three paintings about 40" by 50". They're acrylic on paper. The colors are very bright. It's a series on Columbus, actually. One of them is called Palos, which is the port from which Columbus sailed. It's the figure, the profile of the head. The second is called "Admiral of the Ocean Sea." It is again a profile, but there's a mermaid above it. And then there's the third, a rendition of the place where Columbus made his landfall.

CA: I was assuming that the large figure was someone from the 7th Cavalry and the other one wasn't.
NSM: Actually, it's Columbus with an Indian child. This one is *bright* yellow. The colors in these three paintings are truly vivid. They're in Santa Fe and really special for me. They're larger than most things I've done, and they go together. I don't know what will become of them, but they're interesting pieces.

CA: Would you go back to *The Ancient Child* for one question? Yvor Winters figures into this book. His bear poem opens one of the sections. Is that the entire poem, or is that an excerpt?
NSM: It's an excerpt. And he is relevant in another way; I had Winters very strongly in mind when I was drawing the character of Bent.

CA: Your poetry?
NSM: It goes on. Slowly.

CA: Was it Winters who first encouraged you to write poetry? Were you recruited to Stanford specifically to study with Winters?

NSM: No.

CA: It was a Stegner Fellowship, I believe.

NSM: Right. At the time when I got mine, there were I think four fellowships in fiction and two in poetry. I had been writing poetry as an undergraduate, and I had entered contests. I had even published a poem. In the same year I went to Stanford, I published a poem in the *New Mexico Quarterly*. That was my first publication. But when I was teaching at Dulce on the Jicarilla Reservation the year after I gradua-ted from New Mexico, Bobby Jack Nelson was at Pensacola in the Naval Air Cadet program, and one day I got a letter from him in which he sent me the flyer for the Stanford Stegner Fellowships. He said, "This looks like a good deal; I'm going to apply for it." So I thought, "Well, hell, I'll apply for it too." And so I had an outline of a collection of poems with maybe four or five samples. And I applied, and I won it. I didn't know Yvor Winters at the time—I'd never heard of him—but he's the one who wrote to me and said, "There is only one fellowship in poetry this year—You're it."

CA: Apparently he did think you were "it." He called you a great poet when you were a very young man.

NSM: Well, we became very good friends, and he did give me a lot of encouragement. He seemed to see potential in me when no one else did. When I went to Stanford, I knew very little about poetry. I thought I knew quite a bit; turned out I didn't. But he was patient and directed me to the right classes. I didn't want to take a degree there; instead, I wanted to go back to Dulce. Since I had taken a year's leave of absence, I had a job waiting for me. But once I got to know Winters, he said, "Look, you're here in this high-powered graduate program. Why don't you take an advanced degree? It couldn't hurt." And so I followed his advice, and the first thing I knew I had a master's degree and just sailed right on through. I gave up Dulce forever and became a university teacher. So the course of my life was drastically changed, and Winters had a lot to do with it.

CA: Certain poems of yours are frequently anthologized. "The Bear," "Earth and I Gave You Turquoise," "Comparatives." These have received more attention than some of the others. Which ones would you single out?

NSM: I would include "The Bear," which was my first great success at Stanford. I wrote it, and Winters admired it. I won the Academy of American Poets Prize for it. So I think that's a poem of which I am particularly proud. Beyond that I would name, say, "Angle of Geese," which I think is one of my extraordinary poems.

CA: That's the one that begins with the death of a child?

NSM: Yes. And then Winters admired very much my poem called "Before an Old Painting of the Crucifixion." Technically, it is a solid piece of work, but it's not one of my favorite poems. I like things like "Scaffold Bear" and "On the Cause of a Homely Death"—is that what it's called?—the little epigram that's about the death of a woman. I like the Georgia O'Keeffe poem. There are several that I hold up above the others, but finally it's a matter of taste. If people like "Comparatives," that's great. But if I were anthologizing five or ten of my poems, that wouldn't be on the list. But it's all right. I didn't include "Before an Old Painting of the Crucifixion" in the new collection, *In the Presence of the Sun.* And I'm sure there are some people who wonder why, because Winters said so much about it. But I thought, "Well, I'll do some other things."

CA: Your poetry goes on, you say.

NSM: Yes, slowly. I don't have anything in the works right now, but I'll write a poem soon. That's one of the constants in my life. I keep going back to poetry. Writing slowly, as I say, but it comes.

CA: Your prose is so much like poetry. How do you write any poetry apart from that?

NSM: It is true that I work towards and expect of myself a lyrical quality in the prose. I think there's a closer connection between prose and poetry than most people realize. So when Melville writes with all that lyricism at the end of *Moby Dick,* that is a function of prose. It approaches poetry at its best. So I try for that myself. I'm always in mind of the lyrical quality.

CA: You are known for your voice. Do you read to yourself as you compose?

NSM: Oh, I babble constantly. And I try it that way. If I write

something and I'm not quite sure what it is, I read it aloud to myself,
and I get a better idea of what it is. That's one of the ways in which I
evaluate my work.

CA: You've written a play.
NSM: Yes, you've read it. The first draft. It's going to be premiered
in Syracuse on 8 February [1994]. I never have been involved with a
play before, but it's exciting. I'm really looking foward to seeing
it produced.

CA: You took one of the parts when the play was read last spring?
NSM: There were staged readings at Harvard last February, and I
played the part of one of the six characters. That was great fun too.
Took me back—I was in two plays in college at New Mexico.

CA: You are a bit of an actor.
NSM: Bit of a ham, actually.

CA: What are you working on now? You've told me you're working
on a Manson story. How is that looking?
NSM: All right, I think. I keep getting new slants on it. I keep
changing the focus in my mind. It's a novel set in California in the
60s. I think the main character is a professor. Manson will figure in it,
certainly, though I'm not sure yet to what extent. When I first thought
about it, he was going to have a very large part in it. I think I've now
determined that he's not as large as I once thought, but still there.
He's interesting, and he's important to that decade, and that's really
what I want to evoke, the 60s. So it's begun, and it's going very
slowly, but I'm hoping to pick up the pace pretty soon and get it done.

CA: A couple of the Mansonites visited you in your office at
Stanford, didn't they?
NSM: Yes. Squeaky [Fromme] and Sarah Good came to see me
one day.

CA: They made an impression?
NSM: It was a great moment in my life. These two young girls,
glassy eyed, crosses cut in their foreheads. "Charlie Manson sent us
to talk to you. He would like your permission to live on the land." I
didn't know what to say on this incredible occasion. Then a couple of

days after that I got a call from the FBI in San Francisco. They said, "Your name appears on a list in Charles Manson's possession. We don't know what it means, but we thought you'd like to know." I would have been deeply disturbed had it not been for the visit of the two girls because I'm pretty sure that's what it was about. It wasn't a hit list. My name was there because I think Charlie had read *The Way to Rainy Mountain,* and he decided that I was a custodian of the land and that it would be a good thing to have my Native American permission to live on it. So he knew my name.

CA: I'll ask you the question that you asked Faulkner. Do you have time to read?

NSM: I manage to read certain things. I have to steal time. When I'm on airplanes, I rèad. I've just read a book called *A Violent Act.* I don't know if you've seen it. It has to do with a killer who leads the police on a merry chase for something like three days. And it's well done. It's by a journalist who writes frequently for *The New Yorker,* Alec Wilkinson. And it's a kind of journalistic work, but it's also very perceptive and well-written. I'm reading a biography of Sitting Bull, which Robert Utley is just coming out with. I have the galleys. I'm reading a book-length interview with Louis Malle. And then just bits and pieces here and there. I'm very slow at it. But I do enjoy it; I like to read.

CA: You've been narrating documentaries lately. I've seen the PBS production on the three tribes, entitled *Winds of Change: A Matter of Promises.* You've also done one on Custer's Last Stand, is that right? Are there others?

NSM: I did something on national forests, which is now out on video. I'm doing some narration for a series on the West, which is being done by the people who did the Civil War series. They're doing a series on the American West. They're coming on the 5th of May to interview me. So I'll be on camera in a part of that series. I'm not sure how much. And what else? Just very small things. The thing on Custer is well done, and I really enjoyed that. I'm glad I had a part in it.

CA: Where did you go to do it?

NSM: I recorded it here. The person who made the film, Paul

Stekler, is in Boston. The filming was done at the Little Big Horn, but my narration was recorded in Tucson. It was a great thing to do.

CA: How much can you tell about the Gourd Dancers?

NSM: Well, the Gourd Dance Society is a very old soldier society in the Kiowa tribe. It passed out of existence for a time, and was re-established—I think in the early part of this century, like the 1910s or 20s. Now it's a full-fledged soldier society with over a hundred members. We meet once each year in Oklahoma, on the 4th of July. When I can, I go there; I was made a member in 1969. We, the dancers, wear a certain regalia, and we dance. It's been a very good thing for me because it has been a kind of restoration. I find myself deeply involved in the racial mix when I go and dance. I've been there the last two years. Before that I had missed several in a row. But I would like to keep it up; it's a good thing.

CA: Have you done any ceremonial singing?

NSM: No, I wish I could. That is something I'd like to get into. A lot of the Kiowas know songs, and the drummers and the singers at the society meeting are so much a part of it. I would love to be involved in that at some point. But I don't know any songs. I will need to be taught. And I just haven't got around to that. Maybe in my old age.

CA: I read in the Wheelwright exhibit of your paintings something about the Buffalo Trust.

NSM: I have this dream, which I call the Buffalo Trust. What I imagine doing is setting up a foundation or an institute for the preservation of the sacred in Native American life. At Rainy Mountain, Oklahoma, where there are the ruins of the old school where my grandmother went as a child, there's this wonderful stretch of land with Rainy Mountain here, the ruins here, and then just plains, open plains, grassland. I'd like to build a school there—not a school, a museum—where there are sacred objects rotating all the time from other museums. A danceground where ceremonial dances can be held, where the Gourd Dancers and other tribes from everywhere can come and perform. There would be a library of religious material and sacred matter, where scholars who are interested in the sacred can come and study and lecture and exchange views. But basically it will be a place where Native American people, and especially children, can come into the presence of sacred objects. This seems to me a wonderful idea—to restore the prairie and put buffalo on it. That's what I call the Buffalo Trust, and I have taken some steps—I have talked to people about how you legally set up such a trust. I have talked to some of the Kiowas about the use of the land. It's land owned by the Comanche and Kiowa tribes. But nothing is being done with it. I think it might be possible to lease it. But it's a matter of raising an enormous amount of money to construct the buildings and the library. The easy part of it would be to arrange for exhibits, since I am a member of the National Museum. So I think I could arrange fairly easily to have shields and pipes and wampum displayed on a rotating basis, which would be great for the people, the native people around.

CA: Is that the Museum of the American Indian? Has the name changed?

NSM: It's now called the National Museum of the American Indian because we have affiliated with the Smithsonian. They're building a new museum on the Mall in Washington, D.C.

CA: Several years ago, there was a controversy about who would control which artifacts.

NSM: Yes. It's a great thing for the Museum of the American Indian because we have been housed in that facility in New York, up in the Bronx. It's way up on Audubon Plaza at 155th and Broadway. It's the greatest collection of its kind in the world, but people have not had proper access to it because it was so removed. And now we will have much more exposure in Washington. So it's a good thing.

CA: Are you still working to preserve the Grand Canyon?

NSM: Well, I'm still on the board on the Grand Canyon Trust, which is also concerned to keep the environment clean on the Colorado Plateau. It's a good cause. I'm still involved, but I may have to go off because I just don't have the time to give to it.

CA: I read also in the Wheelwright exhibit that you are "in the process of making a statement about the sacred."

NSM: Yes, I have been asked by several people to write about the sacred. One is a chapter in a book; one was an introduction to a Sierra

Club calendar. A photographer who works with sacred places has asked me to write a book, which I have declined. But I do want to write about the sacred. It's an important concept to me, and so I'd like to set down my ideas in writing, and fairly soon I think.

CA: Tell me about your interest in Billy the Kid.

NSM: I can't remember when I first happened upon Billy the Kid. When I was in the second or third grade, I lived in a town called Hobbs, New Mexico, and I had buddies there. We played war and we played cowboys and Indians. My first real recollection of Billy the Kid is the time my mother and I went to Roswell, which is real Billy the Kid country. I might have gone to a movie that day while my mother visited the daughter of Pat Garrett, the Sheriff of Lincoln County, the man who killed Billy the Kid. The daughter was blind, if I remember rightly, when my mother met her, and she had composed the state song of New Mexico—"O fair New Mexico/ We love, we love you so." Anyway, something about that encounter between my mother and Pat Garrett's daughter gave me a keen interest in Billy the Kid. When I lived in Jemez, which was from 1946 until I went away to school, I had a horse and I rode the range, and in my imagination Billy the Kid accompanied me. We became great friends as we rode the range together, getting into the maddest exploits and saving beautiful young women at every opportunity. He became a very important figure in my imagination.

At some point I began not only to imagine him but to find out everything I could about him. I think there are forty-eight movies about Billy the Kid, and I saw a good number of them when I was growing up. I started reading. I happened across Walter Noble Burns' *The Saga of Billy the Kid*, which I think was really after Pat Garrett's own ghost-written book about the authentic life of Billy the Kid. *The Saga of Billy the Kid* was probably the one book that did create a lot of interest in Billy. It was an exciting story. I don't know whether it was well-written or not, but it was terribly exciting. And so Billy the Kid became more and more important in my life.

When I became a teenager, very impressionable, having to exist on my own so much of the time, Billy the Kid became a kind of companion to me in my mind. And so I imagined all kinds of exploits. Some of them I've written down in "The Strange and True Story of

My Life with Billy the Kid" [in *The Ancient Child* and also *In the Presence of the Sun*] and, as I say, I got interested then in the facts of his life.

I started reading as much as I could. We knew very little about Billy until fairly recently. Now we have a lot of authentic information on his life, though it remains obscure in some ways. He has become, I think, in the last few years more of a personality, and though his legend remains intact, we do know him as a human being now, as a man who did this and that and who went here and there. We can identify places and names and so on. And he remains one of my great glories, and I've written about him. Some of it's imaginative, but in *The Ancient Child*, for example, everything that is written—virtually everything that is written about Billy the Kid there—is based upon fact.

I have gone over the ground he traveled. I've been to Mesilla, where he was convicted, over the Organs to Lincoln, where he was sentenced to be hanged. The courthouse from which he made perhaps the most famous escape in American history is still there. It's very much as it was in his time. So it was a great thing for me to go into the courthouse and climb those stairs on which he killed Bell—the bullethole is still there in the wall—and up to the room in which he was incarcerated—he was chained to the floor at night. And I've been at the window from which he killed Bob Olinger with Olinger's own shotgun. Of course, I've looked down the road towards Fort Stanton—where Billy, after killing his guards and having his chains, his leg irons, cut—got on a horse and rode into legend. I've been to San Patricio, which was one of his favorite places, and is certainly one of the most beautiful villages in New Mexico. And I've been to Fort Sumner, where he was killed by Pat Garrett on the night of July 13, 1881. The house in which he was killed is no longer there, the old fort is vacant, the town has moved to the south. But the grave is there. I've been at his grave. I've been to Stinking Springs, where he was captured by Pat Garrett, and seen the foundation of the little house in which he took refuge. Going over places like that, following legends, is a great thing to do. As I wrote in a piece for the travel supplement of the *New York Times*, I am fortunate to have followed the steps of certain legends. Alexander the Great—I've been on the path where he traveled—and where Tamerlaine walked. I've had these wonderful experiences. And to have followed the steps of Billy the Kid in the last hundred days of his life is to me a great experience, a wonderful act of the imagination. I like that sort of thing.

CA: Billy didn't say much.

NSM: Billy was a man of few words, as far as I can tell, but he did love life. He loved women, he loved dancing, he loved music. But on the whole he was a soft-spoken man, and a cold-blooded killer.

CA: The business of Sister Blandina and the chair shows him to be gentle.

NSM: It demonstrates a side of his personality that we don't generally know. Sister Blandina was a sister of the Mothers of Charity. I think this order was headquartered in Cincinnati. She had come from Italy and joined the order and was missioned to the West. She published a journal which is a wonderful document. As a young nun, she was sent to Trinidad, Colorado, and there she encountered Billy the Kid. It's an interesting story. One of his companions had been mortally wounded. He was alone in a little shack somewhere on the edge of the town, and she visited him in his last days to offer him comfort. One day, according to her journal, he said to her, "Sister, you have been so kind to me. My companions are coming to visit, and I want you to meet them. Will you please come on Friday?" She agreed to come, and the visitors were Billy the Kid and a gang of outlaws. She said that Billy spoke to her in the kindest terms. They had come actually to kill the physicians—three or four physicians in Trinidad, all of whom had refused to minister to this young man because he was an outlaw. When he met Sister Blandina, he thanked her for taking care of his comrade. He said, "If there's anything, ever, anything we can do for you, Sister, just ask." And so she said, "Well, there is one thing. Spare the lives of the physicians of Trinidad." So, according to her diary, she saved the lives of the physicians of Trinidad by speaking kindly to Billy the Kid, who was apparently a very chivalrous man.

Later she was transferred to Santa Fe, and while she was there Billy the Kid was captured and taken to Santa Fe and placed in a room which was a jail, in effect. He was nailed to the floor because he was considered such a dangerous outlaw. She heard of his presence in Santa Fe and went to visit him, and when she entered the room, she saw him on the floor. It must have been a terribly humiliating moment for Billy, and for her. It was a strange moment. But she records that he looked up at her from the floor, unable to rise, and the first thing he said to her was, "I wish I could place a chair for you, Sister." I've always thought that was an unlikely thing to say and that it really did indicate something about Billy's character.

CA: The story of the chewing tobacco, is that yours?

NSM: That one's mine. That's purely out of my own imagination. I imagine that Billy had visited a good friend at Glorieta, an old man, and couldn't make a gift outright of the tobacco because the old man would have been insulted by that. But he could cut off a piece and give it to the old man, pretending that he himself, Billy, would enjoy the other half. In fact, he didn't smoke; he didn't use tobacco at all. So it was a gesture. Riding off, he threw the tobacco away. It was, I thought, a nice touch.

CA: Did you also imagine the dialogue between Billy and Sitting Bear?

NSM: I had such great fun with that. In *The Ancient Child*, Grey, the medicine woman, fantasizes about Billy the Kid throughout, and in one passage she imagines that he encounters Set Angya, Sitting Bear, who is one of the great chiefs in Kiowa tradition. She imagines them talking to each another. It's a funny, funny passage because Billy makes a speech and greatly impresses Sitting Bear with his oratory. And then it comes out that Grey had written the speech for him, and he had memorized it. And all of this is revealed in the confrontation.

CA: But he doesn't sing.

NSM: He can't sing.

Index